S.N. — T. Dicks

1992

CHILDREN'S FICTION SOURCEBOOK

DEDICATION

To Amanda and Christopher
our long-suffering and patient children
with thanks

CHILDREN'S FICTION SOURCEBOOK

A survey of children's books
for 6–13 year olds

Margaret Hobson
Jennifer Madden
Ray Prytherch

Published by
Ashgate Publishing Limited
Gower House
Croft Road
Aldershot
Hants GU11 3HR
England

Ashgate Publishing Co
Old Post Road
Brookfield
Vermont 05036
USA

British Library Cataloguing in Publication Data is available

ISBN: 1 85742 022 5

Printed in Great Britain by
Billing & Sons Ltd, Worcester

CONTENTS

◆

NOTES ON AUTHORS

◆

MARGARET HOBSON

Born in Huddersfield in 1939, she became a library assistant in 1961, eventually specializing in children's work. After qualifying at Liverpool School of Librarianship, she worked first as a children's librarian, then in a college of education library. With one son and one daughter, she currently works as part of a team in the Children's Services Department in Kirklees Cultural Services.

JENNIFER MADDEN

Married with one son. Librarian since 1960, currently in charge of the Children's and Schools' Library Service in Kirklees Cultural Services. Vice-Chairman of the Arts Development Association and Chairman of the local branch of the RSPCA.

RAY PRYTHERCH

Works as an information consultant specializing in bibliographic works, library training, and the international context of research librarianship. His other works for Gower include *Harrod's Librarians' Glossary and Reference Book* (7th edition), *Handbook of Library Training Practice*, and *Sources of Information in Librarianship and Information Science* (2nd edition).

PREFACE

◆

Children's reading is a vital component of education and recreation; parents, teachers and librarians all wish to encourage and foster good reading habits that will provide a sound future base for leisure reading, imaginative skills, and for the everyday requirements of a literate society; all devote much time to the careful selection of a comprehensive stock of children's fiction.

Although advisory guides have been attempted before, they have been, in the main, academic or historical in approach, and reviews, the only other source of guidance, are by their very nature widely scattered and difficult to obtain. We feel a distinct need for a comprehensive source, offering thorough guidance on English-language children's fiction for 6–13-year-olds: a selective survey of the best and most popular children's authors giving a brief biographical note, address and/or agent contact, details of awards and prizes, age range, and versions of their work with essential bibliographical detail.

This volume covers about 140 authors, and for each of their titles or series there is a brief annotation; thus we are offering an evaluative source-book to help in the selection of reading material for children by parents, teachers and librarians. The biographical details will help in the selection and contacting of authors for events, promotional meetings, story-times, literary quizzes and readings.

Not every children's author can be represented: there has been a deliberate selection, mainly those currently writing, and although there is a UK bias, there is also good coverage of North American, Australasian and Commonwealth authors.

Appendices offer a number of valuable features: recommended editions of classic titles that are always important are discussed, together with anthologies of fairy tales; publishers' series are listed, as are television tie-ins from 1985 onwards; lists of winners of major prizes and awards are included.

Inevitably, in a work such as this, there will be errors and omissions. In anticipation of a planned revision, the authors would like to hear from anyone with suggestions for additions or corrections, and particularly from those authors whose biographical details were difficult to trace, and who, therefore, have very short biographical entries in this first edition.

ACKNOWLEDGEMENTS

◆

The authors wish to express their grateful thanks to Woodfield and Stanley Ltd, children's book suppliers of Moldgreen, Huddersfield, for their support and help.

Their thanks are also due to David Madden for his work in preparing and editing the text.

In compiling this volume we have received help, advice and support from many colleagues, libraries and publishers; we should like to record our thanks to all of them.

HOW TO USE THIS BOOK

◆

The main body of the text is a list, in author order, of the selected titles, followed by appendices on classics (also in author order with anthologies at the end), series (in series name order, with lists of authors for each series), and television tie-ins (again in author order). The author index lists every author mentioned, whether the name appears in the main text or in the appendices; similarly every title is included in the title index.

Within the entry for each author, the titles are listed in alphabetical order, unless otherwise indicated. However, where the title is part of a series, the first title is listed in its place in the alphabetical order, and subsequent titles follow it immediately. Such titles are indented to indicate that they are part of the series.

For every title listed, at least one bibliographical citation is given. The format for this citation is:

Publisher, year, no. of pages. – notes. – ISBN

The citations for most entries have the full details as shown above. However, while every title has, of course, been read in the course of compiling this work, not every published edition has been examined. The details are as shown in Whitaker's *British Books in Print*, December 1990.

Within notes, the following abbreviations have been used:

Pbk = Paperback edition
L/P = Large print edition
O/P = Out of print. While this means that the title cannot currently be purchased, the titles chosen are all so well known that this version will almost certainly be available from any good public library.

MAIN AUTHOR LIST

◆

A

ADAMS, Richard

British. Born Newbury, 1920. Educated Bradfield College, Berkshire; Worcester College, Oxford. B.A. Modern History, M.A. British Army WW II. Married Barbara Elizabeth Acland, 1949, two daughters. Civil servant, writer.

Awards: Library Association Carnegie Medal: *Watership Down*, 1972
Guardian Award: *Watership Down*, 1973
Fellow of the Royal Society of Literature, 1975

Address: 26 Church Street, Whitchurch, Hampshire, England

Agent: David Higham Assoc. Ltd, 5–8 Lower John Street, London W1R 4HA, England

WATERSHIP DOWN
A. Lane, 1982, 480p. – 0 7139 1513 7
Ulverscroft, 1981, 683p. – L/P, O/P. –
0 7089 8012 0
Penguin, 1974, 480p. – Pbk. – 0 14 003958 9

A book which deserves a place on every bookshelf, in every home and in every library. It tells the story of a group of rabbits forced to flee their home to save their lives. They journey to a better place, facing untold dangers which not all survive. It is funny, sad, exciting and, above all, totally compelling, making unobtrusive but shrewd observations on life as the story progresses. As with all really excellent novels, it is read to and by adults and children of all ages.
Age range: 8–adult

AHLBERG, Allan

British. Born Croydon, 1938; grew up in Birmingham. Educated Sunderland College of Education. Married Janet Hall, illustrator, 1969, one daughter. Sometime: postman, soldier, schoolteacher, gravedigger and plumber's mate.

Awards: Children's Rights Workshop Other Award: *Miss Plug the Plumber*, 1980
Emil/Kurt Maschler Award: *The Jolly Postman*, 1986
Signal Poetry Award: *Heard it in the Playground*, 1990

Address: 20 Nether Hall Lane, Birstall, Leicestershire LEA 4DT, England

An author with an extraordinary talent. His writing is good, highly original and full of humour. The result is lots of books with enormous appeal to children. His wife has illustrated many of his books, providing complementary illustrations.

THE CLOTHES HORSE AND OTHER STORIES

Penguin, 1989, 32p. – Pbk. – 0 14 032907 2
Viking Kestrel, 1987, 32p. – 0 670 81267 6
illustrated by Janet Ahlberg

Inventive short stories with superb illustrations. They can be read successfully to younger children, and are equally entertaining for older children to read for themselves. As always, they are fresh and amusing.
Age range: 6–10

HAPPY FAMILIES

Viking Kestrel
Penguin. – Pbk.

A series containing many titles all of the highest quality and versatility. Some are about unusual families, for example a bee-keeper; some are more ordinary, like a plumber or a teacher. They are funny, witty and entertaining. The repetition makes them ideal for children mastering the art of reading, yet all the stories move along at a vigorous pace, making them a real delight to read to younger children. Several different illustrators have been used, which adds to the variety.
Age range: 4–7

JEREMIAH IN THE DARK WOODS

Penguin, 1989, 32p. – Pbk. – 0 14 032811 4
Viking Kestrel, 1986, 48p. – 0 670 40637 6
illustrated by Janet Ahlberg

An unusual story woven round traditional tales like *Peter Pan* and *The Queen of Hearts*. An excellent read for children becoming confident readers, as it has clear print and plentiful illustrations.
Age range: 7–9

TEN IN A BED

Chivers Press, 1990, 168p. – L/P. –
0 7451 1244 7
Penguin, 1990, 96p. – Pbk. – 0 14 032531 X
Viking, 1989, 112p. – 0 670 82042 3

Witty parodies of well loved stories like *Goldilocks* and *The Sleeping Beauty*. Amusingly told, the full impact can be felt only if the original stories are already familiar.
Age range: 8–10

THE VANISHMENT OF THOMAS TULL

Black, 1988. – 0 7136 2999 1
Penguin, 1985, 64p. – Pbk. – 0 14 031804 6
illustrated by Janet Ahlberg

At the age of seven, Thomas started to shrink. His parents, alarmed, tried many and varied cures, some of which involved Thomas in exciting adventures. The book has a racy tone which encourages young readers, and the illustrations are, as always, perfect.
Age range: 7–9

WOOF

Penguin, 1987, 160p. – Pbk. – 0 14 031996 4
Chivers Press, 1987, 208p. – L/P. –
0 7451 0487 8
Viking Kestrel, 1986, 156p. – 0 670 80832 6
illustrated by Fritz Wegner

Eric – an ordinary name for an ordinary boy who turns into an ordinary dog who

loves chocolate buttons and chasing cats. How Eric manages his dual life with the help of his loyal friend Roy makes entertaining reading and became an enjoyable television series.
Age range: 9–11

AIKEN, Joan (Delano)

British. Born Rye, Sussex, 1924.
Daughter of Conrad Aiken, writer; sister
of Jane Aiken Hodge, writer. Educated
Wychwood School, Oxford. Married: 1)
Ronald George Brown, 1945 (died
1955), one son, one daughter; 2) Julius
Goldstein, 1976. Information officer,
editor, copywriter, writer.

Awards: Guardian Award for
Children's Fiction: *The
Whispering Mountain*, 1969

Address: The Hermitage, East Street,
Petworth, West Sussex SU28
0AB, England

Agents: A. M. Heath, 40–42 William
IV Street, London WC2N
4DD, England

Brandt & Brandt, 1501
Broadway, New York City,
New York 10036, USA

An author with a special talent – the
ability to create magical fantasy stories
based firmly on historical reality. She
writes for a wide age range, but at all
levels readers need to be proficient as she
maintains a very high standard of writing.
The stories are excellent for reading
aloud and serialization; some have
become successful television
productions.

ARABEL AND MORTIMER
Cape, 1980, 144p. – 0 224 01765 9
Windrush, 1989, 258p. – L/P. – 1 85089 978 9

In the same series:

MORTIMER SAYS NOTHING AND
OTHER STORIES
Cape, 1985, 160p. – 0 224 02335 7

MORTIMER'S CROSS
Cape, 1983, 148p. – O/P. – 0 224 02108 7

TALES OF ARABEL'S RAVEN
Cape, 1974, 160p. – 0 224 01059 X
all illustrated by Quentin Blake

These collections of stories describing the
adventures of Arabel, her raven and her
long-suffering mother were written
specially for BBC's *Jackanory*. When
published with Quentin Blake's amusing
illustrations, they became very popular.
Some of the stories have since been
published separately in paperback. The
large print and plentiful illustrations
combine to provide an excellent, easy
read for children who need practice in the
art of reading.
Age range: 8–10

FAITHLESS LOLLYBIRD AND OTHER
STORIES
Cape, 1977, 224p. – O/P. – 0 224 01332 7

In the same series:

HARP OF FISHBONES
*Penguin, 1975, 240p. – Pbk, O/P. –
0 14 030729 X*
Cape, 1972, 229p. – 0 224 00666 5

MICE AND MENDELSON
*Penguin, 1981, 112p. – Pbk, O/P. –
0 14 031253 6*
Cape, 1978, 144p. – 0 224 01615 6
illustrated by Babette Cole

SMALL PINCH OF WEATHER
*Lutterworth Press, 1988, 192p. –
0 7188 2696 5*
*Penguin, 1972, 192p. – Pbk, O/P. –
0 14 030544 0*

UP THE CHIMNEY DOWN
Cape, 1984, 272p. – 0 224 02198 2

All collections of short stories of endless
invention and variety. Some are simply
amusing, some scary and some exciting –
all are enjoyable and suitable for reading
aloud to children who are experienced
listeners. They are not for filling in the
odd ten minutes, though they are
pleasurable enough to do so. They are so
well written that they will enrich
children's literary experience and provide
an introduction to the author's full length
novels.
Age range: 8–10

FOG HOUNDS, WIND CAT, SEA MICE
Pan Books, 1987, 75p. – Pbk. – 0 330 29511 X
Macmillan, 1984, 64p. – O/P. – 0 333 36574 7
illustrated by John Lawrence

In the same series:

LAST SLICE OF RAINBOW AND OTHER STORIES
Penguin, 1988, 176p. – Pbk. – 0 14 032301 5
Cape, 1985, 128p. – 0 224 02297 0
illustrated by Margaret Watty

Welcome additions to Joan Aiken's collections of stories, as these are aimed at young readers, while remaining at the same high level of writing as her books for older readers.
Age range: 7–9

GO SADDLE THE SEA
Penguin, 1980, 288p. – Pbk. – 0 14 031155 6
Cape, 1978, 304p. – 0 224 01546 X

In the same series:

BRIDLE THE WIND
Penguin, 1986, 272p. – Pbk, O/P. –
0 14 031896 8
Cape, 1983, 272p. – 0 224 02137 0

THE TEETH OF THE GALE
Penguin, 1990, 256p. – Pbk. – 0 14 032934 X
Cape, 1988, 256p. – 0 224 02531 7
illustrated by Pat Marriot.

A trilogy describing an exciting adventure set in Spain in the early nineteenth century. Felix, the young hero, decides to travel to England, to find his father's relatives when his life is made unbearable for him in his dead mother's ancestral Spanish home. The journey leads him into a variety of dangerous situations which make gripping reading. The unfamiliar Spanish names and the background of political unrest form a barrier for some children which requires a sensitive introduction to overcome, but the initial effort is amply rewarded. Serialized on television.
Age range: 10–12

KINGDOM UNDER THE SEA
Penguin, 1973, 112p. – Pbk. – 0 14 030641 2
Cape, 1971, 112p. 0 224 61882 2

In the same series:

NECKLACE OF RAINDROPS
Penguin, 1975, 128p. – Pbk. – 0 14 030754 0
Cape, 1968, 112p. – 0 224 61462 2

PAST EIGHT O'CLOCK: GOODNIGHT STORIES
Penguin, 1990, 128p. – Pbk. – 0 14 032355 4
Cape, 1986, 128p. – 0 224 02856 1

TALE OF A ONE-WAY STREET
Penguin, 1984, 112p. – Pbk. – 0 14 031700 7
Cape, 1978, 128p. – 0 224 01158 8
all illustrated by Jan Pienkowski

These books are a special treat. The stories are excellent – unusual, magical, fantastical – and the silhouette illustrations add a dimension of their own. They make splendid leisure reading, but they can also be read at a deeper level and provide an entry into successful discussion. To accommodate the large print which makes these books accessible to children who want to read for themselves, the hardback edition is larger than average. The paperback, though smaller, is equally attractive.
Age range: 8–10

THE KITCHEN WARRIORS
Hodder, 1984, 96p. – Pbk, O/P. – 0 340 33517 3
BBC, 1983, 95p. – O/P. – 0 563 20216 5
illustrated by Jo Worth

Also written for *Jackanory*, this collection of modern fairy tales is woven around such household appliances as the vacuum cleaner. The elves who live in or near them appeal to young children. The usual blend of magic and reality makes this a really satisfying read.
Age range: 7–9

MIDNIGHT IS A PLACE
Red Fox, 1991, 288p. – Pbk. – 0 09 979200 1
Cape, 1974, 304p. – O/P. – 0 224 00968 0

The loneliness suffered by many children is a recurring theme in Joan Aiken's books, and forms the basis for this fantasy. Lucas is driven to confess 'I'm lonely', setting in motion an extraordinary train of events which eventually transforms his life. It is a fast moving story punctuated by flashes of humour.
Age range: 11–13

MOON'S REVENGE
Red Fox, 1990, 32p. – Pbk. – 0 09 975010 4
Cape, 1987, 32p. – 0 224 02477 9
illustrated by Alan Lee

An unusual, evocative and haunting picture book. The story is about a small child who throws stones at the moon with terrifying consequences. His courage brings the story to a happy conclusion. The illustrations match the mood and atmosphere of the text to perfection.
Age range: 7–11

SHADOW GUESTS
Penguin, 1982, 176p. – Pbk. – 0 14 031388 5
Cape, 1980, 170p. – 0 224 01797 7

A mystery surrounds Cosmo and his family and the way it is resolved makes an unusual story, full of hidden threats. The climax is just as exciting as the build up.
Age range: 11–13

THE WHISPERING MOUNTAIN
Penguin, 1970. – Pbk, O/P. – 0 14 030460 6
Cape, 1968, 240p. – 0 224 61574 2

Set in Wales and peopled by dwarfs, *The Whispering Mountain* is easy to believe in. Owen, once again a lonely boy, proves himself a worthy opponent of the wicked Marquess. An original plot, told with imagination and humour.
Age range: 10–12

THE WOLVES OF WILLOUGHBY CHASE
Chivers Press, 1986, 272p. – L/P. –
0 7451 0299 9

Hutchinson, 1975, 160p. – O/P. – 0 09 124620 2
Penguin, 1971. – Pbk, O/P. – 0 14 030310 3

In the same series:

BLACK HEARTS IN BATTERSEA
Penguin, 1968, 208p. – Pbk. – 0 14 030345 6
Cape, 1965, 192p. – 0 224 60705 7

NIGHT BIRDS ON NANTUCKET
Penguin, 1969, 176p. – Pbk. – 0 14 030346 4
Cape, 1966, 188p. – 0 224 60687 5

THE STOLEN LAKE
Penguin, 1983, 272p. – Pbk. – 0 14 031505 5
Cape, 1981, 272p. – 0 224 01924 4

THE CUCKOO TREE
Penguin, 1973, 247p. – Pbk. – 0 14 030616 1
Cape, 1971, 256p. – O/P. – 0 224 00514 6

DIDO AND PA
Cape, 1986, 252p. – 0 224 02364 0

Set historically in the first half of eighteenth century England, but in the wholly imaginary reign of King James III, the first book in this series has a curiously topical appeal as the Channel Tunnel has just been completed. Among the first to use it is a pack of wolves, starving and savage, who add to the dangers facing Bonnie when a sinister new governess arrives. This series illustrates Joan Aiken's unsurpassable ability to blend history, fantasy and reality into an exciting and really funny whole. To read it is to have a true literary and life-enriching experience. *The Wolves of Willoughby Chase* is currently popular owing to the success of the film version recently released.
Age range: 10–12

ALCOCK, Vivian (Dolores)

British. Born Worthing, Sussex, 1924. Educated at Devizes High School, Wiltshire; Oxford School of Art. Ambulance driver, Auxiliary Territorial Service, WW II. Married Leon Garfield 1948, one adopted daughter. Artist, secretary.

Address: 59 Wood Lane, Highgate, London N6 5UD, England

Agent: John Johnson Ltd, 45–47 Clerkenwell Green, London EC1R 0HT, England

Vivian Alcock's writing is characterized by an ability to deal with issues fundamental to children while at the same time creating an original and enjoyable story. Her books are exciting enough to be read aloud and to provide material for fruitful discussion.

CUCKOO SISTER
Heinemann, 1988, 160p. – 0 435 12327 0
Chivers Press, 1987, 256p. – L/P. –
0 7451 0586 6
Armada Books, 1986, 160p. – Pbk. –
0 00 672690 9

Kate finds it difficult to adjust to the startling revelation that she is not an only child. It is impossible to accept that Rosie, with her spiky hair and tight skirt, could possibly be related to the quiet, polite Setons. The tensions brought about by this situation are well portrayed. Serialized on television.
Age range: 10–12

THE HAUNTING OF CASSIE PALMER
Armada Books, 1982, 160p. – Pbk, O/P. –
0 00 671895 7
Methuen, 1980. – 0 416 89250 7

Because Cassie's Mum is a medium, Cassie is used to the idea of spirits, but she does not want to follow in her mother's footsteps. To prove she has no 'powers', she tries to summon a spirit, and, to her horror, succeeds. Worse still, she cannot free herself of him. The reader experiences with Cassie the feeling of growing menace until the climax relieves the tension. Cassie is an outcast at school, and suffers agonizingly as she comes to the realization that parents are only human, fallible and unsuccessful. The greatest worry is being faced with a serious situation that is beyond one's ability to cope.
Age range: 10–12

MONSTER GARDEN
Chivers Press, 1990, 200p. – L/P. –
0 7451 1063 0
Armada Books, 1989, 128p. – Pbk. –
0 00 673163 5
Methuen, 1988, 144p. – 0 416 09192 X

A moving account of a young girl who 'grows' a monster, and how she comes to accept responsibility for its welfare. The growth of her feelings is well described, but the seriousness of the situation is relieved by the many flashes of humour which combine to make this a well balanced book. It is an exceptionally difficult story to bring to a satisfactory conclusion and there is room for improvement here, but, on the whole, an excellent read.
Age range: 9–11

THE MYSTERIOUS MR ROSS
Chivers Press, 1988, 232p. – L/P. –
0 7451 0759 1
Methuen, 1987, 128p. – 0 416 01312 0

When Felicity saves Mr Ross from drowning, she basks in the acclaim quite naturally afforded to such a heroine. However, there is something mysterious about him, and Felicity's life is transformed by her efforts to unravel the mystery.
Age range: 10–13

THE STONE WALKERS
Armada Books, 1982, 144p. – Pbk. –
0 00 671976 7
Methuen, 1981, 180p. – 0 416 20700 6

'Poppy Brown . . . was a liar' – thus the riveting opening of this story. A storm breathes life into a statue, setting in motion a chain of events. Told with

humour, the book has a characteristic combination to ensure readers are kept interested to the end. Poppy lies to compensate for her unhappy childhood with many foster mothers. Both Poppy and the adults around her have to face and solve their problems, with the reader a closely involved spectator.
Age range: 9–11

THE SYLVIA GAME
Armada Books, 1984, 160p. – Pbk. –
0 00 672138 9
Methuen, 1982, 154p. – 0 416 21930 6

Emily has many problems. She is convalescing, worried about her over-worked mother, lack of money, and, most of all, her father's strange behaviour. When she meets Oliver and learns about Sylvia and her own resemblance to her, her suspicions about her father increase. The characters are realistically drawn and the story carries the reader swiftly along with a highly satisfactory denouement. Serialized on television.
Age range: 10–12

TRAVELLERS BY NIGHT
Armada Books, 1985, 192p. – Pbk. –
0 00 672383 7
Methuen, 1983, 160p. – 0 416 44830 5

Physical disfigurement is an enormous problem to have to face at any age, but Belle succeeds in coping with it. However, when she learns, first that the circus she works in has to close down, and then that her beloved elephant Tessie has to die, she feels it is all too much. Belle is made of stern stuff and rises to the occasion. In spite of the wealth of unhappiness in this story, there are some light moments of humour. A moving story.
Age range: 9–11

THE TRIAL OF ANNA COTMAN
Mammoth, 1990, 176p. – Pbk. – 0 7497 0444 6
Methuen, 1989, 160p. – 0 416 13952 3

Anna's friendship with Linda involves her with a group of organized bullies at her new school. She tries hard not to be frightened, but when she is put on trial, it proves almost too much for her. Serialized on television.
Age range: 10–12

ALLEN, Judy

British. Born Old Sarum, Wiltshire. Educated Southsea, Hampshire. Editor, freelance writer.

Awards: Whitbread Literary Award: *Awaiting Developments*, 1988 Earthworm Children's Book Award: *Awaiting Developments*, 1989

AWAITING DEVELOPMENTS
Walker Books, 1989, 192p. – Pbk. – 0 7445 1321 9
J. MacRae Books, 1988, 176p. – O/P. – 0 86203 356 X

Although published in paperback as part of the 'Teens' series, this book can be appreciated by younger children, especially now it has been televised. It tells the story of a garden about to be redeveloped, and a shy young girl's attempt to save it.
Age range: 11–13

SOMETHING RARE AND SPECIAL
Walker Books, 1989, 144p. – Pbk. – 0 7445 0846 0
J. MacRae Books, 1985, 128p. – O/P. – 0 86203 216 4

Lyn's life is in turmoil – her father has left home, she has to move house, and therefore has to leave her best friend. Describing how Lyn comes to terms with her changed circumstances, Judy Allen shows readers who may be in a similar dilemma that there is always hope.
Age range: 12–14

TRAVELLING HOPEFULLY
Corgi, 1989, 128p. – Pbk. – 0 552 52514 6
J. MacRae Books, 1987, 128p. – O/P. – 0 86203 267 9

An amusingly told story about Clare, who finds herself unexpectedly travelling round Devon with her young aunt, who is a journalist. They are an ill-assorted pair, but gradually they come to accept each other, largely due to a shared sense of humour. A witty book, full of verbal repartee.
Age range: 12–14

ALLEN, Linda

British. Born Huddersfield, West
Yorkshire. Educated Huddersfield.
Married, three children. Secretary, writer.

Address: 51 Churchfields Road,
             Cubert, Newquay, Cornwall,
             England

LIONEL AND THE SPY NEXT DOOR

Pan Books, 1986, 56p. – Pbk, O/P. –
0 330 29528 4
Hamish Hamilton, 1985, 96p. – O/P. –
0 241 11553 1

In the same series:

LIONEL AND THE LONE WOLF

Penguin, 1990, 128p. – Pbk. – 0 14 034183 8
Hamish Hamilton, 1988, 112p. –
0 241 12511 1

LIONEL'S FINEST HOUR

Pan Books, 1986, 90p. – Pbk. –
0 330 29097 5
Hamish Hamilton, 1984, 128p. – O/P. –
0 241 11329 6

Lionel is a boy who knows his own mind,
and this leads him into a series of really
funny adventures. They are well told,
easy to read and well illustrated – books
full of appeal for young readers.
Age range: 9–11

ANTROBUS, John

British. Born Woolwich, 1933. Educated
Bishop Wordsworth Grammar School,
Salisbury; Selhurst Grammar School;
King Edward Nautical College; Sandhurst
Military Academy. East Surrey Regiment,
1952–55. Married Margaret McCormick
1958, three children. Writer.

Agent: Blanche Martin, 21a St. John's
        Wood High Street, London
        NW8 7NG, England

THE BOY WITH ILLUMINATED
MEASLES
Hodder, 1980, 64p. – Pbk. – 0 340 25360 6
Robson Books, 1978, 64p. – 0 86051 028 X

In the same series:

HELP! I AM A PRISONER IN A
TOOTHPASTE FACTORY
Hodder, 1980, 64p. – Pbk, O/P. –
0 340 25359 2
Robson Books, 1978, 64p. – 0 86051 029 8

RONNIE AND THE GREAT KNITTED
ROBBERY
Hodder, 1984, 64p. – Pbk, O/P. –
0 340 35019 9
Robson Books, 1982, 64p. – 0 86051 180 4

RONNIE AND THE HAUNTED
ROLLS ROYCE
Hodder, 1984, 48p. – Pbk, O/P. –
0 340 33988 8
Robson Books, 1982, 48p. – 0 86051 179 0
all illustrated by Rowan Barnes-Murphy

A series of highly original and very
amusing stories designed to encourage
young readers. Short chapters, plenty of
illustrations, and lots of action make these
an undemanding but satisfying read.
Age range: 8–10

APPIAH, Peggy

British. Born Filkins, Gloucestershire, 1921. Daughter of Sir Stafford Cripps (the politician). Educated Norland Place; Queen's College, London; Maltman's Green, Buckinghamshire; Whitehall Secretarial College. Married Joe E. Appiah, 1953, one son, three daughters. Research assistant, secretary.

Address: PO Box 829, Kumasi, Ashanti, Ghana

Agent: David Higham Assoc. Ltd, 5–8 Lower John Street, London W1R 4HA, England

THE PINEAPPLE CHILD, AND OTHER TALES FROM ASHANTI
Deutsch, 1989, 176p. – Pbk. – 0 233 98371 6
Deutsch, 1969, 172p. – O/P. – 0 233 95927 0

In the same series:

TALES OF AN ASHANTI FATHER
Deutsch, 1987, 158p. – Pbk. – 0 233 98126 8
Deutsch, 1967, 160p. – O/P. – 0 233 95927 0
both illustrated by Mora Dickinson

Excellent collections of good traditional folk tales from Ghana, with universal appeal. The paperback edition of *The Pineapple child* is exceptionally well produced, making it a pleasure to handle. Good quality paper, clear print and effective lino cuts combine to give these stories a perfect setting.
Age range: 7–10

ARKLE, Phyllis

British. Born Chester, 1910. Convent school educated; University of Liverpool. Married. Lives near Reading, Berkshire. Secretary, Director of the family firm, writer.

MAGIC AT MIDNIGHT
Penguin, 1974, 112p. – Pbk. – 0 14 030693 5
Hodder, 1972, 96p. – O/P. – 0 340 04068 8

In the same series:

MAGIC IN THE AIR
Penguin, 1980, 88p. – Pbk. – 0 14 031179 3
Hodder, 1978, 88p. – O/P. – 0 340 22195 X
both illustrated by Mike Cole

Two stories, involving exciting magical happenings, which have great appeal to younger children who are just beginning to read with a certain fluency.
Age range: 7–9

THE RAILWAY CAT
Penguin, 1985, 96p. – Pbk. – 0 14 031660 4
Hodder, 1983, 88p. – O/P. – 0 340 32593 3

In the same series:

THE RAILWAY CAT AND DIGBY
Penguin, 1986, 80p. – Pbk. – 0 14 031836 4
Hodder, 1984, 80p. – O/P. – 0 340 35077 6

THE RAILWAY CAT AND THE HORSE
Penguin, 1988, 96p. – Pbk. – 0 14 032488 7
Hodder, 1987, 89p. – 0 340 38844 7

THE RAILWAY CAT'S SECRET
Penguin, 1987, 96p. – Pbk. – 0 14 032110 1
Hodder, 1985, 88p. – O/P. – 0 340 36743 1
all illustrated by Lynne Byrnes

An excellent series of books about Alfie, the cat who lives at the railway station, in spite of the porter's attempts to get rid of him. The stories are basic, but well constructed, and full of humour. They are not too long, so young readers are not deterred, yet they are substantial enough to provide a satisfying read. Recently published in one volume by Puffin as *The Adventures of the Railway Cat.* (Penguin, 1990, 309p. – Pbk. – 0 14 034515 9)
Age range: 8–10

ASHLEY, Bernard

British. Born London, 1935. Educated
Roan School, Blackheath, London; Sir
Joseph Williamson's School, Rochester,
Kent; Trent Park College of Education,
Certificate of Education; Cambridge
Institute of Education, Diploma in
Primary Education. Royal Air Force,
1953–55. Married Iris Holbrook, 1958,
three sons. Teacher.

Awards: Children's Rights Workshop
Other Award: *The Trouble
with Donovan Croft*, 1976

Address: 128 Heathwood Gardens,
London SE7 8ER, England

Having worked with young people,
Bernard Ashley is well placed to know
the issues that currently concern them.
He takes one or more of these issues and
weaves gripping stories around them. He
uses words sparingly and to great effect,
so his books are not an easy read, but
they have great appeal to young readers.
They are tough, set firmly in a harsh
reality that many children are very
familiar with. Many of them concern
runaway children who can no longer face
a person or situation. All are concerned
with growing up and learning to cope,
and all of them offer the reader more than
just a couple of hours' entertainment.

ALL MY MEN
*Penguin, 1979, 160p. – Pbk. – 0 14 031131 9
OUP, 1977, 160p. – 0 19 271390 6*

The problem of trying to settle into a new
school is not exactly an original theme,
but Paul's method of handling this
situation, by trying to get picked for the
football team, seems a good solution.
Learning to deal with the bully who
'controls' the team is a different matter. A
book offering hope to every child who
suffers at the hands of older children.
Age range: 10–12

BAD BLOOD
*Walker Books, 1989, 160p. – Pbk. –
0 7445 0848 7*

*J. MacRae Books, 1988, 176p. – O/P. –
0 86203 316 0*

Determined to save his father, Ritchie sets
out to find the missing brother. Slowly,
with the help of Sadie, he unravels the
mystery that surrounds his father's family.
Intriguing.
Age range: 12–14

A BIT OF GIVE AND TAKE
*Corgi, 1986, 96p. – Pbk. – 0 552 52348 8
Hamish Hamilton, 1984, 96p. – O/P. –
0 241 11301 6
illustrated by Trevor Stubley*

In the same series:

DINNER LADIES DON'T COUNT
*Penguin, 1984, 96p. – Pbk, also including
'Linda's Lie'. – 0 14 031593 4
J. MacRae Books, 1981, 48p. – O/P. –
0 86203 017 X
illustrated by Janet Duchesne*

I'M TRYING TO TELL YOU
*Penguin, 1982, 80p. – Pbk. – 0 14 031337 0
Kestrel Books, 1981, 80p. – O/P. –
0 7226 5725 0
illustrated by Lyn Jones*

YOUR GUESS IS AS GOOD AS MINE
*Corgi, 1987, 80p. – Pbk. – 0 552 52450 6
J. MacRae Books, 1983, 56p. – O/P. –
0 86203 134 6
illustrated by David Parkins*

High quality stories all written for the
young reader just beginning to read full-
length books. The plots are simple, but
well constructed, with their fair share of
humour.
Age range: 7–9

BREAK IN THE SUN
*OUP, 1983, 190p. – 0 19 271476 7
Penguin, 1981, 192p. – Pbk. – 0 14 031341 9*

Like many children today, Patsy has a
terrible life with her new step-father.
When an opportunity to escape presents
itself, she doesn't hesitate. The story of
what happens to her, and the eventual
pursuit by her step-father, keep the
reader engrossed to a very satisfying end.
The book made a very successful
television drama.
Age range: 10–12

DODGEM

Collins, 1983, 222p. – 0 00 330004 8
Penguin, 1983, 224p. – Pbk, O/P. –
0 14 031477 6

Simon has a lot to cope with. He is grieving for his mother; his father suffers from severe depression and cannot be left alone, so Simon stays away from school. This eventually lands him in assessment, where he meets Rose, as tough as they come. Together, they run away and join a travelling fair, where life is harsh indeed. A sensitive novel for young secondary school readers. It will help those children who, like Simon, have more than their fair share of difficulties, and will also give more fortunate children some insight into what life can be like for others.
Age range: 12–14

A KIND OF WILD JUSTICE

OUP, 1989, 192p. – 0 19 271617 4
Penguin, 1988, 192p. – Pbk. – 0 14 032745 2

For four years, Ronnie had lived in fear that, if his father failed to please the master criminals he worked for, he himself would be severely punished. When his father is arrested and his mother abandons him, he feels certain that life 'in care' can only get worse, and he is right. In such a situation a happy ending would be unrealistic, but a satisfying ending is acceptable, and that is what Ronnie achieves, while offering the reader a chance to understand

themselves and others better.
Age range: 11–13

TERRY ON THE FENCE

OUP, 1986, 208p. – 0 19 271537 2
Penguin, 1978, 256p. – Pbk. – 0 14 031092 4
illustrated by Charles Keeping

Self-preservation is a very strong instinct. When faced with a tough gang of hostile boys, fear makes Terry cooperate, however reluctantly. He becomes more and more involved in wrong-doing, until he feels he can no longer cope. Such webs of dishonesty exist in every sphere of life, and ordinary, decent people like Terry are often affected by them. An exciting and compelling read, and an excellent television drama.
Age range: 11–13

THE TROUBLE WITH DONOVAN CROFT

OUP, 1980, 162p. – 0 19 277101 9
Penguin, 1977, 192p. – Pbk. – 0 14 030974 8
illustrated by Fermin Rocker

Donovan's short life has been so traumatic that he has decided that he will not talk any more. This makes life difficult for his new foster family, since no-one can penetrate this defensive barrier. The events in the story move rapidly to the conclusion, with Donovan's silence skilfully woven into the narrative. It is not quite all 'doom and gloom' – the reader's heart is allowed a little lift at the end.
Age range: 10–12

B

BAILLIE, Allan

Scottish. Born Prestwick, Scotland, 1943. Moved to Australia, 1950. Married Agnes Chow, 1972, one son, one daughter. Reporter, writer.

Awards: Kathleen Fidler Award: *Adrift*, 1983
         IBBY Honour Award: *Riverman*, 1988

Address: 49 Prince Alfred Parade, Newport, NSW 2106, Australia

ADRIFT

Mammoth, 1989, 112p. – Pbk. – 0 7497 0016 5
Blackie, 1989, 144p. – 0 216 92717 X
J. Murray, 1988, 112p. – 0 7195 4511 0

A powerful and realistic story about two children playing a harmless game in an old crate by the sea. Suddenly they find themselves in the grip of a strong current rushing out to sea, and fear overwhelms them. Their efforts to maintain a sense of proportion in the face of escalating danger are laudable. The fate of the cat is hard to believe, but another upset would be too much for the hard-pressed children, and for the empathizing reader.
Age range: 9–12

EAGLE ISLAND

Penguin, 1989, 144p. – Pbk. – 0 14 034045 9
Blackie, 1987, 144p. –0 216 92096 5

The plot is based on the difference between two characters – the spoilt Lew, and a petty criminal, Col. Thrown together on a deserted island and unable to resolve their differences, hostilities commence. Exciting and undemanding.
Age range: 10–12

LITTLE BROTHER

Methuen, 1988, 144p. – Pbk, O/P. – 0 416 08302 1

Collins, 1987, 144p. – 0 00 330041 2
illustrated by Elizabeth Honey

Set in Kampuchea, this book paints a realistic portrait of war, without glamour and without heroes, but with a powerful message of harsh times. Many children have had to suffer the various hard consequences of war. This is the story of two brothers separated while trying to escape. Their efforts to get together provide a suspense-filled drama, maintained to the very end.
Age range: 10–12

MEGAN'S STAR

Penguin, 1990, 144p. – Pbk. – 0 14 034046 7
Blackie, 1988, 128p. – 0 216 92390 5

A book of many facets, culminating in a well founded whole. Set in Australia, yet not specifically so, it concerns Megan who is struggling to come to terms with her father's sudden departure. She gradually becomes aware that she is different from 'normal' people – just how different is crystallized when a voice inside her head leads her to rescue the voice's owner, Kel, a boy with similar powers to hers. A well produced book with clear print, ensuring that young readers can cope with this complex, exciting story.
Age range: 10–12

RIVERMAN

Blackie, 1986, 144p. – O/P. – 0 216 91861 8

Tim felt he had proved himself when he helped with the rescue down the mine. When he accompanies his uncle up river, however, he begins to wonder just how tough he has to be. Allan Baillie has created an excellent character in Tim.
Age range: 10–12

BANKS, Lynne Reid

British. Born London, 1929. Educated in Canada where she was evacuated during WW II; Italia Centre Stage School, London; Royal Academy of Dramatic Art, London. Married Chaim Stephenson (the sculptor), 1965, three sons. Actress, teacher, writer. Lived in Israel 1963–71.

Agent: Watson Little Ltd, 26 Charing Cross Road, London WC2H 0DG, England

A capable writer of modern fantasy, Lynne Reid Banks can draw readers effortlessly into a make-believe world. The stories are accessible to less able readers, as linguistically they are not too demanding.

FAIRY REBEL

Cornerstone Books, 1989. – L/P. –
1 55736 124 X
Grafton Books, 1987, 128p. – Pbk. –
0 583 30963 1
Dent, 1985, 128p. – O/P. – 0 460 6178 X
illustrated by William Gaunt

Although slow to start, once launched, this fairy story quickly becomes as exciting as any traditional fairy story. Friendship between the fairy world and adult humans is rare, and the resulting dramatic confrontation puts a child's life at risk. Very easy to read.
Age range: 8–10

THE FARTHEST AWAY MOUNTAIN

Armada Books, 1988, 144p. – Pbk. –
0 00 672998 3
Abelard–Schuman, 1976, 142p. – O/P. –
0 200 72461 4
illustrated by Victor Ambrus

Using the well tried recipe of a young girl encountering and bravely defeating evil during a difficult journey is a successful ploy. Girls will find much to identify with in the character of Dakin, who dreams of a prince, but finds happiness elsewhere.
Age range: 9–11

I, HOUDINI: THE AUTOBIOGRAPHY OF A SELF-EDUCATED HAMSTER

Armada Books, 1989, 128p. – Pbk. –
0 00 673363 8
Mayflower, 1981, 128p. – Pbk. – 0 583 30482 6
Dent, 1978, 120p. – 0 460 06873 3
illustrated by Terry Riley

Amusing, anecdotal episodes about a hamster who refuses to be caged. It is told in the first person, occasioning many asides which are irritating. Despite this, the book will be hugely enjoyed by the many hamster-owning readers.
Age range: 9–11

THE INDIAN IN THE CUPBOARD

Chivers Press, 1987, 280p. – L/P. –
0 7451 0625 0
Mayflower, 1981, 160p. – Pbk. – 0 583 30461 3
Dent, 1980, 160p. – 0 460 06992 6
illustrated by Robin Jacques

In the same series:

THE RETURN OF THE INDIAN

Chivers Press, 1989, 248p. – L/P. –
0 7451 0960 8
Armada Books, 1988, 160p. – Pbk. –
0 00 673052 3
Dent, 1986, 144p. – 0 460 06239 5
illustrated by William Geldert

THE SECRET OF THE INDIAN

Collins, 1991, 144p. – Pbk. – 0 00 673505 3
Chivers Press, 1990, 224p. – L/P. –
0 7451 1232 3
Collins, 1989, 192p. – 0 00 184746 5

Well-sustained fantasies described with wit and the faultless attention to detail which is necessary to make the fantasy world live for the reader. Omri's old cupboard has the magical property of breathing life into plastic toys. The way he comes to understand his responsibility for another life completely dependent on him makes exciting reading.
Age range: 9–11

MAURA'S ANGEL

Penguin, 1985, 128p. – Pbk. – 0 14 031842 9
Dent 1984, 128p. – O/P. – 0 460 06152 6
illustrated by Robin Jacques

An attempt to simplify the situation in

Northern Ireland, to make it accessible to children, but the result is a little too bland. Nevertheless, this is an enjoyable and optimistic story which has much to offer all children who find themselves enduring a harsh life at home, and who would benefit from a little angelic interference.
Age range: 9–11

MELUSINE: A MYSTERY

Penguin, 1990, 192p. – Pbk. – 0 14 032793 2
Hamish Hamilton, 1988, 192p. – 0 241 12548 0

Roger, on holiday in France, feels that he alone can help the strange girl who comes with the château. Gradually he becomes involved with the mystery that surrounds her. Good ending.
Age range: 12–14

BARRY, Margaret Stuart (née Bell)

British. Born Darlington, Co. Durham, 1927. Educated at schools in Richmond, Yorkshire; Teacher Training College, Liverpool, Diploma in Education. Married Pierce Barry, 1957, two daughters, one son. Teacher.

Address: 5 Belvidere Road, Liverpool L8 3TF, England

Agent: Curtis Brown, 162–168 Regent Street, London W1R 5TB, England

SIMON AND THE WITCH
Armada Books, 1978, 80p. – Pbk, O/P. – 0 00 671415 3
Collins, 1976, 78p. – 0 00 184749 X

In the same series:

THE RETURN OF THE WITCH
Armada Books, 1979, 80p. – Pbk. – 0 00 671599 0
Collins, 1978, 80p. – O/P. – 0 00 184702 3

THE WITCH AND THE HOLIDAY CLUB
Armada Books, 1988, 96p. – Pbk. – 0 00 673262 3
Collins, 1988, 96p. – 0 00 184922 0

THE WITCH OF MONOPOLY MANOR
Armada Books, 1981, 80p. – Pbk. – 0 00 671788 8
Collins, 1980, 80p. – O/P. – 0 00 184931 X

THE WITCH ON HOLIDAY
Armada Books, 1984, 80p. – Pbk. – 0 00 672300 4
Collins, 1983, 80p. – 0 00 184932 8

THE WITCH V. I. P.
Armada Books, 1988, 96p. – Pbk. – 0 00 672987 8
Collins, 1987, 96p. – 0 00 184955 7

SIMON AND THE WITCH IN SCHOOL
Armada Books, 1988, 96p. – Pbk. – 0 00 673238 0
Collins, 1987, 96p. – 0 00 184874 7

The first book in this series introduces the reader to an absurd but likeable witch who is befriended by Simon, an eminently sensible little boy. In this and subsequent stories, they come together in a variety of unlikely situations, 'helped' by George, the unfortunate cat. The stories are written in an easy-to-read, flowing style, and contain plenty of humour, both verbal and slapstick. They provide a not too taxing and very satisfactory read. Since their successful adaptation into a television series, they are among the most popular stories with children.
Age range: 8–10

BAWDEN, Nina (née Mabey)

British. Born London, 1925. Educated Ilford County High School, London; Somerville College, Oxford, B.A., M.A. (Modern Greats); Fellow of the Royal Society of Literature. Married: 1) H. W. Bawden, 1946, two sons (one deceased); 2) A. S. Kark, 1954, one daughter, two step-daughters. Reviewer, writer.

Awards: Guardian Award, Children's Fiction: *Peppermint Pig*, 1976

Address: 22 Noel Road, London N1 8HA, England

Nina Bawden has been writing since the 1950s, and is well established as an author of quality for both adults and children. Her books are not for readers lacking fluency, but the storylines are always excellent, often very exciting, and written with humour and a deep understanding of, and faith in, a child's capabilities.

CARRIE'S WAR

Chivers Press, 1985, 248p. – L/P. – 0 7451 0129 1
Penguin, 1974, 144p. – Pbk. – 0 14 030689 7
Gollancz, 1973, 128p. – 0 575 01631 0

Carrie and her younger brother were evacuated from war-torn London to Wales, where they tried hard to combat their natural home-sickness and fit into their new surroundings. Then Carrie does a terrible thing and has to leave the village. Not until she is an adult and takes her own children back for a visit does she learn the final outcome of her action. Serialized for television.
Age range: 10–12

THE FINDING

Chivers Press, 1989, 216p. – L/P. – 0 7451 0922 5
Penguin, 1987, 144p. – Pbk. – 0 14 032023 7
Gollancz, 1985, 128p. – 0 575 03618 4

The drama of this book lies in the skilful handling of events and feelings that can beset an ordinary family. Alex, abandoned by his young mother just after he was born, celebrates his 'Finding Day' rather than guessing his natural birthday. He feels happy and secure with his adoptive family until an old lady dies, leaving him all her possessions. This changes his life to such an extent that he feels he has no choice but to run away, an action which never solves anything. Serialized on television.
Age range: 10–12

A HANDFUL OF THIEVES

Chivers Press, 1990, 232p. – L/P. 0 7451 1247 1
Penguin, 1970. – Pbk. – 0 14 030472 X
Gollancz, 1967, 128p. – 0 575 00152 6

What is a thief? Working on the premise 'if you can't beat 'em, join 'em, then perhaps you can beat 'em!', the five children decide to take the law into their own hands. After all, what could be more important than catching the thief who deprived Gran of her savings? This decision leads to danger of an unexpected degree when the Death Wall threatens to live up to its name. The way the children work together to the exclusion of all adults is reminiscent of Enid Blyton's 'Famous Five'!
Age range: 10–12

KEEPING HENRY

Chivers Press, 1990, 152p. – L/P. – 0 7451 1064 9
Penguin, 1989, 128p. – Pbk. – 0 14 032805 X
Gollancz, 1988, 128p. – 0 575 04256 7
illustrated by Ian Newsham

On a superficial level, a touching story about a baby squirrel, brought up as a pet and loved by the whole family, which finally attains freedom in the wild again. However, there are many issues involved – the shadow cast over the lives of ordinary families by war, coming to terms with bereavement and loss, learning to cope with the inevitable changes that life brings. A good quality, highly satisfying book.
Age range: 10–12

KEPT IN THE DARK

Penguin, 1974, 144p. – Pbk. – 0 14 031550 0
Gollancz, 1982, 160p. – 0 575 03113 1

The combination of an intriguing title and excellent jacket gives a good introduction to an exciting story which holds the reader to the very surprising end. Much of the appeal is provided by the interaction of the characters.
Age range: 10–12

ON THE RUN

Penguin, 1967, 192p. – Pbk. – 0 14 030337 5
Gollancz, 1964, 208p. – 0 575 00634 X

A true adventure story – in order to foil the plan to kidnap Thomas, the son of a Prime Minister, Ben organizes an escape plan. It has to expand to include Lil, a refugee from the 'welfare lady', who wants to put her into care. The three children hide in a cave, and find they need all their resourcefulness in order to survive. A sympathetic view of the way children can manage on their own if they have to.
Age range: 10–12

THE PEPPERMINT PIG

Chivers Press, 1987, 264p. – L/P. –
0 7451 0447 9
Penguin, 1977, 160p. – Pbk. – 0 14 030944 6
Gollancz, 1975, 192p. – 0 575 01927 1

A humorous and delightful story about a pig who lives in a house as part of the family. He is very mischievous and helps to keep the children cheerful even in the midst of all their troubles. A sensitive portrayal of family life.
Age range: 9–12

REBEL ON A ROCK

Penguin, 1980, 128p. – Pbk. – 0 14 031123 8
Gollancz, 1978, 160p. – 0 575 02420 8

Jo feels embarrassed by her odd family. She looks so different with her red hair; since her re-marriage, her Mum is now called Mrs Sandwich, and finally Mr Sandwich is no oil painting. When they go on holiday to Ithaca, she feels very disappointed with the place. But when she makes friends with Alexis, she comes face to face with alarmingly real problems. Coping with these makes an exciting story.
Age range: 10–13

THE ROBBERS

Chivers Press, 1986, 216p. – L/P. –
0 7451 0328 6
Penguin, 1981, 144p. – Pbk. – 0 14 031317 6
Gollancz, 1979, 144p. – 0 575 02695 2

The strength of this story, as so often with Nina Bawden, is the interaction between the main characters. Philip lives with his grandmother in a safe, happy, comfortable routine. Darcy is street-wise and daring. However unlikely, the boys form a close friendship, but this brings difficulties for Philip, who has to make decisions which will change his life.
Age range: 10–12

RUNAWAY SUMMER

Penguin, 1972, 160p. – Pbk. – 0 14 030539 4
Gollancz, 1969, 176p. – 0 575 00337 5

Feeling fed-up at home, Mary is ready for anything. Finding Krishna, an illegal immigrant, seems to be the answer to a prayer. Simon helps him to hide while Mary undertakes to search for his family in London. An enjoyable story – girls will really identify with Mary.
Age range: 10–12

THE SECRET PASSAGE

Penguin, 1979, 160p. – Pbk. – 0 14 031166 1
Gollancz, 1968, 192p. – 0 575 00202 6

The secret passage is an excellent cure for the homesickness and grief which Mary, John and Ben are all suffering from. Trying to unravel the mystery keeps their minds occupied and gives their hearts time to heal and adjust. Told with humour, this story is exciting right to the end.
Age range: 10–12

SQUIB

Collins, 1983, 127p. – 0 00 330011 0
Penguin, 1973, 112p. – Pbk. – 0 14 030581 5
Gollancz, 1971, 128p. – 0 575 00665 X
illustrated by Shirley Hughes

Kate came across Squib in the park, and

was moved by his loneliness. She determined to find out who he was and why he seemed so unhappy. When she succeeds, she can scarcely believe his appalling circumstances. A shockingly realistic description of the home life of a cruelly ill-treated child and the bravery of more fortunate children with a will to help.
Age range: 10–12

THE WHITE HORSE GANG
Penguin, 1972, 160p. – Pbk. – 0 14 030508 4
Gollancz, 1966, 160p. – 0 575 00841 5

A highly readable story about a gang of children who need a lot of money for a good cause, and who set about kidnapping a rich boy, hoping for a substantial ransom. The plot backfires and they find themselves in Gibbet Wood, facing a terrible danger which needs all their courage.
Age range: 10–12

THE WITCH'S DAUGHTER
Chivers Press, 1988, 288p. – L/P. –
0 7451 0654 4
Penguin, 1969, 160p. – Pbk. – 0 14 030407 X
Gollancz, 1966, 160p. – 0 575 00177 1

Nina Bawden has a special gift for describing lonely, unhappy children. Perdita is an orphan and, because her mother was regarded as a witch, everyone avoids her until Janey arrives. Being blind, Janey understands the problems of being 'different'. She shows Perdita the joys and sorrows that friendship brings. This relationship is woven around discovering hidden treasure, but the adventure story is secondary to the story of Perdita's blossoming.
Age range: 10–12

BERG, Leila (Rita)

British. Born Salford, Lancashire, 1917.
Educated Manchester High School;
London University. Married 1940, one
son, one daughter. Children's book
editor.

Awards: Eleanor Farjeon Award, 1974

Address: Alice's Cottage, Brook Street,
            Wivenhoe, near Colchester,
            Essex CO7 9DS, England

A writer who has much experience and
success with writing for the very young.
Her stories are such that they do not date,
but appeal to successive generations.

BOX FOR BENNY

Magnet Books, 1983, 92p. – Pbk, O/P. –
0 416 45350 3
Hodder, 1970, 91p. – O/P. – 0 340 03207 3
illustrated by Jillian Willett

At any age it is a terrible thing to feel an
outcast, but when very young, it is
hardest of all to bear. Benny is not
allowed to play with the other children
because he does not possess a box. How
he succeeds in obtaining this all-
important item makes highly entertaining
reading. It is just as meaningful today as
when first published.
Age range: 5–7

THE LITTLE CAR

Magnet Books, 1985, 96p. – Pbk, O/P. –
0 416 51860 5
Penguin, 1974, 96p. – Pbk, O/P. –
0 14 030682 X
Methuen, 1972, 96p. – 0 416 20250 0
illustrated by Gerald Rose

In the same series:

LITTLE PETE STORIES

Magnet Books, 1984, 96p. – Pbk. –
0 416 48400 X
Methuen, 1952, 78p. – 0 416 11760 0
illustrated by Peggy Fortnum

TALES FOR TELLING

Magnet Books, 1984, 96p. – Pbk, O/P. –
0 416 49280 0
Methuen, 1983, 96p. – O/P. – 0 416 25080 7
illustrated by Danuta Lashowska

TIME FOR ONE MORE

Methuen, 1988, 96p. – Pbk. – 0 416 07452 9
Methuen, 1986, 96p. – 0 416 53440 6
illustrated by Gerald Rose

TOPSY TURVY TALES

Magnet Books, 1984, 112p. – Pbk. –
0 416 45970 6
illustrated by George Him

Collections of short stories and poems for
younger children. Varied, and with a
timeless appeal, they are just the right
length for bedtime stories.
Age range: 4–6

MY DOG SUNDAY

Penguin, 1979, 80p. – Pbk. – 0 14 031083 5
Hamish Hamilton, 1968, 94p. – O/P. –
0 241 01558 8
illustrated by Peter Edwards

A very sensitive story about Ben who
wants a dog more than anything else in
the world. However, living in a high-rise
flat makes this impossible. There is no
easy answer to this problem! Simple
sentences and lots of illustrations make
this an easy book for children who can
read, but who require good, interesting
material to encourage them.
Age range: 7–9

BERRY, James

British. Born Prospect, Jamaica, 1925. Educated at night school and public libraries in England. Married 1948. Overseas telegraphist, Post Office, 1951–77. Writer.

Awards: C. Day Lewis Fellowship
Smarties Prize: *A Thief in the Village*, 1987
Signal Poetry Award: *When I dance*, 1989

Address: C/o Hamish Hamilton, 27 Wrights Lane, London W8 5TZ, England

ANANCY – SPIDERMAN

Walker Books, 1989, 128p. – Pbk. – 0 7445 1311 1
Walker Books, 1988, 128p. – O/P. – 0 7445 0793 6
illustrated by Joseph Olubo

Caribbean folk tales about Anancy the wily spiderman who outwits everyone. Very popular with children.
Age range: 7–10

A THIEF IN THE VILLAGE AND OTHER STORIES

Windrush, 1989, 124p. – L/P. – 1 85089 971 1
Penguin, 1989, 112p. – Pbk. – 0 14 032679 0
Hamish Hamilton, 1987, 144p. – 0 241 12011 X

An excellent collection of short stories so full of atmosphere that the reader feels the heat, smells the cooking, and experiences the fear. Set in the author's native Jamaica, each story vividly portrays children and their view of the world around them in such a way as to cause the reader to query what is happening, not just in their own lives, but in the world generally. A well deserved prize-winner.
Age range: 11–13

BIEGEL, Paul (Johannes)

Dutch. Born Bussum, the Netherlands, 1925. Married, two children.

Awards: Best Children's Book of the
           Year, Holland: *King of the*
           Copper Mountains, 1965
           Nienke van Hichhum Prize for
           Children's Literature, 1973
           Starte Prize, 1974

Address: Keizersgracht 227,
           Amsterdam, The Netherlands

Paul Biegel's interest in, and knowledge of, traditional fairy stories is very evident, and enables him to produce high quality books which are fresh and traditional at the same time.

CROCODILE MAN
Dent, 1982, 96p. – O/P. – 0 460 06091 0
illustrated by Eva Jarnerud

A collection of traditional stories re-told in Paul Biegel's inimitable style.
Age range: 8–10

THE DWARFS OF NOSEGAY
Penguin, 1980, 128p. – Pbk. – 0 14 031217 X
Blackie, 1978, 125p. – O/P. – 0 216 90452 8
illustrated by Babs van Wely

In the same series:

THE FATTEST DWARF OF NOSEGAY
Blackie, 1980, 128p. – O/P. – 0 216 90879 5

VIRGIL NOSEGAY AND THE CAKE HUNT
Blackie, 1981, 128p. – O/P. – 0 216 91088 9

VIRGIL NOSEGAY AND THE HUPMOBILE
Blackie, 1983, 128p. – O/P. – 0 216 91372 1

VIRGIL NOSEGAY AND THE WELLINGTON BOOTS
Blackie, 1984, 128p. – O/P. – 0 216 914957

A popular series of stories about a group of dwarfs and their adventures in the world of 'giants' – alias humans. Full of wry humour, and attractively produced.
Age range: 8–10

THE ELEPHANT PARTY
Kestrel Books, 1977, 112p. – O/P. –
0 7226 5289 5
illustrated by Babs van Wely

A collection of magical stories which are excellent for reading aloud as well as for children to read alone.
Age range: 8–10

THE KING OF COPPER MOUNTAIN
Dent, 1977, 176p. – Pbk, O/P. – 0 460 02742 5
Collins, 1973, 160p. – Pbk, O/P. –
0 00 670480 8
Dent, 1968, 176p. – O/P. – 0 460 05746 4
illustrated by Babs van Wely

Aimed at younger children, this is an excellent introduction to the fantasy genre. In a race against time, the Wonder Doctor searches for a potion to cure the dying King. Each day, the animals come to tell the King stories to ensure his heart keeps beating. The stories they tell are varied – happy, sad, moving. Reading them will keep children's attention from beginning to end.
Age range: 9–11

BLISHEN, Edward

British. Born Whetstone, Middlesex, 1920. Educated Queen Elizabeth Grammar School, Barnet. Married Nancy Smith, 1948, two sons. Teacher, writer.

Awards: Library Association Carnegie Medal (with Leon Garfield): *The God Beneath the Sea*, 1970

Address: 12 Bartrams Lane, Hadley Wood, Barnet, London EN4 0EH, England

A TREASURY OF STORIES FOR FIVE YEAR OLDS
Kingfisher Books, 1989, 160p. – 0 86272 427 9

In the same series:

A TREASURY OF STORIES FOR SIX YEAR OLDS
Kingfisher Books, 1988, 160p. – 0 86272 330 2

A TREASURY OF STORIES FOR SEVEN YEAR OLDS
Kingfisher Books, 1988, 160p. – 0 86272 331 0
all illustrated by Patricia Ludlow

Written in conjunction with his wife, these are really excellent collections of stories, as can be expected from such an experienced couple. They combine traditional and modern stories, and are beautifully illustrated. The clear print on beautiful paper makes them lovely books to be read over and over.
Age range: 5–7

cf. BYARS, B.

BLUME, Judy (née SUSSMAN)

American. Born Elizabeth, New Jersey, 1938. Educated New York University, B.S. in Education. Married 1) John M. Blume, 1959 (divorced), one daughter, one son; 2) Thomas A. Kitchens, 1976 (divorced); 3) George Cooper, 1987, one step-daughter.

Agent: C/o Claire Smith, Harold Ober Associates, 40 East 49th Street, New York City, New York 10017, USA

Undoubtedly one of the most popular authors writing today, and thereby meriting a place. Girls feel that she understands their problems without criticizing them. Her books are written in a chatty style which breaks down the barriers normally felt between maturing children and adults. It is a pity that the understanding she displays is not accompanied by a similar level of literary merit. Her characters tend to be bland, and the plots sketchy.

ARE YOU THERE, GOD? IT'S ME, MARGARET
Chivers Press, 1985, 192p. – L/P, O/P. –
0 7451 0130 5
Pan Books, 1980, 128p. – Pbk. – 0 330 26244 0
Gollancz, 1978, 160p. – 0 575 02433 X

Several common problems are dealt with – moving house and trying to fit in with a new set of people; a mix of religions within the same family; Margaret's overwhelming desire to need a bra.
Age range: 10–12

BLUBBER
Cornerstone Books, 1989. – L/P. –
1 55736 025 1
Pan Books, 1981, 128p. – Pbk. – 0 330 26329 3
Heinemann, 1980, 126p. – O/P. – 0 434 92882 8

The problems of overweight children and the bullying they often attract is the subject of this novel. Of necessity it contains many unpleasant incidents which are not dealt with very satisfactorily. Coming from the pen of someone who has a receptive audience, suggesting a more positive way of coping with this situation would have been preferable to the wishy-washy 'solutions' actually on offer.
Age range: 10–12

IGGIE'S HOUSE
Chivers Press, 1989, 160p. – L/P. –
0 7451 0887 3
Pan Books, 1982, 112p. – Pbk. – 0 330 26682 9
Heinemann, 1981, 112p. – 0 434 92884 4

This book uses the problems that can arise when a black family moves into an all-white street as the basis for a rather slight story.
Age range: 9–11

OTHERWISE KNOWN AS SHEILA THE GREAT
Pan Books, 1980, 128p. – Pbk. – 0 330 26051 0
Bodley Head, 1979, 128p. – 0 370 30170 6

Sheila is afraid of many things, including life, and suffers accordingly. Full of trepidation, she goes to Summer Camp where she meets Mouse, who is a yo-yo champion. Life takes a turn for the better.
Age range: 9–11

TALES OF A FOURTH GRADE NOTHING
Pan Books, 1991, 160p. – Pbk. – 0 330 69935 0
Chivers Press, 1988, 160p. – L/P. –
0 7451 0722 2
Bodley Head, 1979, 128p. – 0 370 30171 4

In the same series:

SUPERFUDGE
Pan Books, 1991, 144p. – Pbk. –
0 330 69936 9
Chivers Press, 1987, 216p. – L/P. –
0 7451 0488 6
Bodley Head, 1980, 128p. – 0 370 30358 X

Peter has problems with his little brother, Fudge, and some of them are serious. In the sequel, the arrival of a new baby increases the problems. Run-of-the-mill family stories.
Age range: 9–11

BOND, (Thomas) Michael

British. Born Newbury, Berkshire, 1926.
Educated Presentation College, Reading.
Royal Air Force, 1943–44, Middlesex
Regiment, British Army, 1944–47.
Married 1) Brenda May Johnson, 1950
(divorced 1981), one daughter, one son;
2) Susan Marfrey Rogers, 1981.
Cameraman, director of Paddington &
Co. (Films) Ltd, writer.

Address: 22 Maida Avenue, London
W2 1SR, England

Agent: Harvey Unna & Stephen
Durbridge Ltd, 24–32 Pottery
Lane, London W11 4LZ,
England

This author's name has become almost
synonymous with his creation
Paddington Bear, who is a firm favourite
with children all over the world. There
are many versions available, from pop-up
books for infants to full-length novels.
However, there are other equally
enjoyable novels by him. The following
list gives some of the best available for
the age range covered by this book.

THE PADDINGTON LIBRARY
*Collins, selected titles by Hutchinson and
Crocodile Books. Selected titles by Windrush
Large Print Children's Books.*

A new version of the original stories, with
an attractive cover and clear print. It
retains the original Peggy Fortnum
illustrations, which are an integral part of
the Paddington tradition.
Age range: 8–10

FONTANA YOUNG LIONS
*Collins, selected titles by Armada Books and Pan
Books, Pbk.*

A paperback version of the same
collections of stories, also attractively
produced.
Age range: 8–10

OLGA DA POLGA
*Longmans
Penguin, Pbk.*

A series of stories about a larger-than-life
hamster, whose adventures are
recounted with the same dry humour as
the Paddington stories. They are
enjoyable and amusing, and provide an
excellent read, but have not achieved
quite the same popularity as Paddington.
Age range: 8–10

PARSLEY THE LION
*BBC
Collins or Penguin, Pbk.*

Parsley first became popular when he
appeared on television, after which
demand for the books increased.
Age range: 5–7

BOSTON, Lucy (Marie, née Wood)

British. Born Southport, Lancashire, 1892. Educated Downs School, Seaford, Sussex; Somerville College, Oxford. Nurse in France in WW I. Married 1917 (dissolved 1935), one son.

Awards: Library Association Carnegie Medal: *A Stranger at Green Knowe*, 1961

Address: The Manor, Hemingford Grey, Huntingdon PE18 9BN, England

THE CHILDREN OF GREEN KNOWE
Chivers Press, 1987, 232p. – L/P. –
0 7451 0626 9
Penguin, 1975, 160p. – Pbk. – 0 14 030789 3
Faber, 1954, 157p. – 0 571 06460 4

In the same series:

THE CHIMNEYS OF GREEN KNOWE
Chivers Press, 1990, 272p. – L/P. –
0 7451 1175 0
Penguin, 1976, 176p. – Pbk. – 0 14 030840 7
Faber, 1958, 186p. – O/P. – 0 571 07030 2

THE RIVER AT GREEN KNOWE
Penguin, 1976, 128p. – Pbk. – 0 14 030861 X
Faber, 1959, 144p. – O/P. – 0 571 06660 7

A STRANGER AT GREEN KNOWE
Penguin, 1977, 176p. – Pbk. – 0 14 030871 7
Faber, 1961, 160p. – O/P. – 0 571 05903 1

AN ENEMY AT GREEN KNOWE
Penguin, 1977, 144p. – Pbk. – 0 14 030910 1
Faber, 1964, 150p. – O/P. – 0 571 05971 6

GUARDIANS OF THE HOUSE
Bodley Head, 1974, 56p. – O/P. –
0 370 10934 1

THE STONES OF GREEN KNOWE
Penguin, 1979, 128p. – Pbk. – 0 14 031061 4
Bodley Head, 1976, 128p. – O/P. –
0 370 11017 X
all illustrated by Peter Boston

Green Knowe is a very old house with happy memories of children who have loved it over the years. The magical atmosphere and the characters form a common thread, but each story is different and enjoyable. In particular, *A Stranger at Green Knowe* will be enjoyed by those who feel compassion for wild creatures caged in zoos. *Guardians of the House* is unusual in that it is set in the future, when the house is empty. The stories have lost nothing over the years, and the first title made an excellent television serial.
Age range: 9–12

BRIGGS, Raymond (Redvers)

British. Born Wimbledon, London, 1934. Educated Rutlish School, Merton, Surrey; Wimbledon School of Art; Slade School of Fine Art, National Diploma in Design; University of London, Diploma in Fine Art. British Army, 1953–55. Married Jean Taprel Clark, 1963 (died 1973). Freelance illustrator and writer, part-time lecturer in illustration.

Awards: Library Association Kate Greenaway Medal: *Mother Goose Treasury*, 1966
Library Association Kate Greenaway Medal: *Father Christmas*, 1973
Boston Globe-Horn Book Award: *The Snowman*, 1979 (for the illustrations)
Children's Rights Workshop Other Award: *When the Wind Blows*, 1982

Address: Weston, Underhill Lane, Westmeston, Hassocks, Sussex BN6 8XG, England

Because so many of his books are lavishly illustrated, Raymond Briggs is generally supposed to create books for the very young. In reality, his picture books have much to offer the older child, as the illustrations are very detailed.

FAIRY TALE TREASURY
Penguin, 1974, 192p. – Pbk, O/P. – 0 14 050103 7
selected by Virginia Haviland

An excellent compilation of traditional fairy stories brought wonderfully to life by Raymond Briggs's illustrations, both black and white and colour. A worth while addition to any child's bookshelf.
Age range: 5–8

FATHER CHRISTMAS
Hamish Hamilton, 1990, 32p – 0 241 13011 5
Penguin, 1975, 32p. – Pbk. – 0 14 050125 8

A story in comic-strip form, without words, about Father Christmas's life with his cat and dog. It is quite long and detailed, requiring a good deal of concentration and several readings to appreciate all it has to offer. It can, of course, be used with younger children, but the humour is best suited to older readers.
Age range: 6–10

FATHER CHRISTMAS GOES ON HOLIDAY
Penguin, 1977, 32p. – Pbk. – 0 14 050187 8
Hamish Hamilton, 1975, 32p. – O/P. – 0 241 89220 1

In comic-strip form again, but more words are used, albeit in the form of conversational 'balloons', and much of it in French. Even an older child may need adult assistance to fully appreciate the humour, although the idea of Father Christmas taking time off has instant appeal.
Age range: 6–10

FUNGUS THE BOGEYMAN
Penguin, 1990, 48p. – Pbk. – 0 14 054235 3
Hamish Hamilton, 1977, 42p. – 0 241 89553 7

A controversial picture book for older children and younger adults, with a certain sense of humour. Fungus awakes as night closes in, and thus begins the story of his 'day', a collection of horrible facts told in Briggs's unique style. Not easy to read.
Age range: 11–adult

GENTLEMAN JIM
Hamish Hamilton, 1981, 30p. – Pbk. – 0 241 10698 2
Hamish Hamilton, 1980, 32p. – 0 241 10281 2

Jim, a cleaner in the public toilets, wants to improve himself, and imagines trying a variety of other jobs. In spite of the usual comic-strip format, some complex issues are dealt with in an unusually (for Raymond Briggs) verbose style. Definitely not a picture book for the young.
Age range: 10–adult

SNOWMAN

Hamish Hamilton, 1990, 24p. – 0 241 13045 X
Penguin, 1980, 32p. – Pbk. – 0 14 050350 1

A book with enormous appeal to children of all ages. It tells of the adventures of a snowman and a little boy, with a realistic, sad ending. It has been produced in a variety of ways in book form, made into a film, and released on video. The illustrations in the original picture-book are pale compared to the vivid colours of the Father Christmas books, making the wordless story a little more difficult to follow.
Age range: 5–10

WHEN THE WIND BLOWS

Penguin, 1983. – Pbk, O/P. – 0 14 006603 3
Hamish Hamilton, 1982, 40p. – 0 241 10721 0

The terrible story of Jim and his wife trying to understand what is happening and what they should do in the face of nuclear war. They follow the official instructions as best they can, but to no avail. The comic-strip format and occasional spots of humour somehow emphasize the poignancy of this story of faith betrayed.
Age range: 10–adult

BRINSMEAD, Hesba (Fay, née Hungerford)

Australian. Born Blue Mountains, New South Wales, 1922. Educated Correspondence School; High School, Wahroonga; Avondale College. Married Reginald Brinsmead, 1943, two sons. Teacher, writer.

Awards: Australian Children's Book Council Book of the Year Award: *Pastures of the Blue Crane*, 1965
Australian Children's Book Council Book of the Year Award: *Longtime Passing*, 1972

Address: Weathertop, Shamara Road, Terranora, New South Wales 2485, Australia

One of Australia's most distinguished story tellers for young readers, she brings humour, understanding and the ability to convey, realistically, differing cultures to her audience. Mainly a writer for teenage girls, but the following are intended for younger children:

THE HONEY FOREST
Hodder, 1980, 60p. – O/P. – 0 340 23048 7
illustrated by Louise Hogan

A simple story, lovingly told, about Mickey and his father, who spend summer together in the rain forest in the Blue Mountains, and about the lessons Mickey learns there.
Age range: 7–9

ONCE THERE WAS A SWAGMAN
OUP, 1979, 62p. – O/P. – 0 19 550549 2
illustrated by Noela Young

This book was written to teach young Australians what a swagman was. Set in the days of the Depression, Teddy has cause to be grateful to Mr Mungo Brodie when she becomes lost in the wild-lands. The sepia illustrations perfectly complement an excellent, deliberately low-key tale.
Age range: 9–12

SOMEPLACE BEAUTIFUL
Hodder, 1986, 152p. – O/P. – 0 340 35776 2
illustrated by Betina Ogden

Miss Dove's Flying Trunk Bookshop is to be demolished, as the Council wants to put a betting shop in its place. For the children of Chapple Road, however, the bookshop is 'someplace beautiful' to go, and so they take action. Humorous and simply told; a joy to read.
Age range: 7–9

BROWN, Jeff

FLAT STANLEY

Ward Lock, 1975, 64p. – Pbk. – 0 7062 3490 1
Methuen, 1974, 75p. – 0 416 80360 1
illustrated by Tomi Ungerer

Although first published in 1968, this extremely funny story is still widely enjoyed. Stanley is flattened when a notice board falls on top of him and life is suddenly completely different.
Age range: 7–9

LAMP FOR THE LAMBCHOPS

Mammoth, 1989, 96p. – Pbk, O/P. –
0 7497 0138 2
Magnet Books, 1986, 96p. – Pbk, O/P. –
0 416 61870 7
illustrated by Quentin Blake

Reprinted as:

STANLEY AND THE MAGIC LAMP

Methuen, 1990, 96p. – 0 416 16852 3
Mammoth, 1990, 96p. – Pbk. – 0 7497 0748 8
illustrated by Quentin Blake

STANLEY IN SPACE

Methuen, 1990, 64p. – 0 416 15862 5
illustrated by Philippe Dupasquier

As sequels to *Flat Stanley*, they are also enjoyable and amusing, but they do not have the same freshness or rollicking sense of humour as the earlier book.
Age range: 7–9

BYARS, Betsy (née Cromer)

American. Born Charlotte, North
Carolina, 1928. Educated Furman
University, Greenville, South Carolina;
Queen's College, Charlotte, B.A.
English. Married Edward Ford Byars,
1950, three daughters, one son.

Awards: American Library
Association, Newbery
Medal: *The Summer of the
Swans*, 1971
Catholic Library
Association, Regina Medal,
1987

Address: 4 Riverpoint, Clemson, South
Carolina 29631, USA

Betsy Byars is one of the most popular
authors currently writing for young
people. She is an able, and, at times,
powerful storyteller, touching on themes
that young people hold dear, as does
Judy Blume, but with none of her
triviality.

AFTER THE GOAT-MAN

Penguin, 1978, 112p. – Pbk. – 0 14 030992 6
Bodley Head, 1975, 112p. – O/P. –
0 370 10951 1

Figgy is a modern child with a liking for
all mod cons, but when he realizes that
the newsworthy 'goat-man' is none other
than his grandfather, who prefers the
simple life in his log-cabin, he has to take
some action.
Age range: 10–12

THE ANIMAL, THE VEGETABLE AND JOHN D. JONES

Penguin, 1984, 144p. – Pbk. – 0 14 031563 2
Bodley Head, 1982, 128p. – 0 370 30914 6

An excellent portrayal of family
relationships and the problems
encountered by the attempts at uniting
two families. The many humorous
passages make this a lively, thoroughly
enjoyable read.
Age range: 10–12

BEANS ON THE ROOF

Bodley Head, 1988, 80p. – 0 370 31257 0
illustrated by Melodye Rosales

The Bean family all end up on the roof
trying to help Anna write a poem for
school. Although short because written
for younger children, it still carries the
hallmark of Betsy Byars and is therefore
a book of quality which can be read again
and again.
Age range: 6–8

THE BURNING QUESTIONS OF BINGO BROWN

Penguin, 1990, 160p. – Pbk. – 0 14 034319 9
Chivers Press, 1989, 232p. – L/P. –
0 7451 0961 6
Bodley Head, 1988, 144p. – 0 370 31186 8

Bingo's questions are all concerned with
the problems life brings to everyone at
one time or another. During the course of
the book, he finds some of the answers.
Organizing the school rebellion against
the ban on T-shirts with words helps him
to realize some fundamental facts, but the
horrific events concerning his teacher
finally teach him to see someone else's
point of view.
Age range: 11–14

THE CARTOONIST

Penguin, 1981, 112p. – Pbk. – 0 14 031182 3
Bodley Head, 1978, 112p. – O/P. –
0 370 30104 8

Alfie, unhappy at home and at school,
takes refuge in the attic, where he spends
his time drawing cartoons. He is unable
to face losing this refuge when his
brother, having some trouble himself,
needs to come and stay for a while. In
spite of the serious plot, this is an
extremely readable story, full of appeal
for young readers.
Age range: 11–14

THE COMPUTER NUT

Penguin, 1986, 144p. – Pbk. – 0 14 031876 3
Bodley Head, 1984, 128p. – 0 370 30835 2

Kate can't decide whether the message

on the computer screen is really from outer space, or just an elaborate joke. Gradually she comes to believe in BB9, and his mission to find the missing element of laughter which has led him to Kate.

Age range: 10–12

CRACKER JACKSON
Chivers Press, 1987, 176p. – L/P. –
0 7451 0493 2
Penguin, 1986, 178p. – Pbk. – 0 14 031881 X
Bodley Head, 1985, 140p. – 0 370 30859 X

A grim story, told with immense perception, yet with a glorious sense of humour. Jackson and his friend Goat are convinced that Alma is in serious trouble at the hands of her violent husband. The 'trouble' is graphically described, just as the attempts to help, which do not always work out, are humorously portrayed. An excellent read.

Age range: 11–14

THE CYBIL WAR
Collins, 1987, 112p. – Pbk. – 0 00 330043 9
Penguin, 1983, 112p. – Pbk. – 0 14 031458 X
Bodley Head, 1981, 112p. – 0 370 30426 8

A realistic look at growing up and first dates. Simon really likes Cybil, but so does his friend Tony. Their struggles have a humorous side, but nevertheless there is a poignancy about the situation which would be lost on younger, inexperienced readers.

Age range: 12–14

THE EIGHTEENTH EMERGENCY
Chivers Press, 1988, 136p. – L/P, O/P. –
0 7451 0691 9
Penguin, 1976, 104p. – Pbk. – 0 14 030863 6
Bodley Head, 1974, 128p. – 0 370 10924 4

Fear of being singled out for a 'beating-up' by fellow pupils is something most children experience at school. Mouse and Ezzie have active imaginations, and work out a detailed plan of action in case of an attack by crocodiles. However, the threat posed by the Hammerman, the biggest bully in the school, is less easy to cope with.

Age range: 10–12

THE GLORY GIRL
Penguin, 1985, 112p. – Pbk. – 0 14 031726 0
Bodley Head, 1983, 128p. – O/P. –
0 370 30997 9

Being left out is one of the worst feelings children have to cope with. They often turn to fellow outcasts for consolation or support. Anna is no exception – unable to join in with her gospel-singing family, she can readily feel sympathy for the rejected ex-con uncle. An exciting story in a rather unlikely setting, and the ending is highly satisfactory.

Age range: 11–14

GOODBYE, CHICKEN LITTLE
Penguin, 1982, 96p. – Pbk. – 0 14 031329 X
Bodley Head, 1979, 96p. – O/P. –
0 370 30212 5

Jimmie's nickname 'Chicken' stems from his fear and embarrassment at the reckless exploits of his family. When his Uncle Pete oversteps the mark, with tragic consequences, Jimmie is overwhelmed by guilt at his own inaction.

Age range: 11–14

THE HOUSE OF WINGS
Penguin, 1977, 112p. – Pbk, O/P. –
0 14 030887 3
Bodley Head, 1973, 136p. – O/P. –
0 370 01247 X

Sammy was fed up with sharing his grandfather's house with all his rare birds, and the resulting mess. He decides to run away, but finds an injured crane which he cannot ignore.

Age range: 9–12

THE MIDNIGHT FOX
Chivers Press, 1989, 184p. – L/P. –
0 7451 0828 8
Penguin, 1976, 128p. – Pbk. – 0 14 030844 X
Faber, 1970, 136p. – O/P. – 0 571 09320 5

A black fox is a rare creature, but it will still cause havoc among livestock. Tom, nevertheless, is determined to prevent his uncle hunting her when she has a cub to care for. A realistic and powerful story, in which Tom learns to rely on himself as his feelings of responsibility for another life

develop. It is not a particularly easy book to read, requiring fluency from the child, but it can successfully be read aloud, as there is sufficient plot, tension and humour to keep the interest of a class of children.
Age range: 9–12

THE NIGHT SWIMMERS
Windrush, 1991, 175p. – L/P. – 1 85089 850 2
Penguin, 1982, 144p. – Pbk. – 0 14 031409 1
Bodley Head, 1980, 112p. – O/P. –
0 370 30317 2

At the age of twelve, Retta is faced with bringing up her two brothers. Her mother is dead, and her father gets on with his own life as if the children did not exist. It takes a real emergency and a terrible fright to make him realize his responsibility to his family. Not lacking in humour, this is, nevertheless, a realistic portrayal of a young girl struggling with a situation that is beyond her ability to deal with, yet coping magnificently.
Age range: 10–14

THE NOT-JUST-ANYBODY FAMILY
Chivers Press, 1988, 200p. – L/P. –
0 7451 0756 7
Collins, 1988, 128p. – Pbk. – 0 00 330038 2
Pan Books, 1988, 144p. – Pbk. – 0 330 29974 3
Bodley Head, 1986, 148p. – O/P. –
0 370 30724 0

In the same series:

THE BLOSSOMS MEET THE VULTURE LADY
Chivers Press, 1988, 168p. – L/P. –
0 7451 0824 5
Pan Books, 1988, 128p. – Pbk. –
0 330 29975 1
Bodley Head, 1986, 126p. – 0 370 30760 7

THE BLOSSOMS AND THE GREEN PHANTOM
Chivers Press, 1989, 184p. – L/P. –
0 7451 0924 1
Pan Books, 1988. – Pbk. – 0 330 30085 7
Bodley Head, 1987, 140p. – 0 370 31041 1

THE BLOSSOM PROMISE
Chivers Press, 1990, 200p. – L/P. –
0 7451 1065 7

Pan Books, 1989, 144p. – Pbk. –
0 330 30730 4
Bodley Head, 1987, 144p. – 0 370 30783 6

A quartet of stories about the Blossom family, written with humour and a sympathetic view of children. They consist of short episodic chapters (a bit like a television 'soap') which appeal to readers who have not developed the ability to concentrate for long. They describe exciting events such as bull-riding at the Rodeo, and making a raft to sail on the flooded creek. Peopled by determined characters, the reader feels compelled to sympathize with them, even when they are engaged in silly activities.
Age range: 9–12

THE PINBALLS
Cornerstone Books, 1988, 186p. – L/P. –
0 55736 028 6
Penguin, 1980, 96p. – Pbk. – 0 14 031121 1
Bodley Head, 1977, 120p. – O/P. –
0 370 30040 8

'The Pinballs' is Carlie's name for herself and the other children in her latest foster home, because she feels they are being tossed about at random by life. It takes a long time and a lot of loving patience from Mrs Mason to show Carlie how to trust and care for people. This sensitive portrayal of what is a common situation today is characterized by a strong sense of humour, provides an excellent read, entertaining and instructive, and has been televised.
Age range: 10–14

THE SUMMER OF THE SWANS
Windrush, 1989, 142p. – L/P. – 1 85089 963 0
Penguin, 1984, 144p. – Phk. – 0 14 031420 2
Kestrel Books, 1984, 144p. – O/P. –
0 7226 5935 0
illustrated by Ted Coconis

Sara finds being a teenager very difficult. She feels out of step with herself and her family, indeed, sometimes, with the whole world. Then her brother goes missing, and suddenly she has to put everything into perspective, and decide just who and what is really important. A

compelling read and justifiable prize winner.
Age range: 11–14

THE TV KID

Chivers Press, 1990, 144p. – L/P. –
0 7451 1179 3
Penguin, 1979, 112p. – Pbk. – 0 14 031065 7
Bodley Head, 1976, 128p. – O/P. –
0 370 11018 8

Lennie is a TV addict. The television allows him to escape from his difficult home life and the poor marks he gets at school. Real life, however, forces itself upon Lennie in a horrifying manner, leaving him to ponder about it from a hospital bed. As always, a contemporary problem dealt with sensitively and with humour.
Age range: 10–12

THE TWO-THOUSAND POUND GOLDFISH

Cornerstone Books, 1989, 160p. – L/P. –
1 55736 131 2
Collins, 1987, 128p. – 0 00 330042 0
Penguin, 1984, 112p. – Pbk. – 0 14 031607 8

A funny yet sensitive novel about Warren who lives with his grandmother, but in the constant hope of his mother's return. He consoles himself, meanwhile, by inventing plots for films, one of which has a giant goldfish as the main character. Fun to read, but a story with a sadness that will find an echo in the heart of the many children who feel, or have felt, abandoned.
Age range: 10–12

C

CAMERON, Ann

American. Born Rice Lake, Wisconsin. Educated Radcliffe College; University of Iowa Writers' Workshop. Lives in New York and Guatemala.

JULIAN, SECRET AGENT
Gollancz, 1989, 64p. – 0 575 04602 3
illustrated by Lis Toft

In the same series:

THE JULIAN STORIES
Armada Books, 1984, 80p. – Pbk. –
0 00 672227 X
Gollancz, 1982, 72p. – 0 575 03143 3

JULIAN'S GLORIOUS SUMMER
Collins, 1990, 64p. – Pbk. – 0 00 673539 8
Gollancz, 1988, 64p. – 0 575 04117 X

MORE STORIES JULIAN TELLS
Armada Books, 1987, 80p. – Pbk. –
0 00 672738 7
Gollancz, 1986, 72p. – 0 575 03676 1
all illustrated by Ann Strugnell

Four books of amusing short stories which are a true delight, either for a child to read, or for reading aloud. Julian is the storyteller (in both senses) and young children may have difficulty in making the connection between the first-person and Julian. Linguistically rich, fresh, and full of a warm family atmosphere.
Age range: 7–10

THE MOST BEAUTIFUL PLACE IN THE WORLD
Doubleday, 1989. – 0 385 26971 4
illustrated by Thomas B. Allen

A simple story told in Ann Cameron's distinctive style, which appeals directly to young readers. Juan is seven and wants to go to school, but he is earning good money as a shoe-shine boy. It is a difficult choice.
Age range: 7–9

CARPENTER, Humphrey
(William Bouverie)

British. Born 1946. Educated
Marlborough College; Keeble College,
Oxford. M.A. Diploma in Education.
Married Mari Christina Pritchard. Writer
and broadcaster.

Address: 6 Farndon Road, Oxford
OX2 6RS, England

MR MAJEIKA
Viking Kestrel, 1988. – 0 670 81975 1
Penguin, 1985, 96p. – Pbk. – 0 14 031677 9

In the same series:

MR MAJEIKA AND THE DINNER
LADY
Penguin, 1990, 96p. – Pbk. – 0 14 032762 2
Viking, 1989, 96p. – 0 670 82294 9

MR MAJEIKA AND THE HAUNTED
HOTEL
Penguin, 1988, 80p. – Pbk. – 0 14 032360 0
Viking Kestrel, 1987, 80p. – 0 670 81706 6

MR MAJEIKA AND THE MUSIC
TEACHER
Penguin, 1987, 96p. – Pbk. – 0 14 032141 1
Viking Kestrel, 1986, 94p. – 0 670 80754 0
all illustrated by Frank Rodgers

Mr Majeika is the new teacher at St Barty.
His arrival on a flying carpet, which turns
into a bicycle at one glance from its
owner, heralds the beginning of many
amusing incidents. The books are not
difficult to read and the vocabulary is
restricted. They are, however, full-length
with amusing, imaginative content, well
illustrated and ideal for encouraging new
readers. The successful television series
ensured the popularity of the books.
Age range: 7–9

CATE, Dick

British. Born Ferryhill, Co. Durham. Educated Spennymore Grammar School, County Durham; Goldsmith's College, London; Bretton Hall, West Yorkshire. Married, four children, two grandchildren. Teacher (retired), full-time writer.

Awards: Children's Rights Other Award: *Old Dog, New Tricks*, 1978

Address: 2 Bank Lane, Denby Dale, Huddersfield, England

An experienced teacher, married to a teacher, Dick Cate has the ability to speak to children in his books in a way that they can understand. He has written many titles, some for particular series listed elsewhere in this book.

GHOST DOG
Yearling, 1989, 128p. – Pbk. – 0 440 86211 6
Gollancz, 1987, 128p. – 0 575 03926 4

In the same series:

TWISTERS
Yearling, 1989, 176p. – Pbk. – 0 440 86213 2
Gollancz, 1987, 160p. – 0 575 04099 8

FOXCOVER
Yearling, 1989, 179p. – Pbk. – 0 440 86214 0
Gollancz, 1988, 160p. – 0 575 04292 3

FLAMES
Gollancz, 1989, 160p. – 0 575 04501 9

FIBS
Gollancz, 1990, 160p. – 0 575 04901 4
all illustrated by Caroline Binch

Set in a mining village outside Durham, these stories are brought to life by the strongly drawn characters. They are centred around everyday events in the boys' lives, the football team, playing for the school, belonging to the gang. Told with authenticity and humour, they have immense appeal for boys, although Emma is able to fly the flag for the equality of girls.
Age range: 10–12

CHAMBERS, Aidan

Also writes as Malcolm Blacklin. British. Born Chester-le-Street, Co. Durham, 1934. Educated Queen Elizabeth I Grammar School, Darlington; Borough Road College, London. Royal Navy, 1953–55. Married Nancy Harris Lockwood, 1968. Teacher, radio presenter, editor, proprietor and publisher, Thimble Press and Signal: approaches to children's books.

Awards: Eleanor Farjeon Award, 1982

Address: Lockwood, Station Road, South Woodchester, Stroud, Gloucestershire GL5 5EQ, England

Agent: Pat White, Deborah Rogers Ltd, 20 Powis Mews, London W11 1JN, England

Aidan Chambers is a well-known name in the field of children's literature. There are several excellent collections of stories edited by him, as well as the following two books written by him.

THE PRESENT TAKERS
Magnet Books, 1985, 128p. – Pbk, O/P. –
0 416 51000 0
Bodley Head, 1983, 128p. – 0 370 30967 7

Bullying in schools is currently an issue much discussed by the media, but for many years adults have refused to acknowledge the seriousness of the problem. This book was one of the first attempts to fictionalize the problem. There is a horrible realism in the description of Melanie and the tortures she inflicts. The solution offered here gives the reader an important lesson in the power of peer cooperation. The book, unfortunately, appears to condone the childhood ethic 'don't tell or it will get worse' by allowing the children to succeed in putting a stop to the bullying where the adults had failed miserably to have any effect.
Age range: 10–12

SEAL SECRET
Hippo Books, 1984, 112p. – Pbk. –
0 590 70302 1
Bodley Head, 1980, 128p. – 0 370 30296 6

An unwilling holiday friendship is forced upon William and Gwyn, but the outcome changes William forever. Gwyn has a baby seal, but his plans for it sicken William, who is determined to rescue it. The seal, however, is not at all cooperative. A powerful book.
Age range: 11–13

CHRISTOPHER, John

Pseudonym for Christopher Samuel Youd; has also written as Hilary Ford, William Godfrey, Peter Graaf, Peter Nichols and Anthony Rye. British. Born Knowsley, Lancashire, 1922. Educated Peter Symonds School, Winchester. Royal Corps of Signals, WW II. Twice married, four daughters and a son from the first marriage.

Awards: Guardian Children's Fiction Award: *The Guardians*, 1971

Address: La Rochelle, Rye, East Sussex, England

Over the years, John Christopher has produced some excellent science fiction for older children. He is able to create imaginative yet believable worlds, peopled by memorable characters. Reading stamina is required to enjoy his novels.

FIREBALL
Penguin, 1983, 144p. – Pbk, O/P, –
0 14 031498 9
Gollancz, 1981, 192p. – O/P – 0 575 02974 9

In the same series:

NEW FOUND LAND
Penguin, 1984, 128p. – Pbk, O/P. –
0 14 031683 3
Gollancz, 1983, 160p. – O/P. –
0 575 03222 7

Brad and Susan learn the hard way that to survive, they must forget their differences and work together. The dangers they face in both books are overwhelming, and keep the reader engrossed to the end.
Age range: 12–14

THE GUARDIANS
Penguin, 1973, 176p. – Pbk. – 0 14 030579 3
Hamish Hamilton, 1970, 160p. – O/P. –
0 241 01795 5

When Rob's father dies, Rob has to live in a state boarding school, where the regime is harsh and bullying is rife. When he cannot stand any more, he runs away to safety, but he is not as safe as he hoped. A tense, exciting story.
Age range: 12–14

THE LOTUS CAVES
Penguin, 1971, 176p. – Pbk. – 0 14 030503 3
Hamish Hamilton, 1969, 160p. – O/P. –
0 241 01729 7

Overwhelmed by the boredom of life on the moon, Marty and Steve break the rules and take a moon vehicle beyond the legal limits. They fall through the crust into a strange land of caves where their troubles really begin.
Age range: 12–14

THE PRINCE IN WAITING
Collins, 1983, 160p. – 0 00 330010 2
Penguin, 1973. – Pbk, O/P. – 0 14 030617 X

In the same series:

BEYOND THE BURNING LANDS
Penguin, 1973, 160p. – Pbk, O/P. –
0 14 030625 0
Hamish Hamilton, 1971, 160p. – O/P. –
0 241 02033 6

THE SWORD OF THE SPIRITS
Penguin, 1973, 144p. – Pbk, O/P. –
0 14 030630 7
Hamish Hamilton, 1972, 160p. – O/P. –
0 241 02137 5

An excellent trilogy, available both separately and in one volume (Penguin, 1983, 464p. – Pbk. – 0 14 031654 X). Set in a fragmented England in the future, where violence is the norm, someone is urgently needed to unite the country. Luke is heir to one of the settlements, but it would appear that such a task is beyond him. A frightening vision of the future.
Age range: 12–14

THE WHITE MOUNTAINS
Chivers Press, 1989, 256p. – L/P. –
0 7451 1043 6
Kestrel Books, 1984, 160p. – O/P. –
0 7226 5909 1
Penguin, 1984, 160p. – Pbk, O/P. –
0 14 031684 1

In the same series:

THE CITY OF GOLD AND LEAD
Chivers Press, 1990, 280p. – L/P. –
0 7451 1100 9
Kestrel Books, 1984, 160p. – 0 7226 5910 5
Penguin, 1984, 160p. – Pbk, O/P. –
0 14 031685 X

THE POOL OF FIRE
Chivers Press, 1990, 280p. – L/P. –
0 7451 1176 9
Kestrel Books, 1984, 160p. – O/P. –
0 7226 5915 6
Penguin, 1984, 160p. – Pbk, O/P. –
0 14 031686 8

The Tripods trilogy, published separately and in one volume (Penguin, 1984, 448p. – Pbk. – 0 14 031722 8) was a thoroughly enjoyable television serial, and is probably the best of John Christopher's work. Earth is ruled by the Tripods, until Will, an unlikely hero, is sent to the rescue. It is dangerous, but Will and his companions fight on through the three novels to win in an exciting climax.
Age range: 12–14

WILD JACK
Hamlyn, 1978, 160p. – Pbk, O/P. –
0 600 39405 0
Longman, 1975, 80p. – Pbk, O/P. –
0 582 53791 6
Hamish Hamilton, 1974, 160p. – O/P. –
0 241 89070 5

A future ruled by an energy crisis seems a real possibility to current readers. Clive is taken prisoner by Wild Jack, a savage who has to live outside the protected city in the Outlands. Here Clive learns a different viewpoint, and finally makes his own decision.
Age range: 12–14

CLEARY, Beverly

Born McMinnville, Oregon, 1916.
Educated University of California,
Berkeley, B.A.; University of Washington,
Seattle, B.A. (Librarianship). Married
Clarence Cleary, 1940, twin daughter
and son. Librarian.

Awards: American Library Association
Laura Ingalls Wilder Award,
1975
Catholic Library Association
Regina Medal, 1980
American Library Association
Newbery Medal: *Dear Mr
Henshaw*, 1984

Address: C/o William Morrow Inc, 105
Madison Avenue, New York
City, New York 10016, USA

Beverly Cleary has the ability to view
young children clearly and shrewdly, and
yet lovingly. She also has the fortunate
ability to re-create what she sees in the
characters in her books, resulting in
funny, readable and thoroughly
enjoyable stories with lots of appeal to
the young reader. The book jackets do
not have instant appeal, and therefore,
some children will need a personal
introduction to these excellent books.

BEEZUS AND RAMONA
Penguin, 1981, 160p. – Pbk. – 0 14 031249 8
Hamish Hamilton, 1978, 192p. – O/P. –
0 241 10014 3
illustrated by Thelma Lambert

In the same series:

RAMONA AND HER FATHER
Cornerstone Books, 1988, 168p. – L/P. –
1 55736 076 6
Penguin, 1981, 144p. – Pbk. – 0 14 031303 6
Hamish Hamilton, 1978, 192p. – O/P. –
0 241 89752 1
illustrated by Alan Tiegreen

RAMONA AND HER MOTHER
Penguin, 1982, 176p. – Pbk. – 0 14 031328 1
Hamish Hamilton, 1979, 192p. – O/P. –
0 241 10280 4
illustrated by Alan Tiegreen

RAMONA FOREVER
Cornerstone Books, 1990, 192p. – L/P. –
1 55736 139 8
Penguin, 1986, 160p. – Pbk. – 0 14 031916 6
J. MacRae Books, 1984, 144p. – O/P. –
0 86203 167 2
illustrated by Alan Tiegreen

RAMONA QUIMBY, AGE EIGHT
Cornerstone Books, 1989. – L/P. –
1 55736 000 6
Penguin, 1984, 160p. – Pbk. – 0 14 031560 8
Hamish Hamilton, 1981, 192p. – O/P. –
0 241 10665 6
illustrated by Alan Tiegreen

RAMONA THE BRAVE
Windrush, 1990, 184p. – L/P. –
1 85089 830 8
Penguin, 1978, 112p. – Pbk. – 0 14 031059 2
Hamish Hamilton, 1975, 190p. –
0 241 89257 0
illustrated by Alan Tiegreen

RAMONA THE PEST
Windrush, 1990, 152p. – L/P. –
1 85089 825 1
Penguin, 1976, 160p. – Pbk. – 0 14 030774 5
Hamish Hamilton, 1974, 192p. –
0 241 02412 9
illustrated by Louis Darling

Ramona is a wonderful, memorable
character who, being accident prone,
leads a life full of hilarious escapades
which cause children to laugh out loud.
New editions are being brought out with
more attractive jackets, using
photographs from the television serial.
Age range: 7–9

DEAR MR HENSHAW
Cornerstone Books, 1987, 150p. – L/P. –
1 55736 001 4
Penguin, 1985, 144p. – Pbk. – 0 14 031797 X
J. MacRae Books, 1983, 144p. – O/P. –
0 86203 147 8

As part of a class exercise, Leigh writes a
letter to the author of his favourite book.
Thus begins a correspondence between
them in which Leigh confides the exploits
of his family and his highly unusual dog.
Completely in letter form, some children
may be put off, but others will find the
easy, chatty style a welcome change from

the formal arrangement of most books.
Age range: 9–11

HENRY AND BEEZUS
Penguin, 1990, 208p. – Pbk. – 0 14 032821 1
Hamish Hamilton, 1980, 192p. – O/P. –
0 241 10431 9

In the same series:

HENRY AND RIBSY
Penguin, 1989, 128p. – Pbk. – 0 14 032820 3
Hamish Hamilton, 1979, 192p. – O/P. –
0 241 10020 8

HENRY AND THE CLUBHOUSE
Penguin, 1989, 128p. – Pbk. – 0 14 032819 X
Hamish Hamilton, 1981, 192p. – O/P. –
0 241 10618 4
all illustrated by Thelma Lambert

A highly entertaining set of stories about a small boy's exploits told in a marvellously funny style. The humorous illustrations perfectly complement the text.
Age range: 7–9

MOUSE AND THE MOTORCYCLE
Windrush, 1990, 160p. – L/P. – 1 85089 960 6
Penguin, 1977, 144p. – Pbk. – 0 14 030970 5
Hamish Hamilton, 1974, 160p. – O/P. –
0 241 89020 9
illustrated by Louis Darling

In the same series:

RALPH S. MOUSE
Windrush, 1990, 134p. – L/P. –
1 85089 800 6
Penguin, 1984, 128p. – Pbk. – 0 14 031669 8
Hamish Hamilton, 1982, 139p. – O/P. –
0 241 10883 7
illustrated by Paul O. Zelinsky

RUNAWAY RALPH
Penguin, 1978, 144p. – Pbk. – 0 14 031020 7
Hamish Hamilton, 1974, 176p. – O/P. –
0 241 89112 4
illustrated by Louis Darling

Through watching television, Ralph has learned to talk. His happiness is complete when he meets a boy with a toy motorbike – just the right size for a mouse. He has many adventures, making this a series of delightful and amusing stories.
Age range: 7–9

COLLINSON, Roger

British. Born London, 1936. Educated Durham University, County Durham. Teacher.

Address: 231 Carlton Avenue,
             Westcliffe-on-Sea, Essex
             SS0 0QD, England

GET LAVINIA GOODBODY

Hippo Books, 1985, 128p. – Pbk, O/P. –
0 590 70351 X
Andersen Press, 1983, 128p. – 0 86264 054 7
illustrated by John Shelley

Figgy is convinced that a girl with a name like Lavinia is certain to be snooty and superior. He persuades his gang to help him teach her a lesson. Written in a conversational style with plenty of humour, this book has lots of appeal.
Age range: 9–11

HANKY PANKY

Penguin, 1989, 160p. – Pbk. – 0 14 032659 6
Andersen Press, 1986, 160p. – 0 86264 134 9
illustrated by Tony Rais

An extremely funny school story beginning with a practical joke at the Autumn Fayre. The headmaster found the joke distinctly unfunny – hence the hanky-panky.
Age range: 11–13

COLWELL, Eileen

Educated University College, London. Pioneer children's librarian. Began children's library service in Hendon, 1926; helped found the Association of Children's Librarians, 1937. Chairman for five years of the International Federation of Library Associations' committee on library work with children. Member of the Carnegie Medal Committee since its inception until her retirement. Librarian, lecturer.

Awards: MBE, 1965
           Honorary Fellow of
           Manchester Polytechnic, 1974
           Loughborough University
           Honorary Degree of Doctor of
           Letters, 1975

BAD BOYS
Kestrel Books, 1975, 172p. – O/P. –
0 7226 5027 2
Penguin, 1972, 176p. – Pbk. – 0 14 030530 0
illustrated by John Riley

In the same series:

HIGH DAYS AND HOLIDAYS
Penguin, 1989, 144p. – Pbk. – 0 14 032300 7
Viking Kestrel, 1988, 144p. – O/P. –
0 670 81928 X
illustrated by Maureen Bradley

MORE STORIES TO TELL
Penguin, 1979, 160p. – Pbk. – 0 14 031062 2
illustrated by Caroline Sharpe

TELL ME A STORY
Penguin, 1970, 176p. – Pbk. – 0 14 030159 3
illustrated by Judith Bledsoe

TELL ME ANOTHER STORY
Penguin, 1969, 256p. – Pbk. – 0 14 030210 7

A pioneer and champion of children's librarians, Eileen Colwell was also a master storyteller, able to captivate large or small audiences from the youngest child to adults. Who better, then, to put together collections of stories suitable for telling or reading aloud? Contained in these four volumes is a wide variety of authors, styles and themes, ranging from Joan Aiken and Margaret Mahy to Edward Lear.
Age range: 5–14

CORBALIS, Judith

New Zealander. Educated at University in New Zealand and L.A.M.D.A., London. Moved to London at age of 29 and has lived there ever since. Lives with Philip King, the sculptor, one son. Actress, writer.

OSKAR AND THE ICE-PICK

Hodder, 1989, 160p. – Pbk. – 0 340 49910 9
Deutsch, 1988, 176p. – 0 233 98181 0
illustrated by David Parkins

Oskar has undertaken to deliver an ice-pick to his mother who is a world-famous mountaineer presently climbing in the Himalayas. Very amusing.
Age range: 8–10

THE WRESTLING PRINCESS

Hodder, 1987, 159p. – Pbk. – 0 340 40860 X
Deutsch, 1986, 160p. – 0 233 97852 6
illustrated by Helen Craig

A very light-hearted book designed specifically to make fun of the conventional roles of men and women. Princesses who drive a fork-lift truck, challenge a dragon, or aspire to become astronauts, make a refreshing change, although readers need a sound knowledge of traditional fairy stories to appreciate fully the jokes.
Age range: 7–9

CORRIN, Sara and Stephen

British. Retired teachers, Sara Corrin latterly senior lecturer in education at Hertfordshire College of Education, Stephen Corrin a teacher of French and Russian. Both now write and Stephen translates.

THE FABER BOOK OF FAVOURITE FAIRY TALES
Faber, 1988, 256p. – 0 571 14854 9
illustrated by J. Wijngaard

In the same series:

IMAGINE THAT! FIFTEEN FANTASTIC TALES
Penguin, 1988, 176p. – Pbk. – 0 14 032393 7
Faber, 1986. – 0 571 13843 8

MODERN FAIRY TALES
Penguin, 1983, 224p. – Pbk. – 0 14 031546 2
Faber, 1981, 312p. – 0 571 11768 6
illustrated by Ann Strugnell

THE PUFFIN BOOK OF CHRISTMAS STORIES
Penguin, 1986, 192p. – Pbk, O/P. – 0 14 031967 0

THE PUFFIN BOOK OF PET STORIES
Penguin, 1987, 208p. – Pbk. – 0 14 032117 9

ROUND THE CHRISTMAS TREE
Penguin, 1985, 144p. – Pbk. – 0 14 031777 5
Faber, 1983, 134p. – O/P. – 0 571 13151 4

STORIES FOR UNDER-FIVES
Penguin, 1979, 160p. – Pbk. -- 0 14 031100 9
Faber, 1974, 157p. – 0 571 10371 5

MORE STORIES FOR UNDER-FIVES
Penguin, 1988, 112p. – Pbk. – 0 14 032529 8
Faber, 1988, 96p. – 0 571 15058 6

STORIES FOR FIVE YEAR OLDS AND OTHER YOUNG READERS
Penguin, 1976, 160p. – Pbk. – 0 14 030839 3
Faber, 1973. – 0 571 10162 3

STORIES FOR SIX YEAR OLDS AND OTHER YOUNG READERS
Penguin, 1976, 176p. – Pbk. – 0 14 030785 0
Faber, 1967, 198p. – 0 571 08114 2

STORIES FOR SEVEN YEAR OLDS
Penguin, 1976, 192p. – Pbk. – 0 14 030882 2
Faber, 1964, 188p. – 0 571 05823 X

MORE STORIES FOR SEVEN YEAR OLDS
Penguin, 1982, 192p.   Pbk. – 0 14 031347 8
Faber, 1978, 183p. – O/P. – 0 571 11196 3

STORIES FOR EIGHT YEAR OLDS AND OTHER READERS
Penguin, 1977, 224p. – Pbk. – 0 14 030975 6
Faber, 1971, 192p. – 0 571 09332 9

STORIES FOR NINE YEAR OLDS AND OTHER YOUNG READERS
Penguin, 1981, 224p. – Pbk. – 0 14 031342 7
Faber, 1979, 159p. – 0 571 11409 1

STORIES FOR TENS AND OVER
Penguin, 1982, 208p. – Pbk. – 0 14 031364 8
Faber, 1976, 240p. – 0 571 10873 3

TIME TO LAUGH: FIFTEEN FUNNY STORIES
Faber, 1989, 116p. – Pbk. – 0 571 15499 9
illustrated by Gerald Rose

Specialists in collecting folk and fairy tales, both traditional and modern, the Corrins have put together various collections loosely round a theme, for example, heroes and heroines for the eight year olds, humour for the nines. Although they have tried to match the theme to the age group most likely to appreciate it, the stories can, in fact, be used with a variety of age groups. Occasionally extracts are included, for example *The Iron Man* in *Modern Fairy Tales*. These volumes are reprinted time after time as they have proved their value. *The Faber Book of Favourite Fairy Tales* is a particularly attractive volume. *Age range:* 5–12

COUNSEL, June

British. Born Carshalton, 1926. Parents lived in Malaya. Educated at schools in Sussex; Royal Holloway College, B.A. English, (Hons). WRNS, 1945–46. Married Alan Counsel, one son. Secretary, teacher.

Address: 17 Andrew Close, Ailsworth, Peterborough PE5 7AD, England

A DRAGON IN CLASS 4
Corgi, 1986, 112p. – Pbk. – 0 552 52313 5
Faber, 1984, 102p. – O/P. – 0 571 13249 9

In the same series:

A DRAGON IN SPRING TERM
Faber, 1988, 112p. – 0 571 15026 8

DRAGON IN SUMMER
Faber, 1990, 112p. – 0 571 14342 3
all illustrated by Jill Bennett

Humorous fantasy stories which will enhance any bookshelf. The books are well produced, clearly printed without being too big, copiously illustrated, and with an excellent story-line. Scales, a dragon, is trapped, and Sam rescues him. As a reward, Scales accompanies Sam to school, where the adventures really begin.
Age range: 6–9

CRESSWELL, Helen

British. Born Nottinghamshire, 1934.
Educated Nottingham Girls' High School;
King's College, London University. B.A.
(Hons) English. Married Brian Rowe,
1962. Worked as a literary assistant,
fashion buyer, teacher.

Address: Old Church Farm, Eakring,
           Newark, Nottinghamshire
           NG22 0DA, England

Agent: A. M. Heath, 79 St. Martin's
           Lane, London WC2N 4AA,
           England

The secret of Helen Cresswell's
popularity is the originality of her plots,
combined with an odd sense of humour
which corresponds with a child's. She
writes for a wide age range, but all to the
same high standard.

THE BAGTHORPE SAGA comprising:
  ABSOLUTE ZERO
  Penguin, 1979, 168p. – Pbk. – 0 14 031177 7
  Faber, 1978, 168p. – 0 571 11155 6

  BAGTHORPES ABROAD
  Penguin, 1986, 192p. – Pbk. – 0 14 031972 7
  Faber, 1984, 186p. – 0 571 13350 9

  BAGTHORPES HAUNTED
  Penguin, 1987, 208p. – Pbk. – 0 14 032172 1
  Faber, 1985, 208p. – 0 571 13585 4

  BAGTHORPES LIBERATED
  Penguin, 1990, 208p. – Pbk. – 0 14 034428 4
  Faber, 1989, 176p. – 0 571 15402 6

  BAGTHORPES UNLIMITED
  Penguin, 1980, 192p. – Pbk. – 0 14 031178 5
  Faber, 1978, 176p. – 0 571 11245 5

  BAGTHORPES VERSUS THE
  WORLD
  *Penguin, 1982, 192p. – Pbk, O/P. –
  0 14 031324 9*
  Faber, 1979, 192p. – 0 571 11446 6

  ORDINARY JACK
  *Windrush, 1987, 252p. – L/P. –
  1 85089 929 3*
  Penguin, 1979, 192p. – Pbk. – 0 14 031176 9
  Faber, 1977, 192p. – O/P. – 0 571 11114 9
all illustrated by Jill Bennett

The Bagthorpe family are definitely
eccentric. Pandemonium reigns, helped
on many occasions by Zero, the dog.
They stagger from crisis to crisis,
providing both hilarious reading and
viewing, as the saga became a popular
television serial.
Age range: 10–12

THE BARGE CHILDREN
White Lion, 1976, 88p. – O/P. – 0 85686 270 3

Billy and Betsy Moon live on a barge. As
the story unfolds, the reader is given a
clear picture of what life was like for the
bargees in the heyday of Britain's
waterways. It is not a long story, but very
entertaining.
Age range: 7–9

THE BEACHCOMBERS
*Chivers Press, 1987, 192p. – L/P. –
0 7451 0546 7*
*Penguin, 1978, 144p. – Pbk, O/P. –
0 14 031026 6*
Faber, 1972, 128p. – O/P. – 0 571 09932 7
illustrated by Errol le Cain

An unusual story about a boy whose only
hope of a holiday is to agree to
accompany an only child, when he
becomes involved in the rivalry of the
beachcombers. In spite of the rising
tension, there is no shortage of humour,
and the final denouement brings the
book to a highly satisfactory close. An
excellent book for reading aloud.
Age range: 10–12

THE BONGLEWEED
Penguin, 1981, 176p. – Pbk. – 0 14 031272 2
Faber, 1973, 157p. – O/P. – 0 571 10374 X
illustrated by Ann Strugnell

Owing to the perfect blend of fantasy and
realism personified by Becky's pragmatic
parents, this book is a first-rate example
of the comic fantasy genre. The fantasy
element is provided by a new species of
plant which, besides threatening to
overrun everything, displays more sinister
powers. Even if the reader fails to draw
the parallels between the blossoming of
Becky and the Bongleweed, the sheer

vitality of the story pulls them along to the immensely satisfactory ending.
Age range: 10–12

DEAR SHRINK

Penguin, 1988, 160p. – Pbk. – 0 14 032636 7
Windrush, 1987, 236p. – L/P, O/P. –
1 85089 903 7
Faber, 1982, 221p. – O/P. – 0 571 11912 3

A graphic portrayal of the difference between a loving, sheltered home and the bleakness of being fostered by uncaring people. The reader experiences this with the Saxon family whose parents are working abroad, leaving the children in the care of an elderly baby-sitter, who unfortunately dies. There are many problems, both practical and emotional, to cope with before the moving climax releases the children and the reader.
Age range: 10–12

ELLIE AND THE HAGWITCH

Lutterworth Press, 1987, 80p. – 0 7188 2672 8
Corgi, 1987, 128p. – Pbk. – 0 552 52411 5
illustrated by Jonathon Heap

A strange, chilling fantasy about a little girl struggling alone to combat the witch. Quite easy to read.
Age range: 8–10

GAME OF CATCH

Red Fox, 1990, 80p. – Pbk. – 0 09 975260 3
Chatto, 1969, 64p. – O/P. – 0 7011 0303 5
illustrated by Gareth Floyd

Although not very long because it is intended for young children, this excellently crafted story captures the carefree games of childhood and weaves into them a ghostly echo from a painting. The result is a compelling read.
Age range: 8–10

A GIFT FROM WINKLESEA

Penguin, 1971, 80p. – Pbk. – 0 14 030493 2
Hodder, 1969, 88p. – O/P. – 0 340 10472 4
illustrated by Janina Ede

A seaside souvenir which hatches into something else altogether is the unlikely hero of this unusual and delightful fantasy.
Age range: 7–9

GREEDY ALICE

Corgi, 1989, 64p. – Pbk. – 0 552 52524 3
Deutsch, 1986, 44p. – 0 233 97951 4
illustrated by Kate Simpson

Written for children newly experiencing the delights of reading alone, this is a delightful story. Greedy and curious, Alice decides to eat the cake in the box, and, like her famous namesake, she grows and grows, with equally disastrous results.
Age range: 6–8

LIZZIE DRIPPING

Windrush, 1990, 104p. – L/P. – 1 85089 991 6
Penguin, 1985, 96p. – Pbk. – 0 14 031751 1
BBC, 1973, 96p. – O/P. – 0 563 12411 3

In the same series:

LIZZIE DRIPPING AGAIN
BBC, 1974, 127p. – O/P. – 0 563 12687 6

LIZZIE DRIPPING AND THE LITTLE ANGEL
BBC, 1990, 31p. – Pbk. – 0 563 20908 9

LIZZIE DRIPPING BY THE SEA
BBC, 1990, 64p. – Pbk. – 0 563 20907 0
all illustrated by Faith Jacques

A series of stories about a rather irritating little girl who actively seeks out adventure. Very popular on television.
Age range: 8–10

MOONDIAL

Faber, 1987, 220p. – 0 571 14805 0
illustrated by P. J. Lynch

Specially written for television, the story takes place around Belton House, a National Trust property in Lincolnshire. Minty has supernatural powers which allow her to work out the secret of the moondial. Suspenseful, it is easier to watch than read.
Age range: 9–11

THE NIGHT-WATCHMEN

Chivers Press, 1990, 168p. – L/P. –
0 7451 1102 5
Penguin, 1976, 128p. – Pbk, O/P. –
0 14 030851 2
Faber, 1969, 148p. – O/P. – 0 571 08903 8
illustrated by Gareth Floyd

Not a book for those of a nervous disposition, as it is a story with decidedly frightening overtones. Henry is curious about the so-called night-watchmen, and sets out to find out exactly what they do. As the mystery unfolds, Henry's mounting fear is shared by the reader.
Age range: 10–12

THE PIEMAKERS

Faber, 1988, 160p. – 0 571 14761 5
Penguin, 1976, 128p. – Pbk. – 0 14 030868 7
illustrated by V. H. Drummond

Light-hearted and amusing, the story centres on Gravella, feeling fed-up with her never-ending job – helping with the family business of pie-making. When the pie competition is announced, they have a splendid idea, which gradually loses its splendour!
Age range: 9–11

THE SECRET WORLD OF POLLY FLINT

Penguin, 1984, 178p. – Pbk, O/P. –
0 14 031542 X
Faber, 1982, 176p. – 0 571 11939 5

Polly believes in magic, and knows that anything is possible, even the disappearance of a whole world. This intriguing story made a highly successful television series.
Age range: 9–11

TIME OUT

Lutterworth Press, 1987, 76p. – 0 7188 2658 2
illustrated by Tessa Hamilton

Written specifically for the television programme *Jackanory*, this funny story about a green cat and a butler with magic powers has been granted a new lease of life. It is now available in an attractive new edition.
Age range: 7–9

WHERE THE WIND BLOWS

Faber, 1990, 96p. – Pbk. – 0 571 14425 X
Faber, 1966, 63p. – O/P. – 0 571 06854 5
illustrated by Peggy Fortnum

A delightful book for younger children. The story is simple but appealing. Kirstine feels a little bored living with her grandfather by the slow river. When, by chance, she is shown the boat, she sets off at once on a fairy tale adventure.
Age range: 7–9

CROSS, Gillian (Clare, née Arnold)

British. Born London, 1945. Educated North London Collegiate School; Somerville College, Oxford, B.A., M.A.; University of Sussex, D.Phil (Eng). Married Martin Cross, 1967, two sons, two daughters.

Awards: Junior Education Best Historical Fiction: *A Whisper of Lace*, 1981

Address: 41 Essex Road, Gravesend, Kent DA11 0SL, England

Children are fortunate that a novelist of this stature should choose to write for them. She has evolved from a competent writer with exceptionally good ideas for stories into a first-rate author, writing equally well for different age groups.

THE DARK BEHIND THE CURTAIN
Hippo Books, 1985, 208p. – Pbk. – 0 590 70349 8
OUP, 1984, 160p. – 0 19 271500 3
illustrated by David Parkins

An above average thriller. The rehearsals for the school play are not progressing well, and there is a real menace lurking behind the stage curtain. The writing is powerful enough to render the book sometimes very frightening, and is a gripping read at all times.
Age range: 10–12

THE DEMON HEADMASTER
OUP, 1990, 96p. – Pbk. – 0 19 831270 9
Chivers Press, 1990, 208p. – L/P. – 0 7451 1150 5
OUP, 1986, 176p. – 0 19 271553 4
illustrated by Gary Rees

In the same series:

THE PRIME MINISTER'S BRAIN
OUP, 1990, 196p. – 0 19 271641 7
Penguin, 1987, 160p. – Pbk. – 0 14 032312 0
illustrated by Sally Burgess

The Demon Headmaster has proved to be an exceptionally popular book. Linguistically accessible to most children, the story has a remarkable appeal. The headmaster is a thoroughly evil man, controlling pupils and staff by fear. Dinah, an exceptional child in many ways, is the only one immune to his hypnotic ministerings. How she succeeds in defeating him makes an exciting and believable story, told with humour. The sequel is equally funny and exciting, but has lost some of the freshness of the original.
Age range: 9–11

THE IRON WAY
OUP, 1990, 138p. – 0 19 271642 5

The beginning of the railway is the setting for this excellent book, full of period detail and atmosphere. Unfortunately, historical novels are not very popular, and without a knowledgeable adult to bridge the gap, many children will miss a very exciting story. The human drama, culminating in a threat to the lives of the children as resentment against the 'navvies' spoiling the countryside with the railway lines reaches fever pitch, is strongly portrayed.
Age range: 11–14

THE MINTYGLO KID
Magnet Books, 1985, 128p. – Pbk, O/P. – 0 416 47850 6
Methuen, 1983, 128p. – O/P. – 0 416 25420 9
illustrated by Gareth Floyd

Dreadful Denzil amazes everyone by arriving with a five years' supply of toothpaste. Not all of it is destined for his toothbrush, and the situation rapidly gets out of hand so that drastic measures are required. Clipper, Barney and Spag are not short of ideas. A lively style and lots of humour guarantee a good read.
Age range: 9–11

ON THE EDGE
OUP, 1989, 176p. – 0 19 271606 9
Penguin, 1987, 176p. – Pbk. – 0 14 032053 9

The title is an apt description of the readers of this tense thriller, the tension

being maintained until the last page. Tug is kidnapped, and very frightened of his captors. Bravely, he tries to attract attention to his plight. Meanwhile, attempts to rescue him fail, putting him in more danger. The television serialization had children glued to their sets.
Age range: 10–14

RESCUING GLORIA
Methuen, 1989, 128p. – O/P. – 0 416 13402 5
illustrated by Gareth Floyd

Leo is appalled to learn that the gentle goat has to be put to sleep, and rescues her. The reality of looking after her proves rather more difficult than he anticipated. Then the ducks arrive, and his problems increase. A lively, funny story, well told and attractively produced.
Age range: 7–9

REVOLT AT RATCLIFFE'S RAGS
OUP, 1983, 146p. – 0 19 271477 5
OUP, 1980, 144p. – O/P. – 0 19 271439 2

Reissued as:

STRIKE AT RATCLIFFE'S RAGS
Methuen, 1987, 144p. – Pbk, O/P. –
0 416 97100 8

The slight alteration in the title indicates the main theme of this story. As a school project, the class was studying the working conditions in Ratcliffe's, a small clothing factory. Eventually the parents become involved, taking sides, and a strike results. The subject indicates that this is not an easy, lightweight book, but it is a thought-provoking introduction to the problems of management and workers, albeit as seen through the simplistic eyes of the children.
Age range: 11–14

ROSCOE'S LEAP
Penguin, 1990, 176p. – Pbk. – 0 14 034013 0
OUP, 1987, 160p. – 0 19 271557 7

As expected of this author, the plot is original and enthralling. The setting is an unusual house, built by Samuel Roscoe, which is rapidly going to rack and ruin in spite of the efforts of Stephen and

Hannah. Gradually the reader realizes that there is a reason for the children living in one half, almost cut off from the occupants of the other half, and that the reason is some terrible event in the past. The clues are tantalizingly revealed chapter by chapter. A compelling read.
Age range: 12–14

THE RUNAWAY
Magnet Books, 1986, 176p. – Pbk. –
0 416 52100 2
Methuen, 1979, 176p. – O/P. – 0 416 87230 1
illustrated by Reginald Gray

A subject currently receiving media attention is the increasing number of children running away from home, which is also the subject of this book. Children (and some adults) do not find it easy to empathize without personal experience, but a well written book can be the next best thing. This is such a book, describing how so many things go wrong for Denny that he feels he has no other option. Abandoned by his parents, the one stable adult in his life, Gran, has to go to hospital. Victimized by Bouncer Bradley, the school bully, having to live in the same children's home proves to be the last straw. As, in reality, running away is no solution, so it is in the book, and finding an alternative is a painful process.
Age range: 10–12

SAVE OUR SCHOOL
Methuen, 1983, 111p. – Pbk, O/P. –
0 416 30110 X
Methuen, 1981, 112p. – O/P. – 0 416 89800 9

In the same series:

SWIMATHON
Magnet Books, 1987, 128p. – Pbk, O/P. –
0 416 04502 2
Methuen, 1986, 128p. – O/P. – 0 416 59700 9

More hilarious adventures involving the little gang from *The Mintyglo Kid*. Their loyalty to their school surfaces at times of crisis. Never short of ideas, even if sometimes their plans go wrong, the lads race through the books with their readers in a thoroughly enjoyable partnership.
Age range: 9–11

TWIN AND SUPER-TWIN
OUP, 1990, 176p. – 0 19 271594 1
illustrated by Maureen Bradley

Ben and Mitch are twins, and between them they have a strange power – Ben is able to change Mitch's arm into anything he chooses – just by thinking hard. Sometimes it is useful, sometimes a nuisance. An amusing read, but rather slight.
Age range: 8–10

A WHISPER OF LACE
OUP, 1981, 143p. – O/P. – 0 19 271447 3

A story centred around the harm to the local lacemakers when Chantilly lace was smuggled in. Lame and weak, Dan nevertheless triumphs when he becomes dangerously involved with the smugglers to save his sister. An excellent read.
Age range: 12–14

CROSSLEY-HOLLAND,
Kevin (John William)

British. Born Mursley, Buckinghamshire, 1941. Educated Bryston School; St Edmund's Hall, Oxford, B.A. (Hons). Married: 1) Caroline Tendall Thompson, 1963, two sons; 2) Ruth Marris, 1972; 3) Gillian Cook, 1982, two daughters. Worked as editor, radio producer and university lecturer in Britain and America.

Awards: Arts Council Award 1968, 1977 and 1978
Carnegie Medal Winner: *Storm*, 1986

Address: The Old Vicarage, Walsham-le-Willows, Bury St. Edmunds, Suffolk, England

Agent: Rogers, Coleridge & White, 20 Powis Mews, London W11 1JN, England

Well known for his interest in mythology and folklore, this author has produced many volumes of collected folk and fairy tales. Many of them require adult introduction or assistance, but some can be tackled directly and with pleasure.

BOO!
Orchard Books, 1988, 64p. – 1 85213 091 1

In the same series:

DATHERA DAD
Orchard Books, 1988, 64p. – 1 85213 092 X

PIPER AND POOKA
Orchard Books, 1988, 64p. – 1 85213 093 8

SMALL-TOOTH DOG
Orchard Books, 1988, 64p. – 1 85213 094 6
all illustrated by Peter Melynczuk

Small books, published so far in a uniform edition, containing very short fairy tales or short stories. Illustrated on every page, they may well be acceptable to the reluctant reader.
Age range: 9–12

BRITISH AND IRISH FOLK TALES
Orchard Books, 1990, 160p. – 1 85213 265 5

Selected very much with children's enjoyment in mind, this collection contains the more popular stories, which children will certainly not find too difficult.
Age range: 9–11

THE DEAD MOON AND OTHER TALES FROM EAST ANGLIA AND THE FEN COUNTRY
Deutsch, 1990, 108p. – Pbk. – 0 233 98572 7
Deutsch, 1982, 104p. – O/P. – 0 233 97478 4
illustrated by Shirley Felts

Eleven folk tales from East Anglia showing an excellent and varied mixture of funny and scary stories.
Age range: 9–12

THE FABER BOOK OF NORTHERN FOLK TALES
Faber, 1983, 157p. – Pbk, O/P. – 0 571 13166 2
Faber, 1980, 157p. – 0 571 11519 5
illustrated by Alan Howard

A splendid collection of traditional stories from Scandinavia, Germany, the British Isles and Iceland. They are carefully arranged to follow on easily from each other.
Age range: 9–12

WULF
Faber, 1988, 105p. – 0 571 15100 0
illustrated by Gareth Floyd

A revised version of a trilogy published much earlier, it tells the story of an Anglo-Saxon boy, converted to Christianity, whose new faith is tested to the full. An excellent book, but a minority choice, in spite of being translated to the television screen in an engrossing serial.
Age range: 10–12

CURTIS, Philip

British. Born Westcliffe-on-Sea, 1920. Married, two children. Now lives in Leigh-on-Sea. Teacher, writer.

BEWARE OF THE BRAIN SHARPENERS
*Beaver Books, 1987, 144p. – Pbk. –
0 09 954080 0
Andersen Press, 1983, 136p. – O/P. –
0 86264 055 5*

In the same series:

BEWITCHED BY THE BRAIN SHARPENERS
*Beaver Books, 1988, 128p. – Pbk. –
0 09 956780 6
Andersen Press, 1986, 128p. – 0 86264 153 5*

BRAIN SHARPENERS ABROAD
Andersen Press, 1987, 128p. – 0 86264 183 7

CHAOS COMES TO CHIVY CHASE
Andersen Press, 1988, 128p. – 0 86264 193 4

MR BROWSER AND THE BRAIN SHARPENERS
*Penguin, 1982, 80p. – Pbk. – 0 14 031526 8
Andersen Press, 1979, 96p. – 0 905478 59 2*

MR BROWSER AND THE COMET CRISIS
*Penguin, 1983, 112p. – Pbk, O/P. –
0 14 031527 6
Andersen Press, 1981, 118p. – O/P. –
0 86264 004 0*

MR BROWSER AND THE MINI-METEORITES
*Beaver Books, 1986, 128p. – Pbk, O/P. –
0 09 943670 1
Andersen Press, 1983, 127p. – 0 86264 030 X*

MR BROWSER AND THE SPACE MAGGOTS
*Penguin, 1990, 128p. – Pbk. – 0 14 034394 6
Andersen Press, 1989, 126p. – 0 86264 244 2*

MR BROWSER IN THE SPACE MUSEUM
*Beaver Books, 1988, 144p. – Pbk. –
0 09 956770 9
Andersen Press, 1985, 144p. – 0 86264 095 4*

MR BROWSER MEETS THE BURROWERS
*Beaver Books, 1986, 128p. – Pbk. –
0 09 943680 9*

*Andersen Press, 1980, 128p. – O/P. –
0 905478 88 6*

MR BROWSER MEETS THE MIND SHRINKERS
Andersen Press, 1989, 128p. – 0 86264 261 2

REVENGE OF THE BRAIN SHARPENERS
*Beaver Books, 1987, – Pbk. – 0 09 954090 8
Andersen Press, 1982, 120p. – 0 86264 013 X
all illustrated by Tony Ross*

A series of science fiction stories involving the children of Chivy Chase school and their teacher, Mr Browser. The books are funny, with lots of action, maintaining the reader's interest, not just to the end of the book, but throughout the series. Tony Ross's amusing illustrations add the finishing touch.
Age range: 8–10

A PARTY FOR LESTER
*Andersen Press, 1984, 146p. – 0 86264 066 0
illustrated by Sarah Parker*

Quite different to the *Mr Browser* series, this story concerns Lester, a retarded child, and his struggle to be accepted at school and in society. He undergoes a fundamental change when told he has to attend a special school. Aided by his friend Billy, they go into hiding in the church until a solution can be found. A tense and moving story.
Age range: 10–12

THE QUEST OF THE QUIDNUNCS
*Andersen Press, 1985, 128p. – O/P. –
0 86264 113 6
illustrated by Tony Ross*

Along the same lines as *Mr Browser*, this science fiction story is set in Austria, where the holiday of a lifetime is not all it promised. Exciting and funny, this will not disappoint Mr Curtis's many fans.
Age range: 8–10

D

DAHL, Roald

British. Born Llandaff, Glamorganshire, Wales, 1916, died 23 November 1990. Educated Repton School, Yorkshire. RAF in WW II. Wing Commander, 1943–45. Married: 1) Actress Patricia Neal, 1953, divorced 1983, one son, four daughters (one deceased); 2) Felicity Ann Crosland, 1983.

Awards: Federation of Children's Book Groups award: *The Witches*, 1983
Whitbread Award: *The Witches*, 1983
Federation of Children's Book Groups award: *Matilda*, 1988
Smarties' Prize for Children's Books: *Esio Trot*, 1990

Undisputedly the most popular children's author of today. The reason for this is the combination of original and ingenious plots, which appeal to the reluctant reader, and a verbal competence which satisfies the more demanding reader. Roald Dahl allied himself with the child reader in much the same way as Enid Blyton. The books are full of crude, even rude humour, which causes raised adult eyebrows, but guarantees delighted readers.

THE BFG
Windrush, 1988, 288p. – L/P. – 1 85089 957 6
Penguin, 1984, 208p. – Pbk. – 0 14 031597 7
Cape, 1982, 224p. – 0 224 02040 4
illustrated by Quentin Blake

Sophie befriends the friendly giant and together they plot to put an end to the other bogthumping giants. Excellent on television.
Age range: 9–11

CHARLIE AND THE CHOCOLATE FACTORY
Windrush, 1986, 184p. – L/P. – 1 85089 902 9
Allen & Unwin, 1985, 159p. – 0 04 823303 X
Penguin, 1985, 160p. – Pbk. – 0 14 031824 0
illustrated by Michael Foreman

Charlie's winning ticket enabling him to inspect the chocolate factory leads him into some astonishing situations. Many versions are available, including a play; has been filmed and televised.
Age range: 8–10

CHARLIE AND THE GREAT GLASS ELEVATOR
Windrush, 1987, 240p. – L/P. – 1 85089 907 X
Allen & Unwin, 1986, 160p. – 0 04 823342 0
Penguin, 1986, 160p. – Pbk. – 0 14 032043 1
illustrated by Michael Foreman

The sequel to *Charlie and the Chocolate Factory.* Instead of stopping at the correct place, the elevator goes off into space, where they cope as best they can.
Age range: 8–10

DANNY, THE CHAMPION OF THE WORLD
Windrush, 1989, 276p. – L/P. – 1 85089 982 7
Penguin, 1977, 176p. – Pbk, O/P. – 0 14 030912 8
Cape, 1975, 208p. – 0 224 01201 0
illustrated by Jill Bennett

Danny is unusual, in that, at the age of five, his knowledge of cars is second to none. This knowledge comes in useful when he has to rescue his Dad, who has an accident while out poaching. He earns his title by proving that he is a champion poacher, the equal of his Dad. A film version has been shown on television.
Age range: 9–11

ESIO TROT
Cape, 1990, 64p. – 0 224 02786 7
illustrated by Quentin Blake

Mr Hoppy woos his lady-love by the unlikely means of a tortoise. Amusing as always, with large print and lots of

illustrations, this makes an excellent easy reading book.
Age range: 9–10

FANTASTIC MR FOX
Windrush, 1989, 96p. – L/P. – 1 85089 980 0
Penguin, 1988, 96p. – Pbk. – 0 14 032671 5
Allen & Unwin, 1970, 63p. – 0 04 823096 0

Wily Mr Fox manages to outwit the combined brains of three farmers, Boggins, Bunce and Bean, who are determined to put an end to him.
Age range: 7–9

GEORGE'S MARVELLOUS MEDICINE
Windrush, 1989, 152p. – L/P. – 1 85089 985 1
Penguin, 1982, 112p. – Pbk. – 0 14 031492 X
Cape, 1981, 96p. – 0 224 01901 5

George finds his unpleasant Grandma too much to bear, so he concocts a medicine which he hopes will 'cure' her. Also televised.
Age range: 8–11

THE GIRAFFE AND THE PELLY AND ME
Penguin, 1987, 32p. – Pbk. – 0 14 050566 0
Cape, 1985, 32p. – 0 224 02999 1

An unlikely trio set up a window cleaning business, and embark upon some hilarious escapades.
Age range: 6–9

JAMES AND THE GIANT PEACH
Unwin Hyman, 1990, 136p. – 0 04 440621 5
Penguin, 1990, 144p. – Pbk. – 0 14 034269 9
Windrush, 1988, 144p. – L/P. – 1 85089 931 2

James travels the world inside an outsize peach, having fantastic adventures.
Age range: 8–10

MATILDA
Chivers Press, 1989, 320p. – L/P. –
0 7451 1044 4
Penguin, 1989, 240p. – Pbk, O/P. –
0 14 032759 2
Cape, 1988, 192p. – 0 224 02572 4

Matilda is a child prodigy who is not appreciated by her parents. She develops her mental powers to a very high degree, and uses them to defeat her cruel headmistress. Televised, and also a very successful play.
Age range: 8–11

THE TWITS
Windrush, 1990, 112p. – L/P. – 1 85089 870 7
Penguin, 1982p, 96p. – Pbk. – 0 14 031406 7
Cape, 1980, 80p. – 0 224 01855 8

An amusing anecdotal story about an unpleasant couple who spend their time playing revolting tricks on each other.
Age range: 7–9

THE WITCHES
Windrush, 1990, 196p. – L/P. – 1 85089 890 1
Penguin, 1985, 208p. – Pbk. – 0 14 031730 9
Cape, 1983, 192p. – 0 224 02165 6

At last – an explanation for the curious fact that most people have never met a black-cloaked witch accompanied by a broomstick. 'Real' witches look the same as everyone else, at first glance, but once you have learned to recognize them, terrible things can happen. The book has been televised and made into a film.
Age range: 9–11

DANN, Colin (Michael)

British. Born Richmond, Surrey, 1943. Educated Richmond and East Sheen Grammar School. Married Elizabeth Stratton, 1977. Writer.

Awards: Arts Council National Award for Children's Literature: *The Animals of Farthing Wood,* 1980

Address: The Old Forge, Whatlington, East Sussex, England

ANIMALS OF FARTHING WOOD
Mammoth, 1989, 320p. – Pbk. – 0 7497 0035 1
Magna, 1981, 496p. – L/P. – 0 86009 338 7

In the same series:

FLIGHT FROM FARTHING WOOD
Heinemann, 1988. – 0 434 93398 8

FOX CUB BOLD
Magna, 1986, 256p. – L/P. – 1 85057 016 7
Magna, 1986, 256p. – Pbk, L/P. –
1 85057 017 5
Beaver Books, 1984, 176p. – Pbk. –
0 09 937520 6
Hutchinson, 1983, 164p. – O/P. –
0 09 153860 2
illustrated by Terry Riley

FOX'S FEUD
Magna, 1985, 271p. – L/P. – 0 86009 690 4
Arrow Books, 1983, 176p. – Pbk. –
0 09 932260 9
Hutchinson, 1982, 174p. – O/P. –
0 09 149400 1

IN THE GRIP OF WINTER
Sparrow Books, 1982, 176p. – Pbk. –
0 09 929220 3
Hutchinson, 1981, 168p. – O/P. –
0 09 146340 8
illustrated by Terry Riley

SIEGE OF WHITE DEER PARK
Magna, 1987, 252p. – L/P. – 0 86009 983 0
Magna, 1987, 252p. – Pbk, L/P. –
0 86009 984 9
Beaver Books, 1986, 160p. – Pbk. –
0 09 944760 6
Hutchinson, 1985, 160p. – 0 09 161700 6

A series of books about the animals living in the threatened Farthing Wood. The first story tells how they decide to find a safer home and describes their perilous journey, depending on each other for help and support. Subsequent books reveal that there is to be no 'happy ever after', for the animals find that they still have to work together to survive. The books reflect Colin Dann's deep concern for conservation issues and his knowledge of wild life. They do require a degree of reading competence, but any effort is richly rewarded by exciting, tense adventure stories of an unusual kind.
Age range: 10–12

THE BEACH DOGS
Beaver Books, 1989, 144p. – Pbk. –
0 09 961380 8
Hutchinson, 1988. – 0 09 173623 4

Jack belongs to the ferryman and has to spend each winter marooned on his island home. One year he persuades two friends to take the last ferry with him, but life in hiding is not all fun, and they have some hair-raising adventures. Thoroughly enjoyable, with really attractive covers for both the hardback and paperback editions.
Age range: 9–12

A GREAT ESCAPE
Hutchinson, 1990, 164p. – 0 09 174437 7

Unable to bear the sight of live animals in the pet shop, Eric opens all the cages and sets them free. Thus the amazing troop of monkeys, rabbits and tortoises, etc., make for their meeting place – the windmill.
Age range: 10–12

JUST NUFFIN
Red Fox, 1990, 248p. – Pbk. – 0 09 966900 5
Hutchinson, 1989, 144p. – 0 09 174092 4

Not a very original plot, but the story is tackled without the usual accompanying sentimentality. Roger is bored on holiday until his father finds an abandoned puppy. He is only allowed to keep it until a home can be found, and so he lives in constant fear of losing his beloved friend.

A little overlong, it is nevertheless a good story, well handled.
Age range: 9–12

KING OF THE VAGABONDS
Beaver Books, 1988, 160p. – Pbk. –
0 09 957190 0
Hutchinson, 1987, 128p. – 0 09 171960 7

An unusual story about a curious kitten determined to find out who his father is. Attractively produced.
Age range: 9–12

RAM OF SWEETRIVER
Beaver Books, 1987, 224p. – Pbk. –
0 09 951240 8
Hutchinson, 1986, 160p. – 0 09 165070 4

A graphic description of a devastating flood opens this story, which relates how a flock of sheep, led by a courageous and resourceful ram, struggle to survive.
Age range: 10–12

DAVIES, Andrew (Wynford)

British. Born Cardiff, Glamorganshire, Wales, 1936. Educated Whitchurch Grammar School, Glamorgan; University College, London. B.A. (Eng.). Married Diana Huntley, 1960, one son, one daughter. Teacher and lecturer.

Awards: Guardian Award for Children's Fiction: *Conrad's War*, 1979
Boston Globe–Horn Award: *Conrad's War*, 1980

Address: 21 Station Road, Kenilworth, Warwickshire CV8 1JJ, England

Agent: Harvey Unna and Stephen Durbridge Ltd, 24–32 Pottery Lane, London W11 4LZ, England

CONRAD'S WAR
Blackie, 1989, 128p. – 0 216 92564 9
Chivers Press, 1987, 192p. – L/P. – 0 7451 0489 4
Hippo Books, 1980, 144p. – Pbk. – 0 590 70010 3

War books are not unusual, but there are few for younger readers. Conrad, fascinated by the war, suddenly finds he is taking part, and comes to realize that war at first hand is much less glamorous. *Age range:* 9–11

DAVIES, (Edward) Hunter

British. Born Renfrew, Scotland, 1936. Educated University of Durham. B.A., Dip. Ed. Married the novelist Margaret Forster, two daughters, one son. Columnist and broadcaster.

Address: 11 Boscastle Road, London NW5, England

COME ON, OSSIE
Armada Books, 1987, 132p. – Pbk, O/P. – 0 00 672739 5
Bodley Head, 1985, 132p. – 0 370 30895 6
illustrated by Malou

In the same series:

OSSIE GOES SUPERSONIC
Armada Books, 1988, 144p. – Pbk, O/P. – 0 00 672894 4
Bodley Head, 1986, 144p. – 0 370 31007 1

OSSIE THE MILLIONAIRE
Bodley Head, 1987, 144p. – 0 370 31111 6

FLOSSIE TEACAKE AGAIN
Armada Books, 1985, 128p. – Pbk. – 0 00 672384 5
Bodley Head, 1982, 128p. – O/P. – 0 370 30554 X

FLOSSIE TEACAKE'S FUR COAT
Armada Books, 1984, 144p. – Pbk. – 0 00 672178 8
Bodley Head, 1982, 144p. – O/P. – 0 370 30933 2

FLOSSIE TEACAKE STRIKES BACK
Armada Books, 1986, 128p. – Pbk. – 0 00 672555 4
Bodley Head, 1984, 128p. – O/P. – 0 370 30622 8
all illustrated by Laurence Hutchins

Two series to encourage new readers to tackle full length books. Originality and humour, combined with large clear print, makes them ideal.
Age range: 7–9

DEJONG, Meindert

American. Born Wierum, Netherlands, 1906; moved to the USA when aged 8. Educated Calvin College, Grand Rapids, Michigan; University of Chicago. US Army Corps, WW II. Married: 1) Hattie Overeinter, 1932; 2) Beatrice de Claire McElwee, 1962 (died 1969). Step-children. Worked as college lecturer and farmer.

Awards: American Library Association Newbery Medal: *The Wheel on the School*, 1955
Hans Christian Andersen International Medal Award, 1962
Catholic Library Association Regina Medal, 1972

Address: 351 Grand Street, Allegan, Michigan 49010, USA

A gifted writer whose books are read less than they deserve. The book jackets are plain and unattractive, and do not, therefore, appeal to children, but the stories are excellent.

THE ALMOST ALL-WHITE RABBITY CAT
Penguin, 1977, 96p. – Pbk, O/P. – 0 14 030674 9
illustrated by Gioia Fiammenghi

Barney was heart-broken at leaving his rabbits behind. The new city flat was boring until in walked the cat which changed his life.
Age range: 8–10

ALONG CAME A DOG
Collins, 1971, 128p. – Pbk, O/P. – 0 00 670478 6
Illustrated by Maurice Sendak

A wonderful story about a black dog who befriends and protects an unpopular hen. When she hatches some chicks, the family is complete.
Age range: 9–11

THE HOUSE OF SIXTY FATHERS
J. Murray, 1988, 160p. – 0 7195 4510 2
Penguin, 1971. – Pbk. – 0 14 030276 X
illustrated by Maurice Sendak

Based on a true story, this tense book tells of a small boy, very frightened by the destruction of his village by Japanese soldiers, who becomes separated from his parents. Accompanied by his dog, he begins his search for them, while the dangers surrounding him increase.
Age range: 10–12

HURRY HOME, CANDY
Armada Books, 1977, 159p. – Pbk. – 0 00 671352 1
Lutterworth Press, 1962. – 0 7188 0452 X
illustrated by Maurice Sendak

A story in which the first chapter brings a lump to the throat that stays throughout the book. Candy is a stray dog, longing for love which never seems to materialize. It's a relief to reach the end!
Age range: 9–11

JOURNEY FROM PEPPERMINT STREET
Collins, 1973, 192p. – Pbk, O/P. – 0 00 670748 3
Lutterworth Press, 1969, 242p. – 0 7188 1587 4
illustrated by Emily Arnold McCully

Set in Holland at the turn of the century, this story has to surmount the barrier of historical fiction. With the right introduction, many children empathize with the anxious Siebren, who, fed up with looking after his baby brother, is allowed to accompany Grandpa on his visit to his great-aunt. This journey brings many surprises, good and bad. Siebren learns (as does the reader) many lessons about life. The book has a highly satisfying ending.
Age range: 9–11

THE WHEEL ON THE SCHOOL
Penguin, n.d. – Pbk. – 0 14 030152 6
illustrated by Maurice Sendak

Although not read very much now, this remains an excellent book in many ways. By puzzling over the absence of storks, a solution is found to the nesting problem. Highly satisfactory for all concerned.
Age range: 10–12

DICKINSON, Peter (Malcolm de Brissac)

British. Born Livingston, Zambia, 1927. Educated Eton College (King's Scholar); King's College, Cambridge, B.A. British Army. Married Mary Rose Barnard 1953 (died 1988), two daughters, two sons. Editor and reviewer.

Awards:	Guardian Children's Fiction Award: *Blue Hawke*, 1977
	Whitbread Award: *Tulku*, 1979
	Library Association Carnegie Medals: *Tulku*, 1979
	Library Association Carnegie Medals: *City of Gold*, 1980
	Whitbread Award: *AK*, 1990
Address:	Brendeen Lodge, near Alresford, Hampshire SO24 0JN, England

The books produced for children by this author are quite outstanding. His ability as a story-teller is second to none; add his strong characterization, all constructed by a highly intelligent mind, and the result is some very powerful novels, many for older teenagers. Intelligent children will find them a challenging and absorbing read.

ANNERTON PIT
Penguin, 1979, 176p. – Pbk. – 0 14 031042 8
Gollancz, 1977, 192p. – 0 575 02239 6

Twelve-year-old Jake is blind, but compensates for his lack of sight by a highly developed sixth sense. It is this attribute which he and his brother heavily rely on when they set off to find their grandfather whose hobby, ghost-hunting, has landed him in a terrifying dangerous situation. Superbly told through Jake's senses, it is a tense thriller.
Age range: 11–13

A BOX OF NOTHING
Chivers Press, 1987, 208p. – L/P. –
0 7451 0547 5
Magnet Books, 1987, 128p. – Pbk. –
0 416 96630 6
Gollancz, 1985, 144p. – 0 575 03530 7
illustrated by Ian Newsham

An unusual adventure story set in motion by the purchase of a box of nothing for the princely sum of nothing from nowhere else but the Nothing Shop. Children too young or too reluctant to be able to tackle the fairly dense text and small print will nevertheless enjoy having it read to them.
Age range: 9–12

THE DEVIL'S CHILDREN
Penguin, 1972, 160p. – Pbk. – 0 14 030546 7

In the same series:

HEARTSEASE
Penguin, 1971, 192p. – Pbk. – 0 14 030498 3
Gollancz, 1969, 192p. – 0 575 00223 9

THE WEATHERMONGER
Gollancz, 1984, 144p. – 0 575 03475 0
Penguin, 1970, 176p. – Pbk, O/P. –
0 14 030433 9

Now published by Penguin in a single volume (1985, 348p. – O/P. – 0 14 031846 1) this trilogy is one of the most memorable works of fiction ever produced for children. Successive generations are captivated by the horrifying portrait of a future England in which people have rejected machines, but whose lives have been reduced to hardship and fear. Nicky is convinced that somewhere a machine has been resurrected. Absorbing, right to the final, optimistic chapter of the third book.
Age range: 12–14

THE GIFT
Penguin, 1975, 176p. – Pbk. – 0 14 030731 1
Gollancz, 1973, 176p. – 0 575 01630 2
illustrated by Gareth Floyd

Davy's life is not exactly wonderful, in spite of his ability to see beyond the face into what people are thinking and feeling. It can be just a nuisance, and sometimes, downright dangerous. His Granny always warned him not to make use of the things he learned this way, but the day comes when he has a terrible choice to make. A nail-biting television serial made this book accessible to lots of children who would not otherwise have felt able to tackle it.

Age range: 11–13

DICKS, Terrance

British. Born London, 1935. Educated East Ham Grammar School; Downing College, Cambridge.

A prolific writer capable of producing imaginative stories with great appeal to children. Full of action and easy to read, they are suitable for reluctant readers.

ASK OLIVER
Hodder
Piccadilly Press, Pbk.
illustrated by Valerie Littlewood

Mystery stories aimed at younger children. Oliver and his gang are good at solving mysteries. The reader is given clues, and can try to solve them first. Enjoyable and fun, they encourage new readers to gain confidence.
Age range: 7–9

BAKER STREET IRREGULARS
Blackie
Magnet Books, Pbk.

A series of modern Sherlock Holmes detective stories in which children solve mysteries using the same methods as their hero. Characterization is weak, but the plots are sound.
Age range: 10–12

A CAT CALLED MAX
Piccadilly Press
Piccadilly Press, Pbk.
illustrated by Toni Goffe

Max is no ordinary cat: although he has no home he is well-mannered and exudes a magical aura. An interesting and amusing story, doubtless with more to follow.
Age range: 6–8

DAVID AND GOLIATH
Hodder
Piccadilly Press, Pbk.
illustrated by Valerie Littlewood

Goliath is a huge, happy dog. Together, he and David embark on a series of adventures providing amusing yet short reads for beginners.
Age range: 6–8

THE MACMAGICS
Piccadilly Press, 1991, 64p. – 1 85340 155 2
Piccadilly Press, 1990, 96p. – 1 85340 080 7

In the same series:

MEET THE MACMAGICS
Piccadilly Press, 1990, 96p. – 1 85340 070 X
both illustrated by Celia Canning

Mike, trying hard to be a normal, boring schoolboy, is constantly embarrassed by his family displaying their various magical powers. Funny, easy to read, with plenty of illustrations.
Age range: 7–9

T. R. BEAR
Piccadilly Press
Corgi, Pbk.
illustrated by Susan Hellard

Jimmy and his Teddy have many little adventures, amusingly told in large print. Ideal for first time readers.
Age range: 6–8

DOHERTY, Berlie

British. Born Liverpool, 1943. Educated
Durham University, County Durham,
B.A. (Hons) English; Liverpool
University, Post-Graduate Certificate in
Social Sciences; Sheffield University,
Post-Graduate Certificate in Education.
Married Gerard Adrian Doherty, 1966,
two daughters and one son. Social
worker and teacher.

Awards: Library Association Carnegie
           Medal: *Granny was a Buffer
           Girl*, 1986

Address: 38 Banner Cross Road,
           Sheffield S11 9HR, South
           Yorkshire, England

A writer with an outstanding ability to
create vivid pictures in words, as well as
absorbing stories.

CHILDREN OF WINTER
*Armada Books, 1986, 128p. – Pbk. –
0 00 672583 X
Methuen, 1985, 128p. – O/P. – 0 416 51130 9*

Three children are sent away by their
parents to live in safety in a cave when
their village is struck by the plague. There
is humour, suspense and sensitivity in
every page. An excellent television
drama.
Age range: 9–12

GRANNY WAS A BUFFER GIRL
*Chivers Press, 1988, 232p. – L/P. –
0 7451 0725 7
Armada Books, 1988, 128p. -- Pbk. –
0 00 672792 1
Methuen, 1986, 128p. – 0 416 53590 9*

An unusual framework illustrates how
Jess's life is interwoven with her Granny.
It is a love story, an historical novel
describing a life of industrial toil, a story
of growing up, and is completely
compelling.
Age range: 12–14

HOW GREEN YOU ARE
*Methuen, 1982, 144p. – 0 416 20940 8
Armada Books, 1983, 144p. – Pbk. –
0 00 672210 5
illustrated by Eunice McGregor Turney*

In the same series:

THE MAKING OF FINGERS FINNIGAN
*Armada Books, 1985, 144p. – Pbk. –
0 00 672340 3
Methuen, 1983, 128p. – O/P. – 0 416 23610 3
illustrated by John Hayson*

Stories about a group of children who
live in the same street. Everyday
happenings vividly described with
laughter, sadness and, sometimes, a
serious tone combine to provide highly
enjoyable reads.
Age range: 9–11

SPELLHORN
*Collins, 1990, 192p. – Pbk. – 0 00 673500 2
Hamish Hamilton, 1989, 160p. – 0 241 12624 X*

A fantasy firmly based on experience and
reality. Laura is blind, and therefore 'sees'
the world through her hands and ears,
which is how she finds the lost unicorn.
The story of her life with the unicorn and
his people is utterly compelling.
Age range: 10–14

TILLY MINT TALES
*Armada Books, 1986, 96p. – Pbk. –
0 00 672557 0
Methuen, 1984, 96p. – 0 416 48220 1
illustrated by Thelma Lambert*

In the same series:

TILLY MINT AND THE DODO
*Collins, 1989, 112p. – Pbk. – 0 00 673250 X
Methuen, 1988, 128p. – 0 416 04622 3*

When Tilly's babysitter, Mrs Hardcastle,
falls asleep, it is a signal for the magic to
begin for Tilly. Fantasy stories, excellent
for reading aloud.
Age range: 7–9

WHITE PEAK FARM

*Armada Books, 1986, 112p. – Pbk. –
0 00 672431 0
Methuen, 1984, 112p. – 0 416 47020 3*

Describing life on a remote Derbyshire farm, this can be read as one long story, or as individual stories as they were when treated on television and radio. There is something for everyone from the age of 12 to adults, dealing with life and death issues.

Age range: 12–15

E

EADINGTON, Joan

British. Born Egham, Surrey, 1926.
Educated Open University, B.A., Arts.
Nurse, writer.

Address: C/o BBC Book Publicity
Department, Room A3125,
BBC Enterprises, Woodlands,
80 Wood Lane, London W12
0TT, England

Here is an example of the influence that
television has on the reading habits of
children.

THE ADVENTURES OF JONNY
BRIGGS
BBC, 1979, 159p. – O/P. – 0 563 17728 4
illustrated by William Marshall

In the same series:

JONNY BRIGGS
Hodder, 1983, 80p. – Pbk, O/P. –
0 340 33118 6
BBC, 1977, 80p. – Pbk, O/P. – 0 563 17268 1

JONNY BRIGGS AND THE
GALLOPING WEDDING
BBC, 1983, 96p. – 0 563 20140 1
Hodder, 1983, 96p. – Pbk, O/P. –
0 340 33022 8

JONNY BRIGGS AND THE GHOST
Hodder, 1984, 80p. – Pbk, O/P. –
0 340 35338 4
BBC, 1978, 80p. – Pbk, O/P. – 0 563 17462 5
illustrated by William Marshall

JONNY BRIGGS AND THE GIANT
CAVE
Hodder, 1982, 96p. – Pbk. – 0 340 28042 5

JONNY BRIGGS AND THE GREAT
RAZZLE DAZZLE
BBC, 1981, 96p. – O/P. – 0 563 17931 7
Hodder, 1981, 96p. – Pbk. – 0 340 27532 4

JONNY BRIGGS AND THE JUBILEE
CONCERT
BBC, 1984, 96p. – O/P. – 0 563 20234 3
Hodder, 1984, 96p. – Pbk, O/P. –
0 340 34837 2

JONNY BRIGGS AND THE SECRET
SUNFLOWERS
Hodder, 1988, 80p. – O/P. – 0 340 42528 8

JONNY BRIGGS AND THE SILVER
SURPRISE
Hodder, 1989, 80p. – 0 340 49713 0

JONNY BRIGGS AND THE WHITBY
WEEKEND
Hodder, 1985, 80p. – Pbk, O/P. –
0 340 37187 0
BBC, 1979, 80p. – Pbk, O/P. – 0 563 17700 4

STAND UP JONNY BRIGGS
Hodder, 1988, 128p. – Pbk, O/P. –
0 340 39976 7
BBC, 1986, 144p. – 0 563 20535 0

THE WORLD OF JONNY BRIGGS
Hodder, 1985, 80p. – Pbk. – 0 340 38718 1
BBC, 1985, 126p. – O/P. – 0 563 20430 3

A series of family stories first told on BBC
television's popular *Jackanory*
programme. They were later published
and are much in demand. Some of the
books have also been dramatized for
television.
Age range: 7–10

EDWARDS, Dorothy (née Brown)

British. Born Teddington, Middlesex, 1914 (died 9 August 1982). Educated Teddington and Sunbury. Married Francis P. Edwards, 1942, one daughter, one son. Worked as secretary, freelance editor, radio producer, lecturer and broadcaster.

Awards: Children's Rights Workshop Other Award: *A Strong and Willing Girl*, 1981

The mention of Dorothy Edwards's name immediately brings to mind the *My Naughty Little Sister Stories*, which, after 30 years, still claim a place on nursery bookshelves, in spite of being a little old-fashioned now. She is a competent storyteller, and her books are well worth reading.

KING DICKY BIRD AND THE BOSSY PRINCESS
Magnet Books, 1988, 64p. – Pbk. – 0 416 07502 9
Methuen, 1987, 60p. – 0 416 96100 2

A modern, humorous fairy tale about a princess who marries a most unusual beggar.
Age range: 7–9

THE MAGICIAN WHO KEPT A PUB AND OTHER STORIES
Armada Books, 1981, 160p. – Pbk. – 0 00 671785 3
Kestrel Books, 1975, 128p. – O/P. – 0 7226 5452 9
illustrated by Jill Bennett

In the same series:

MARK THE DRUMMER BOY
Magnet Books, 1986, 96p. – Pbk, O/P. – 0 416 61860 X
Methuen, 1983, 96p. – 0 416 26130 2
illustrated by Thelma Lambert

THE OLD MAN WHO SNEEZED: READ ALOUD STORIES
Magnet Books, 1985, 96p. – Pbk. – 0 416 51920 2
Methuen, 1983, 96p. – O/P. – 0 416 26120 5
illustrated by Thelma Lambert

Books of short stories, excellent for reading aloud, of the sort which Dorothy Edwards excels in writing. They are extremely varied, and appeal to both boys and girls.
Age range: 5–7

MISTS AND MAGIC
Armada Books, 1985, 160p. – Pbk, O/P. – 0 00 672357 8
Lutterworth Press, 1983, 160p. – 0 7188 2537 3
illustrated by Jill Bennett

An excellent and wide-ranging collection of stories and poems chosen and edited by Dorothy Edwards. Equally effective, whether read aloud or silently.
Age range: 9–11

A STRONG AND WILLING GIRL
Magnet Books, 1982, 112p. – Pbk. – 0 416 24590 0
Methuen, 1980, 128p. – 0 416 88630 2

The story of a young girl in service, the Victorian age is revealed on every page. Entertaining to read as well as instructive in period detail.
Age range: 12–14

F

FARJEON, Eleanor

Also wrote as 'Tomfool'. British. Born London, 1881 (died 5 June 1965). Daughter of novelist Benjamin Leopold Farjeon; sister of the writers Herbert and Joseph Jefferson Farjeon and the composer Harry Farjeon. Educated privately. Columnist, poet, writer.

Awards: Library Association Carnegie Medal: *The Little Bookroom*, 1955
Hans Andersen International Medal, 1956
Catholic Library Association Regina Medal, 1959

Eleanor Farjeon wrote many books for children, for which she received an award. They are now generally considered to be out of date, but it is good that these books, aptly illustrated by Edward Ardizzone, still find a place on the bookshelves.

THE LITTLE BOOKROOM
OUP, 1979, 314p. – O/P. – 0 19 277099 3
OUP, 1972, 226p. – Pbk, O/P. – 0 19 272035 X
illustrated by Edward Ardizzone

A collection of stories for older children. They are varied in length and subject, with something for everyone. Magic, fairies, tales of bygone childhood – quite spellbinding.
Age range: 7–9

THE OLD NURSE'S STOCKING BASKET
Penguin, 1981, 80p. – Pbk, O/P. –
0 14 031220 X
OUP, 1980, 108p. – O/P. – 0 19 277093 4
illustrated by Edward Ardizzone

Although first published in 1931, this book is still re-issued because it has a timeless quality that ensures it can be passed from one generation to another. There are 13 short stories for reading aloud, varied in content, but uniformly rich in the poetic use of language, making them a delight to listen to.
Age range: 3–7

FINE, Anne

British. Born Leicester, 1947. Educated Northampton High School for Girls; University of Warwick, B.A. (Hons) History and Politics. Married Kit Fine, 1968, two daughters. Teacher and information officer.

Awards: Scottish Arts Council Award, 1986
Guardian Children's Fiction Award: *Bill's New Frock*, 1989
Smarties Award: *Bill's New Frock*, 1989
Library Association Carnegie Medal: *Goggle-Eyes*, 1990
Guardian Children's Fiction Award: *Goggle-Eyes*, 1990

Agent: Murray Pollinger, 4 Garrick Street, London WC2E 9BH, England

A writer of great originality, Anne Fine's books are a true delight to read. She has an extraordinary ability to pitch them at just the right level and she can put across a serious point while at the same time making a joke of it. Every story skilfully combines humour with a deep understanding of the situation portrayed in a straightforward manner.

ANNELI THE ART-HATER
Methuen, 1986, 128p. – O/P. – 0 416 61550 3
illustrated by Vanessa Julian–Ottie

Art is Anneli's most hated subject at school, but one day she finds an old oil painting which makes her see things very differently. A good read.
Age range: 8–10

BILL'S NEW FROCK
Mammoth, 1990, 96p. – Pbk. – 0 7497 0305 9
Methuen, 1989, 96p. – 0 416 12152 7
illustrated by Philippe Dupasquier

Bill wakes up one morning to find he is a girl, but only he seems to notice that there has been a change. Everyone acts as if he has always been a girl. This dilemma is skilfully maintained to the very end, causing many hilarious situations.
Age range: 8–10

THE COUNTRY PANCAKE
Methuen, 1989, 96p. – 0 416 14982 0
illustrated by Philippe Dupasquier

Intended for younger readers, this delightful story will amuse and interest children to the last page. Easy to read.
Age range: 7–9

CRUMMY MUMMY AND ME
Penguin, 1989, 112p. – Pbk. – 0 14 032876 9
Deutsch, 1988, 96p. – 0 233 98059 8
illustrated by David Higham

Poor Minna has a difficult time trying to behave sensibly when her 'punk' Mum behaves so outrageously. All she wants is a 'normal' Mum like her friends. Excellent light entertainment.
Age range: 9–11

GOGGLE-EYES
Penguin, 1990, 144p. – Pbk. – 0 14 034071 8
Hamish Hamilton, 1989, 144p. – 0 241 12617 7

Divorce is the subject of many books designed to help children come to terms with events in their own life, but good books which deal specifically with a prospective re-marriage and the problems it can cause are less easy to find. Here is one of the best. The story is told by Kitty, the elder daughter, and it realistically portrays the emotional and practical problems that arise when an unwelcome 'outsider' becomes part of the family. The conclusion and the warmth and humour of the telling make this a delightful and useful book to read.
Age range: 11–14

THE GRANNY PROJECT
Mammoth, 1990, 128p. – Pbk. – 0 7497 0186 2
Collins, 1986, 80p. – Pbk. – 0 00 330234 2
Methuen, 1983, 160p. – O/P. – 0 416 44400 8

A moving but unsentimental look at a problem facing many families today – what to do for old people who can no

longer care for themselves. The children want to keep Granny at home; the parents want to put her in a home. The ensuing battle makes highly entertaining reading.
Age range: 10–12

MADAME DOUBTFIRE
Chivers Press, 1990, 272p. – L/P. –
0 7451 1228 5
Penguin, 1989, 192p. – Pbk. – 0 14 032633 2
Hamish Hamilton, 1987, 176p. – 0 241 12001 2

A gem among children's books, this novel shows how the troubles of divorce can be overcome, given the will and a sense of humour. The children's father, out of work, appears incognito for the job of cleaning lady to his ex-wife. It works well at first, but then the inevitable complications set in. This sensitive yet funny story will appeal to everyone, but speaks particularly meaningfully to young people who have experienced divorce.
Age range: 10–12

A PACK OF LIARS
Penguin, 1990, 128p. – 0 14 032954 4
Hamish Hamilton, 1988, 128p. – 0 241 12229 5

A common dilemma – telling lies is wrong, but sometimes expediency makes them necessary. Oliver is unable to resolve this dilemma which eventually leads him into an exciting adventure, related with much humour.
Age range: 10–12

ROUND BEHIND THE ICE-HOUSE
Penguin, 1990, 112p. – Pbk. – 0 14 034067 X
Methuen, 1981, 112p. – O/P. – 0 416 20820 7

This book can be read on two levels. There is the storyline, with the twins pitting themselves against Jamieson and his cruelty. Underlying this is the story of the twins, once so close, now approaching adolescence and painfully growing apart. An exceptionally well written, sensitive story.
Age range: 12–14

THE STONE MENAGERIE
Methuen, 1980, 128p. – O/P. – 0 416 88640 X

Unusually set in a mental hospital, this moving story tells how Ally comes to understand the acrimonious relationship he has with his parents. Characteristically full of humour and sadness, this book lives in the memory.
Age range: 12–14

FISK, Nicholas

Pseudonym for David Higginbottom.
British. Born London, 1923. Educated
Ardingly College, Sussex. RAF WW II.
Married Dorothy Antoinette Richold,
1949, twin daughters, two sons. Actor,
journalist, musician, editor and publisher,
former advertising creative director and
consultant.

Address: 59 Elstree Road, Bushey
           Heath, Hertfordshire WD2
           3QX, England

Agent: Laura Cecil, 17 Alwyne Villas,
           London N1 2HG, England

Often underestimated, perhaps because
he is such a prolific writer, Nicholas Fisk
has written some really excellent novels.
He writes in a chatty style which makes
his books readily accessible to all
children. The plots are both exciting and
thought–provoking, and can make a real
contribution to the maturing process
which so many children find difficult.

ANTIGRAV
Penguin, 1982, 128p. – Pbk, O/P. –
0 14 031416 4
Kestrel Books, 1978, 128p. – O/P. –
0 7226 5322 0

The classic dilemma of good versus bad,
with the outcome dependent on the
integrity of three children, who find an
apparently harmless red pebble on the
beach. It quickly becomes obvious that it
is an extra-special pebble which, in the
wrong hands, would have evil
consequences. Exciting and easy to read.
Age range: 8–11

DARK SUN, BRIGHT SUN
Blackie, 1986, 128p. – O/P. – 0 216 92024 8

An unusual science fiction story set on the
distant planet of Merci. The festival of
Dany's Day is approaching, and evil
forces are about to be unleashed against
the unsuspecting children.
Age range: 7–11

GRINNY
Chivers Press, 1989, 168p. – L/P. –
0 7451 0827 X
Collins, 1984, 162p. – 0 00 330020 X
Penguin, 1975, 96p. – Pbk – 0 14 030745 1

Tim and Beth are shocked when they
realize that Great-aunt Emma is, in fact,
an alien and highly dangerous. The
ensuing battle provides a gripping story,
while helping children to come to terms
with the realization that adults, even
one's parents, are not infallible.
Age range: 10–13

LEADFOOT
Hodder, 1982, 128p. – Pbk, O/P. –
0 340 26809 3
Pelham Books, 1980, 128p. – O/P. –
0 7207 1199 1

An intriguing title for an action-packed
thriller, in which a classy Alvis is pitted
against a loud Pontiac. It has a special
appeal for boys with some knowledge of
cars.
Age range: 10–13

MINDBENDERS
Penguin, 1988, 112p. – Pbk. – 0 14 032164 0
Viking Kestrel, 1987, 114p. – 0 670 81244 7

A nest of ants is an unusual and a rather
disappointing present. Gradually Vinny
and Toby become fascinated, then
virtually hypnotized. Mindbending
becomes a habit, but there is danger in
store, as there must be when people can
be controlled. An excellent read.
Age range: 10–13

MONSTER MAKER
Mammoth, 1989, 144p. – Pbk. – 0 7497 0049 1
Chivers Press, 1986, 200p. – L/P, O/P. –
0 7451 0301 4
Pelham Books, 1979, 142p. – O/P. –
0 7207 1111 8

Matt is fascinated by the mechanics of
constructing monsters for films, and is
delighted when Chauncey lets him help.
He identifies with the creations to such an
extent that he is convinced they are real
and he cannot leave them. Local

hooligans breaking into the studio, as a result of Matt's actions, bring him back to a frightening reality. A gripping read, for the plot is exciting; a little more difficult to understand are the underlying complexities of Matt's character which shape the story. The book made a strange, compelling television drama.
Age range: 10–13

ON THE FLIP SIDE

Chivers Press, 1987, 200p. – L/P. –
0 7451 0587 4
Penguin, 1985, 128p. – Pbk, O/P. –
0 14 031556 X
Kestrel Books, 1983, 160p. – O/P. –
0 7226 5825 7

A world catastrophe is threatening and can be averted only by Letty, who has an extraordinary affinity with animals. A topical theme with an unusual slant.
Age range: 10–12

A RAG, A BONE AND A HANK OF HAIR

Penguin, 1982, 128p. – Pbk. – 0 14 031417 2
Kestrel Books, 1980, 126p. – O/P. –
0 7226 5550 9

The title is a list of 'ingredients' from which 'reborns' are made. Reborns are necessary since the nuclear accident wiped out so many people. Brin has the job of controlling these newly created children, but his plans go wrong. A chilling portrayal of human engineering at its worst. An exceptional book.
Age range: 10–13

ROBOT REVOLT

Penguin, 1983, 128p. – Pbk, O/P. –
0 14 031551 9
Pelham Books, 1981, 128p. – O/P. –
00 7207 1332 3

Max the robot helps the children in a plot against their father, but when it suits him he stops obeying and makes his own dangerous plans. Not the most original story, but, well written, it makes a good, exciting read.
Age range. 10–12

SNATCHED

Hodder, 1984, 128p. – Pbk, O/P. –
0 340 35847 5
Hodder, 1983, 117p. – O/P. – 0 340 28455 2

Two children are kidnapped because their father is an important ambassador. They are exceptionally brave, and refuse to give way to the fear that their situation naturally inspires. Realistically described in Nicholas Fisk's characteristic colloquial style.
Age range: 10–12

SPACE HOSTAGES

Kestrel Books, 1984, 144p. – 0 7226 5917 2
Penguin, 1970, 144p. – Pbk. – 0 14 030439 8

A top-secret spacecraft with nine children on board is adrift in space. Their struggle to get home, and all the dangers they have to face without adult help provide the ingredients for an exciting read.
Age range: 10–12

STARSTORMER SAGA:

STARSTORMERS

Blackie, 1984, 112p. – O/P. – 0 216 91691 7
Hodder, 1980. – Pbk, O/P. – 0 340 24878 5

SUN BURST

Hodder, 1980. – Pbk, O/P. – 0 340 24879 3
Blackie, 1985, 128p. – O/P. – 0 216 91692 5

CATFANG

Blackie, 1985, 112p. – O/P. – 0 216 91693 3
Hodder, 1981, 96p. – Pbk, O/P. –
0 340 26529 9

EVIL EYE

Blackie, 1986, 112p. – O/P. – 0 216 91694 1
Hodder, 1982, 112p. – Pbk, O/P. –
0 340 27076 4

This is a lengthy and complicated science fiction series. Committed readers of this genre will enjoy it immensely, and will read it strictly in order. However, each volume gives a precis of 'the story so far', so it is possible to read individual books.
Age range: 10–14

TRILLIONS

Kestrel Books, 1984, 128p. – O/P. –
0 7226 5918 0
Penguin, 1973, 128p. – Pbk. – 0 14 030633 1

First published almost 20 years ago, this is still a firm favourite with science fiction fans, and is hugely enjoyed by many who would not normally read science fiction. The army wants to destroy the hordes of brittle, hard bright 'things' which have invaded. The children are horrified, and try to rescue them. An excellent television drama.
Age range: 9–12

WHEELIE IN THE STARS
Penguin, 1979, 96p. – Pbk. – 0 14 031066 5

Brave space cadets succeed, against overwhelming odds, in saving the population of a doomed planet. The basic story is derivative, but it is handled with ingenuity.
Age range: 10–12

THE WORM CHARMERS
Walker Books, 1990, 192p. – Pbk. – 0 7445 1448 7
Walker Books, 1989, 192p. – 0 7445 0837 1

An adventure story, full of action, realistic children, and an exciting plot about kidnapping. With clear print, this is an excellent read.
Age range: 10–12

FOX, Paula

American. Born New York City, 1923, the daughter of the writer Paul Hervey Fox. Educated Columbia University, New York. Married: 1) Richard Sigerson 1948 (divorced 1954), two sons; 2) Martin Greenberg, 1962. Now lives in Brooklyn. News Service correspondent, teacher of writing workshops.

Awards: Guggenheim Fellowship 1972
American Academy Award, 1972
American Library Association Newbery Medal: *The Slave Dancer*, 1974
National Endowment of the Arts Award, 1974
Hans Christian Andersen International Medal, 1978
Christopher Award: *One–eyed Cat*, 1985

Agent: Robert Lescher, Lescher and Lescher, 67 Irving Place, New York City, New York 10009, USA

An exceptionally perceptive writer whose books seem to have limited appeal to children, yet they have much to offer any child willing to make the effort to meet the author half-way. They are not light-hearted, easy reads, but the stories are original and give the reader an insight into aspects of life which would otherwise pass them by.

HOW MANY MILES TO BABYLON

Penguin, 1972, 112p. – Pbk, O/P. –
0 14 030561 0
Macmillan, 1968, 128p. – O/P. – 0 333 08968 5

James, an innocent in the city, is no match for the gang who recognize his potential. They make him help them with stealing, and his life becomes a nightmare. A sad story with an optimistic ending.
Age range: 11–13

IN A PLACE OF DANGER

Orchard Books, 1989, 144p. – 1 85213 176 4
Orchard Books, 1989, 144p. – Pbk. –
1 85213 166 7

The two weeks that Emma has to stay with her strange Aunt Bea while Emma's father is in hospital seem to her to stretch out forever. Luckily she makes friends with Bertie, which helps a lot until the night of the big row.
Age range: 10–12

THE LOST BOY

Pan Books, 1989, 160p. – Pbk. – 0 330 30775 4
Chivers Press, 1989, 240p. – L/P. –
0 7451 0890 3
Dent, 1987, 156p. – 0 460 06271 9

A sensitive book of feelings and emotions rather than actions. Lily and Paul become friends, but Lily is hurt when Jack, newly arrived, steals Paul away from her.
Age range: 11–13

THE ONE-EYED CAT

Cornerstone Books, 1988, 172p. – L/P. –
1 55736 071 5
Collins, 1988, 128p. – Pbk. – 0 00 330037 4
Pan Books, 1988, 144p. – Pbk. – 0 330 29646 9
Dent, 1985, 176p. – 0 460 06186 0

One moment of mischief leads Ned into a nightmare situation. Coming to terms with his feelings of guilt about the injured cat makes a moving story. Light relief is there in the person of the horrible housekeeper who gets her come-uppance.
Age range: 10–12

FURLONG, Monica

British. Born 1930. Educated Harrow County Girls' School; University College, London. Married John William Knights (dissolved 1977), one son, one daughter. Journalist, writer.

Address: C/o Anthony Sheil Assoc.,
43 Doughty Street, London
WC1, England

How privileged children are that this talented author should use her attributes to produce such excellent novels. She combines atmosphere, memorable settings and characters, and believable stories into whole books of outstanding stature, from which every reader emerges wiser.

WISE CHILD
Corgi, 1990, 208p. – Pbk. – 0 552 52597 9
Gollancz, 1987, 192p. – 0 575 04046 7

There is so much packed into this novel that it needs another one to do it justice. The story tells of the childhood of Wise Child on the Isle of Mull, in the seventh century, when superstition is rife, and times are hard. She is 'adopted' by Juniper, a kind, wise woman, suspected to be a witch, with whom she learns how to live. Told with vitality, sympathy, warmth and understanding, the book comes close to sharing the essence of life with discerning readers.
Age range: 12–15

A YEAR AND A DAY
Gollancz, 1990, 224p. – 0 575 04591 4

This is the prequel to *Wise Child*, telling Juniper's story, which proves to be just as absorbing and moving.
Age range: 12–15

G

GARDAM, Jane (née Pearson)

British. Born Coatham, Yorkshire, 1928. Educated Saltburn High School for Girls; Bedford College, London, B.A. (Hons), Graduate Study. Married David Gardam, 1952, two sons and one daughter. Sub-editor and literary editor.

Awards: Fellow, Royal Society of Literature, 1976
Whitbread Award: *The Hollow Land*, 1981

Address: Haven House, Sandwich, Kent, England

Agent: Bruce Hunter David Higham Assoc., 5–8 Lower John Street, London W1R 4HA, England

Here is another author whose skill is of the highest quality, and who is able to bring that skill to books for a wide age range, although many are for teenagers. Her character portrayal of both adults and children is superb. The books are interlaced with verbal humour requiring a degree of competence in the reader, even at the youngest level. Reading Jane Gardam's novels is an enriching experience that concerned adults should endeavour to give to every child.

BILGEWATER

Sphere, 1985, 208p. – Pbk. – 0 349 11402 1
Penguin, 1979, 208p. – Pbk, O/P. –
0 14 005368 9
Hamish Hamilton, 1976, 200p. – O/P. –
0 241 89398 4

Marigold Daisy Green, a name to conjure with, feels she is truly ugly, a feeling confirmed by the horrible boys at the school where her father is headmaster. As she and the boys grow older, things change, but with painful slowness. A witty, introspective book for avid girl readers.
Age range: 12–15

BRIDGET AND WILLIAM

Penguin, 1984, 96p. – Pbk. – 0 14 031592 6
J. MacRae Books, 1981, 48p. – O/P. –
0 86203 012 9
illustrated by Janet Rawlins

An easy-to-read story in large print. Bridget's father has no time for the fat pony until his courage in the snow-storm earns him the respect he deserves.
Age range: 6–8

A FEW FAIR DAYS

Walker Books, 1989, 128p. – Pbk. –
0 7445 1337 5
J. MacRae Books, 1987, 120p. – O/P. –
0 86203 302 0

Amusing little anecdotes of Lucy's childhood, told with such humour that children laugh out loud. Easier to listen to than read.
Age range: 8–10

THE HOLLOW LAND

Chivers Press, 1987, 272p. – L/P. –
0 7451 0495 9
Penguin, 1983, 160p. – Pbk, O/P. –
0 14 031552 7
J. MacRae Books, 1981, 160p. – O/P. –
0 86203 023 4
illustrated by Janet Rawlins

Heart-warming stories about two families, one born and bred in Cumbria, the other moved there from London. It is the superb characterization that gives these stories their appeal. Jane Gardam's love of the Cumbrian fells and the farming communities is much in evidence.
Age range: 12–14

HORSE

J MacRae Books, 1982, 48p. – O/P.
0 86203 066 8
illustrated by Janet Rawlins

Another easy-to-read novel with large print, but very interesting. The villagers

put up a fight to save the 'White Horse'
cut into the hills .
Age range: 6–8

KIT

*J MacRae Books, 1983, 56p. – O/P. –
0 86203 132 X
illustrated by William Geldart*

In the same series:

KIT IN BOOTS

*J MacRae Books, 1986, 64p. – O/P. –
0 86203 258 X
illustrated by William Geldart*

KIT IN BOOTS: 'KIT' AND 'KIT IN BOOTS'

Penguin, 1988, 112p. – Pbk. – 0 14 032394 5

Aimed at younger readers, these novels
are not very long, but they are,
nevertheless, superbly written. Kit is a
memorable seven-year-old who lives on
a farm. Her escapades, first with the farm
bull, and second with a visiting artist, are
told in a lively, colloquial style.
Age range: 7–9

THE SWAN

*J MacRae Books, 1987, 64p. – O/P. –
0 86203 263 6
illustrated by John Dillow*

Henry Wu refuses to speak and appears
not to listen. Pratt is given the task of
trying to draw him out, but in vain, and
the swans in the park have more success.
A moving, forthright story.
Age range: 9–11

GARFIELD, Leon

British. Born Brighton, Sussex, 1921. Educated Brighton Grammar School. Royal Army Medical Corps, WW II. Married Vivien Alcock, children's author, 1948, one daughter. Biochemical technician, 1946–69, writer.

Awards: Guardian Children's Fiction Award: *Devil-in-the-fog*, 1966
Library Association Carnegie Medal: *The God beneath the Sea*, 1970
Whitbread Award: *John Diamond*, 1980
Prix de la Foundation de France, 1984
Fellow of the Royal Society of Literature, 1985
Golden Cat Award, Sweden, 1985
Children's Literature Association Phoenix Award, 1987

Address: 59 Wood Lane, London N6, England

Agent: John Johnson Ltd, 45–47 Clerkenwell Green, London EC1R 0HT, England

International Creative Management, 40 West 57th Street, New York, New York 10019, USA

An author whose command of words is absolute. He is able to create an atmosphere of mystery and suspense, which lingers long after the book is finished, yet there are lots of witty jokes. He weaves several different threads together to make one completely gripping story, peopled by memorable characters.

APPRENTICES
Penguin, 1984, 316p. – Pbk. – 0 14 031595 0
Heinemann, 1982, 316p. – O/P. – 0 434 94044 5

Life for apprentices in eighteenth century London is hard. This book tells the story of twelve of them, one for each month, with their hopes, disappointments, and, above all, the realities of their respective situations.
Age range: 12–14

BLACK JACK
Penguin, 1971, 192p. – Pbk. – 0 14 030489 4
Kestrel Books, 1975, 192p. – O/P. – 0 7226 5092 2
illustrated by Antony Maitland

This book caused quite a stir when it was runner-up for the Carnegie Medal – unusual for a first novel. It is exciting, unusual, and quite compelling, and bestowed respectability on historical novels. It has an effective beginning, with a coffin containing a live person, and goes on to weave a tale of adventure and evil together with love and understanding.
Age range: 12–14

THE CONFIDENCE MAN
Kestrel Books, 1978, 320p. – O/P. – 0 7226 5407 3

An incident in eighteenth century Germany in which Protestants were persecuted provides Leon Garfield with a basis for this superb adventure story. A young boy, journeying to a better future in America, has to face many obstacles.
Age range: 12–14

THE DECEMBER ROSE
Chivers Press, 1987, 344p. – L/P. – 0 7451 0588 2
Viking Kestrel, 1986, 208p. – O/P. – 0 670 81054 1
Penguin, 1986, 208p. – Pbk. – 0 14 032070 9

Originally written for television, this story is set in Victorian London, and is a typical mystery. Barnacle is a likeable lad, and the reader follows his fortune and misfortune with avid interest.
Age range: 12–14

DEVIL-IN-THE-FOG
Kestrel Books, 1975, 188p. – O/P. – 0 7226 5089 2
Penguin, 1970. – Pbk, O/P. – 0 14 030353 7

It is difficult for George to learn at

fourteen that he is not a humble Treet, but the son of Sir John Dexter, and must now take his rightful place. This obviously cannot be achieved without some difficulties, but when it leads to attempted murder, George finds out just what he is made of.
Age range: 12–14

THE EMPTY SLEEVE

Penguin, 1989, 176p. – Pbk. – 0 14 032686 3
Viking Kestrel, 1988, 192p. – O/P. –
0 670 80118 6

As the title suggests, this is a ghost story concerning twin boys and their different fortunes. It is full of atmosphere, and has an intriguing plot climaxing with murder most foul.
Age range: 12–14

THE GHOST DOWNSTAIRS

Kestrel Books, 1975, 96p. – O/P. –
0 7226 5094 9
Penguin, 1975, 96p. – Pbk. – 0 14 030788 5
illustrated by Antony Maitland

Rather more than 'just a ghost story', this book has the capacity to enable readers to experience real horror. Mr Frost and Mr Fishbone, so aptly and wittily named, are characters not easily forgotten.
Age range: 12–14

JACK HOLBORN

Kestrel Books, 1984, 200p. – O/P. –
0 7226 5088 4
Penguin, 1970. – Pbk. – 0 14 030318 9
illustrated by Antony Maitland

Jack is an orphan who falls into the hands of a pirate crew. The captain is a mysterious character who influences Jack's life to the very exciting end.
Age range: 12–14

JOHN DIAMOND

Chivers Press, 1988, 304p. – L/P. –
0 7451 0757 5
Penguin, 1981, 192p. – Pbk. – 0 14 031366 4
Kestrel Books, 1980, 180p. – O/P. –
0 7226 5619 X

Set in the familiar territory of the backstreets of Victorian London, this is the tale of an honest young man trying to put right the wrongs committed by his father, actions easier to plan than to execute. Amusing, yet shocking.
Age range: 12–14

MR CORBETT'S GHOST, AND OTHER STORIES

Kestrel Books, 1982, 88p. – O/P. –
0 7226 5806 0
Penguin, 1971, 144p. – Pbk. – 0 14 030510 6
illustrated by Antony Maitland

Three shorter stories, very much in the same vein as his full-length novels, but not so daunting. The first story was made into an excellent film.
Age range: 12–14

THE PRISONERS OF SEPTEMBER

Kestrel Books, 1975, 256p. – O/P. –
0 7226 5097 3

The French Revolution is not the easiest period in which to set a popular story, but it gives an opportunity for an adventure story which Leon Garfield exploits to the full, combining excitement with comedy and romanticism. As always, the characters are vividly portrayed and the conclusion gives an opportunity for discussion about ideals and how they should dictate one's actions. Not an easy book to read.
Age range: 12–14

SMITH

Chivers Press, 1987, 320p. – L/P. –
0 7451 0448 7
Kestrel Books, 1977, 192p. – O/P. –
0 7226 5090 6
Penguin, 1970, 176p. – Pbk. – 0 14 030349 9
illustrated by Antony Maitland

Smith is a pick-pocket in eighteenth century London, where murder is commonplace. Uncharacteristically, he feels sorry for a blind man and helps him – an act of charity which changes his whole life.
Age range: 12–14

THE STRANGE AFFAIR OF ADELAIDE HARRIS

Kestrel Books, 1977, 176p. – O/P. –
0 7226 5095 7
Penguin, 1974, 176p. – Pbk, O/P. –
0 14 030671 4
illustrated by Fritz Wegner

In the same series:

BOSTOCK AND HARRIS

Kestrel Books, 1979, 176p. – O/P. –
0 7226 5529 0
illustrated by Martin Cottam

Entertainment at its best, these amusing and original novels show Leon Garfield at his most inventive. Harris puts his history lesson to the test by taking his baby sister to use in an experiment which goes wrong, with horrifying consequences. The sequel is equally gripping.
Age range: 12–14

GARNER, Alan

British. Born Congleton, Cheshire, 1934. Educated Alderly Edge Primary School, Cheshire; Manchester Grammar School; Magdalen College, Oxford. Second Lieutenant, Royal Artillery. Married: 1) Ann Cook, 1956 (marriage dissolved), one son, two daughters; 2) Griselda Greaves, 1972, one son, one daughter.

Awards: Guardian Children's Fiction
          Award: *Owl Service*, 1968
          Library Association Carnegie
          Medal: *Owl Service*, 1968

Address: Blackden, Holmes Chapel,
          Crewe, Cheshire CW4 8BY,
          England

Alan Garner has an unique gift for storytelling, coupled with an erudite grasp of language. His books all have a compelling story to tell, but are sometimes inaccessible to readers because of the very high literary standard. This can be overcome by being read out loud by a sympathetic reader.

BAG OF MOONSHINE
Collins, 1988, 144p. – Pbk. – 0 00 184449 0
Collins, 1986, 160p. – 0 00 184403 2
illustrated by Patrick James Lynch

A book of folk tales retold to make them accessible to his young audience. Large print and lots of varied illustrations give hours of pleasure.
Age range: 8–10

ELIDOR
Windrush, 1989, 244p. – L/P. – 1 85089 945 2
Collins, 1980, 160p. – Pbk. – 0 00 671674 1
Collins, 1965, 160p. – 0 00 184202 1
illustrated by Charles Keeping

Fantasy at its best. Roland finds himself separated from his friends in the old church and in a different world, where evil holds sway. Even when safely back in Manchester, Elidor's power affects him and his friends, until the dramatic climax.
Age range: 10–12

THE STONE BOOK QUARTET
Collins, 1983, 224p. – Pbk, O/P. –
0 00 184289 7
Collins, 1983, 224p. – 0 00 184282 X
illustrated by Michael Foreman

Experienced and confident readers will enjoy these demanding stories about craftsmen and their children. Although short, they are beautifully written.
Age range: 10–12

THE WEIRDSTONE OF BRISINGAMEN
Collins, 1983, 224p. – Pbk. – 0 00 671672 5
Collins, 1965, 224p. – 0 00 183104 6

In the same series:

THE MOON OF GOMRATH
Collins, 1972, 160p. – Pbk. – 0 00 670543 X
Collins, 1963, 160p. – 0 00 184503 9

Both books are a wonderful mixture of legend and fact, culled from the Cheshire countryside. They each tell a classic story of the struggle between good and evil, as the wizard's last magic-store turns up in a bracelet. As with Tolkien, there is initial difficulty in getting used to the strange names, but the stories are powerful and compelling.
Age range: 10–12

GAVIN, Jamila

Born in India of an Indian father and English mother. Studied music in London, Paris and Berlin. Married, two children. Works in TV and radio.

Being born of mixed parentage has given Jamila Gavin a deeper understanding of the two cultures. She is able, therefore, to convey the differences naturally in her stories. There is nothing artificial to spoil the flow of the plots.

DIGITAL DAN

Methuen, 1984, 128p. – O/P. – 0 416 46050 X
illustrated by Patrice Aitken

Dan daydreams that he has a motor-bike with all the gadgets, so that he can have fantastic adventures. Easy to read.
Age range: 7–9

DOUBLE DARE

Methuen, 1982, 144p. – O/P. – 0 416 21540 8
illustrated by Simon Willby

Four stories verging on the supernatural, without being very frightening.
Age range: 8–10

HIDEAWAY

Methuen, 1987, 128p. – O/P. – 0 416 02382 7

Effie, the unhappy victim of a bitter divorce, is delighted when his Dad gives him a bike, but his mother uses it as a weapon, finally taking it away. For Pete, this is the final straw, so he runs away to the only place where he has been able to find any peace, the hideaway he shares with Jack.
Age range: 9–11

THE HINDU WORLD

MacDonald, 1986, 48p. – Religions of the world series – 0 356 11509 7

A collection of traditional Hindu stories, retold with attention to detail and meaning, yet with imagination. Beautifully illustrated, the stories are made accessible to all children, with or without previous knowledge of Hindu religion.
Age range: 9–11

KAMLA AND KATE

Magnet Books, 1986, 112p. – Pbk, O/P. – 0 416 50450 7
Methuen, 1983, 96p. – O/P. – 0 416 22780 5
illustrated by Thelma Lambert

The two friends are mischievous, yet at the same time they explore the differences in each other's lives. A very popular book with girls.
Age range: 7–9

THE MAGIC ORANGE TREE AND OTHER STORIES

Magnet Books, 1987, 96p. – Pbk. – 0 416 07322 0
Methuen, 1979, 96p. – O/P. – 0 416 86240 3
illustrated by Ossie Murray

A book of short stories about a group of children living in a city. They have diverse cultural backgrounds, and different experiences to share.
Age range: 9–11

THREE INDIAN PRINCESSES: THE STORIES OF SAVITRI, DAMAYANTI AND SITA

Methuen, 1987, 128p. – 0 416 97030 3

Indian folk tales re-told to make them accessible and enjoyable for children. The story of Rama and Sita is particularly moving.
Age range: 9–11

GEE, Maurice (Gough)

New Zealander. Born Whakatare, 1931. Educated Avondale College, Auckland; University of Auckland, M.A. (Hons) English. Married Margaretha Garden, 1970, one son (previous marriage) and two daughters. Teacher, librarian, writer.

Address: 125 Cleveland Terrace, Nelson, New Zealand

Agent: Richards Literary Agency, P.O. Box 31240, Milford, Auckland 9, New Zealand

It is always a pleasure to see an author, successful in his own country, being accepted and enjoyed by children in different parts of the world. Maurice Gee's books have become immensely popular, perhaps because some of them have been shown on television, revealing what exciting and dramatic plots they contain.

THE CHAMPION
Penguin, 1990, 176p. – Pbk. – 0 14 034160 9

Jackson Coop, an American soldier in New Zealand during WW II, is wounded and comes to stay with Rex's family to recuperate. There are people who do not welcome black soldiers into their community, and events that take place during Jackson's fortnight in Kettle Week change it forever.
Age range: 11–13

THE HALFMEN OF O
Penguin, 1984, 192p. – Pbk. – 0 14 031712 0
OUP, 1982, 208p. – O/P. – 0 19 558081 8

In the same series:

THE PRIESTS OF FERRIS
Penguin, 1987, 192p. – Pbk, O/P. –
0 14 032061 X
OUP, 1985, 180p. – O/P. – 0 19 558112 1

MOTHERSTONE
Penguin, 1988, 184p. – Pbk, O/P. –
0 14 032361 9
OUP, 1986, 184p. – O/P. – 0 19 558130 X

The planet O is in danger of being destroyed by the evil Halfmen, who have lost all trace of any human virtues. They send a sign to Susan, who bears a special mark on her wrist, asking for help. Together with her cousin, Nick, she sets about the task of restoring the balance of good and evil. Having faced unknown terrors in defeating the Halfmen of O, Susan and Nick are dismayed to learn that a new tyranny, in the form of cruel priests, is threatening to overrun the planet. They are determined to set O free. Just as they are convinced they have succeeded, a new leader with an entirely new weapon arrives, and the hard-won peace is threatened yet again. In the final part of this trilogy, Susan and Nick face one last task, from which they do not flinch.
Age range: 12–14

UNDER THE MOUNTAIN
Penguin, 1982, 160p. – Pbk, O/P. –
0 14 031389 3
OUP, 1979, 164p. – O/P. – 0 19 558040 0

A similar idea of a world being taken over, in this case by evil giants living under extinct volcanoes. Less complicated than his trilogy, the book became an engrossing television serial.
Age range: 10–12

THE WORLD AROUND THE CORNER
Penguin, 1983, 96p. – Pbk. – 0 14 031580 2
OUP, 1981, 80p. – O/P. – 0 19 558061 3
illustrated by Garry Webley

Caroline finds a pair of special spectacles, and is determined to return them. Equally determined to stop her are the evil Grimbles, who have their own plans for the spectacles.
Age range: 8–10

GERAS, Adele (Daphne, née Weston)

British. Born Jerusalem, Israel, 1944. Educated St Hilda's College, Oxford, B.A. (Hons), Modern Languages. Married Norman Geras, 1967, two daughters. Teacher, writer.

Address: 10 Danesmoor Road, Manchester M20 9JS, England

Agent: Laura Cecil, 17 Alwyne Villas, London N1 2HG, England

Undoubtedly at her best writing for teenagers, Adele Geras can nevertheless write stories which appeal to younger children, and keep their interest.

APRICOTS AT MIDNIGHT
Armada Books, 1989, 192p. – Pbk. –
0 00 673225 9
Hamish Hamilton, 1977, 144p. – O/P. –
0 241 89479 4
illustrated by Doreen Caldwell

A collection of stories reflecting Edwardian England. They are connected by the various materials which make up Aunt Pinny's patchwork quilt. An enjoyable way of learning about everyday life in a bygone age.
Age range: 9–11

THE FANTORA FAMILY FILES
Collins, 1990, 128p. – Pbk. – 0 00 673348 4
Hamish Hamilton, 1988, 128p. – 0 241 12467 0
illustrated by Tony Ross

This book contains sparks of true originality. The story is related by the Fantora cat, who has a nice turn of phrase. Other members of the family have different claims to fame: Aunt Varrora is a vegetarian vampire, others possess strange powers. The short, anecdotal chapters are verbally funny.
Age range: 9–11

THE GIRLS IN THE VELVET FRAME
Armada Books, 1988, 160p. – Pbk. –
0 00 672879 0
Hamish Hamilton, 1978, 160p. – O/P. –
0 241 10011 9

Naomi and her sisters are anxious to hear from Isaac, who is living in America, but has not contacted them. Their aunt arranges for them to be photographed as a birthday present for their mother, hoping it will cheer her up. It proves to be far more significant in helping to reunite Isaac and the family. The romances of the eldest girls will be enjoyed by older girls.
Age range: 13–15

LETTERS OF FIRE AND OTHER UNSETTLING STORIES
Armada Books, 1986, 160p. – Pbk. –
0 00 672556 2
Hamish Hamilton, 1984, 154p. – O/P. –
0 241 11268 0

A masterly collection of mysteries and macabre stories that send shivers down the spine, and cause readers to glance fearfully over their shoulders.
Age range: 12–14

GORDON, John (William)

British. Born Jarrow, Co. Durham, 1925. Educated Wisbech Grammar School, Cambridgeshire. Royal Navy, 1943–47. Married Sylvia Ellen Young, 1954, one son and one daughter. Worked as newspaper reporter and sub-editor.

Address: 99 George Barrow Road, Norwich, Norfolk NR4 7HU, England

John Gordon is a writer able to create a compelling story, full of atmosphere and chilling menace, yet maintaining the action at a pace guaranteed to draw the reader to the end.

CATCH YOUR DEATH AND OTHER GHOST STORIES
Magnet Books, 1985, 128p. – Pbk, O/P. – 0 416 54540 8
P. Hardy Books, 1984, 128p. – 0 7444 0029 5

Sinister and scary ghost stories for older readers with good nerves. Very enjoyable.
Age range: 12–14

THE EDGE OF THE WORLD
Armada Books, 1985, 192p. – Pbk, O/P. – 0 00 672249 0
P. Hardy Books, 1983, 192p. – 0 7444 0005 8

Ghost stories are always popular, but this book is above average. Completely believable, the children draw the reader into the web of mystery. Together, reader and characters are led on a chillingly frightening journey to the edge of the world.
Age range: 12–14

THE GIANT UNDER THE SNOW
Penguin, 1971, 192p. – Pbk. – 0 14 030507 6
Hutchinson, 1968, 192p. – O/P. – 0 09 088370 5

John Gordon's first story proved an instant success. Atmospheric, the hidden menace threatens to erupt at any minute. Jonquil, in possession of the brooch, is constantly aware of it. An exciting and inventive story, but not for those of 'a nervous disposition'.
Age range: 11–13

THE HOUSE ON THE BRINK
Penguin, 1989, 192p. – Pbk. – 0 14 032629 4
P. Hardy Books, 1983, 192p. – 0 7444 0004 X

A most unusual story, as always, filled with a feeling of foreboding. A stump of wood, washed up by the tide, moves about, leaving a silvery trail, just like a giant slug. Full of evil and menace, it affects all within its radius. A really superb climax.
Age range: 11–13

THE QUELLING EYE
Armada Books, 1988, 160p. – Pbk, O/P. – 0 00 672841 3
Bodley Head, 1986, 140p. – 0 370 31011 X

A compelling, tense story with many threads. Chuck's mother feels that Tessa is an unsuitable friend for her son, and tries to separate them. Chuck and Tessa share a secret, a knowledge of magic, that makes them inseparable. Percy Falconer poses a great threat to all, and the young people feel ill-equipped to deal with this.
Age range: 12–14

RIDE THE WIND
Bodley Head, 1989, 140p. – 0 370 31279 1

The sequel to *The Giant Under the Snow*, when the menace of the warlord is resurrected even more strongly than before, and the counter-magic is less effective. Good to read if you enjoyed the first story, but it does not have the same impact.
Age range: 11–13

GRANT, Gwen(doline Ellen)

British. Born Worksop, Nottinghamshire, 1940. Educated Open University, B.A.; Diploma in Adult Education. Married Ian Grant, 1964, two sons. Having left school at 15, has had a variety of jobs; now a full-time writer.

Address: 95 Watson Road, Worksop, Nottinghamshire, England

Gwen Grant's books are light-hearted easy-to-read romps which do not demand too much from the reader.

THE LILY PICKLE BAND BOOK
Armada Books, 1983, 160p. – Pbk. – 0 00 672081 1
Heinemann, 1982, 160p. – O/P. – 0 434 94137 9
illustrated by Margaret Chamberlain

Lily is made leader of the band, and is told she must write down everything that happens – which is how the book came to be written. The large print, coupled with the colloquial style, makes this a jolly read, full of fun and enjoyment.
· *Age range:* 8–10

PRIVATE – KEEP OUT!
Armada Books, 1980, 144p. – Pbk. – 0 00 671652 0
Heinemann, 1978, 144p. – O/P. – 0 434 94170 0
illustrated by Faith Jacques

In the same series:

KNOCK AND WAIT
Armada Books, 1981, 144p. – Pbk, O/P. – 0 00 671762 4
Heinemann, 1979, 112p. – O/P. – 0 434 94138 7
illustrated by Gareth Floyd

ONE WAY ONLY
Armada Books, 1985, 128p. – Pbk. – 0 00 672290 3
Heinemann, 1983, 144p. – O/P. – 0 434 94136 0
illustrated by Faith Jacques

A series of anecdotal stories set in Nottinghamshire in the 1950s. Large families, no money, hiding from the rent man – it's all part of everyday life. In spite of being so realistic, they are amusing to read. Excellent 'period' books.
Age range: 12–14

GREAVES, Margaret

British. Born Birmingham, 1914.
Educated Alice Ottley School, Worcester;
St Hugh's College, Oxford, B.A. (Hons),
English, B.Litt., M.A. British Women's
Land Army, WW II. Teacher and lecturer.

Address: 8 Greenways, Winchcombe,
Cheltenham, Gloucestershire
GL54 5LG, England

CHARLIE, EMMA AND ALBERIC
*Magnet Books, 1984, 96p. – Pbk, O/P. –
0 416 46990 6*
*Methuen, 1980, 96p. – Pbk, O/P. –
0 416 87950 0*

In the same series:

CHARLIE, EMMA AND DRAGONS
TO THE RESCUE
*Magnet Books, 1988, 94p. – Pbk, O/P. –
0 416 10292 1*
Methuen, 1986, 96p. – O/P. – 0 416 54260 3

CHARLIE, EMMA AND THE
DRAGON FAMILY
*Magnet Books, 1985, 96p. – Pbk. –
0 416 47870 0*
Methuen, 1982, 96p. – 0 416 21580 7

CHARLIE, EMMA AND THE
JUGGLING DRAGONS
Mammoth, 1990, 80p. – Pbk. – 0 7497 0191 9
Methuen, 1989, 80p. – 0 416 08112 6

CHARLIE, EMMA AND THE
SCHOOL DRAGON
Mammoth, 1990, 96p. – Pbk. – 0 7497 0192 7
Methuen, 1984, 96p. – O/P. – 0 416 46090 9
series illustrated by Eileen Brown

Charlie is so desperate for a pet, he is
pleased to adopt the little lizard he and
Emma find. When they realize he is really
a dragon, they are delighted – thus begins
a series of adventures which make
inventive and hilarious reading.
Age range: 8–10

HETTY PEGLER, HALF WITCH
Methuen, 1987, 96p. – O/P. – 0 416 00312 5
illustrated by Derek Crowe

An intriguing title for a story about a
family who invite a deprived child to go
on holiday with them, much to the disgust
of the children. However, they change
their minds when they realize she can cast
spells. The trouble is that, being only half
a witch, the spells only half-work, with
surprising results.
Age range: 7–9

GREEN, Roger J.

British. Born Buxton, Derbyshire, 1944. Educated Bakewell; University of London, B.A. (History); Teacher Training College, Sheffield. Married, two children. Teacher.

THE FEAR OF SAMUEL WALTON
OUP, 1984, 252p. – 0 19 271474 0

In the same series:

LENGTHENING SHADOW
OUP, 1986, 220p. – 0 19 271509 7

DEVIL FINDS WORK
OUP, 1987, 180p. – 0 19 271556 9

THEY WATCHED HIM DIE
OUP, 1988, 208p. – 0 19 271573 9
all illustrated by David Parkins

An intriguing quartet of quite extraordinary dramatic tension, which, at times, becomes quite unbearable. Set in Derbyshire at the turn of the century, the central 'character' is the Stone, which in each book is the catalyst for many unpleasant happenings, and which inspires great fear. Excellent for reading to a class.
Age range: 11–13

H

HALAM, Ann

Pseudonym for Gwyneth A. Jones.
British. Born Manchester, 1952.
Educated Sussex University, B.A. (Hons).
Married Peter Gwilliam, 1976, one son.
Civil servant.

Agent: Herta Ryder, C/o Toby Eady
Assoc., 7 Gledhow Gardens,
London SW5 0BL, England

Another writer with an exceptional talent
for creating fantasy worlds which can
seem as real as our own. Her books are
not purely entertainment, but require
some thought on the part of intelligent
readers, who may glean some insight into
the meaning of life itself.

ALLY, ALLY, ASTER
Penguin, 1990, 160p. – Pbk. – 0 14 032924 2
Allen & Unwin, 1981, 144p. – O/P. –
0 04 823192 4

A mixture of reality and fantasy, so well
blended that it becomes impossible to
separate them. Powerful descriptions of
Ally and her element make it seem as if
the cold is actually emanating from the
page. Richard and Laura try hard to
combat the encroachment of a distant
past, but the witchcraft is very strong. A
thoroughly enjoyable read.
Age range: 11–13

THE DAYMAKER
Penguin, 1989, 176p. – Pbk, O/P. –
0 14 032779 7
Orchard Books, 1987, 174p. – 1 85213 019 9

In the same series:

TRANSFORMATIONS
Penguin, 1990, 224p. – Pbk. – 0 14 034186 2

THE SKYBREAKER
Orchard Books, 1990, 192p. – 1 85213 183 7
Orchard Books, 1990, 192p. – Pbk. –
1 85213 201 9

A trilogy of extraordinary depth set in the
future. Zanne possesses powers she is
unable to control, and must be trained so
that she can destroy the Daymaker before
it destroys the peace of Inland. Four years
later, she undertakes a new task, to
discover the secret hidden by the people
of Minith. The conclusion to this book is
both surprising and frightening. Both
Zanne and the reader embark on the last
voyage, to Magia, with some trepidation.
A monster, buried for years, is beginning
to stir, threatening once again the fabric
of their society. Each book is totally
compelling, involving the reader deeply.
Age range: 13–15

KING DEATH'S GARDEN
Chivers Press, 1988, 232p. – L/P. –
0 7451 0657 9
Penguin, 1988, 128p. – Pbk, O/P. –
0 14 032292 2
Orchard Books, 1986, 160p. – 1 85213 003 2

Maurice finds himself moving between
two worlds. There is the 'real' world of
school, where he is a loner, and the
supernatural world of the cemetery,
which begins to encroach more and more
on his life. Where does Moth belong? As
his fear increases, tension rises and the
book draws to a dramatic conclusion.
Very satisfying and enjoyable.
Age range: 11–13

HALL, Willis

British. Born 1929. Educated Cockburn
High School, Leeds. Married Valerie
Shute, 1973, four sons, (three by
previous marriage). Writer, playwright.

Address: C/o London Management,
235–241 Regent Street,
London W1A 2JT, England

THE 'ANTELOPE' COMPANY ASHORE
Bodley Head, 1986, 156p. – 0 370 30775 5
Armada Books, 1986, 160p. – Pbk. –
0 00 672765 4

In the same series:

THE 'ANTELOPE' COMPANY AT LARGE
Armada Books, 1988, 160p. – Pbk, O/P. –
0 00 672926 6
Bodley Head, 1987, 160p. – 0 370 31151 5

THE RETURN OF THE 'ANTELOPE'
Chivers Press, 1990, 256p. – L/P. –
0 7451 1103 3
J. Murray, 1988, 176p. – 0 7195 4508 0
Armada Books, 1985, 176p. – Pbk. –
0 00 672550 3
Bodley Head, 1985, 180p. – 0 370 30693 7
illustrated by Rowan Barnes-Murphy

Originally written as a serial for television,
it proved so popular that the plot was
turned into a series of novels. Willis Hall
is able to maintain the suspense very well
as the little people battle against
overwhelming odds, helped by two
children trying to protect them from the
evil Harwell. Period detail adds an extra
dimension.
Age range: 9–12

DR JEKYLL AND MR HOLLINS
Bodley Head, 1988, 144p. – 0 370 31040 3

In the same series:

DRAGON DAYS
Chivers Press, 1991, 200p. – L/P. –
0 7451 1294 3
Armada Books, 1987, 142p. – Pbk. –
0 00 672614 3
Bodley Head, 1985, 132p. – O/P. –
0 370 30626 0

HENRY HOLLINS AND THE DINOSAUR
Bodley Head, 1988, 192p. – 0 370 31255 4
Target Books, 1979, 192p. – Pbk, O/P. –
0 426 20043 8

THE INFLATABLE SHOP
Armada Books, 1986, 128p. – Pbk. –
0 00 672436 1
Bodley Head, 1984, 128p. – 0 370 30807 7

THE LAST VAMPIRE
Chivers Press, 1987, 232p. – L/P. –
0 7451 0589 0
Armada Books, 1984, 160p. – Pbk. –
0 00 672248 2
Bodley Head, 1982, 160p. – O/P. –
0 370 30503 5

SUMMER OF THE DINOSAUR
Bodley Head, 1977, 216p. – O/P. –
0 370 30003 3
all illustrated by Maggie Ling

Henry is a lovable and appealing small
boy, to whom the most extraordinary and
original things happen. Each book has its
own individual adventure, always told
with great humour. Readers need a
certain linguistic competence, but the
stories are sufficiently enjoyable to
encourage children to tackle these full-
length novels.
Age range: 9–11

HALLWORTH, Grace

West Indian. Born Trinidad. Schools and children's librarian, now full-time storyteller and writer.

LISTEN TO THIS STORY: TALES FROM THE WEST INDIES
Methuen, 1978, 80p. – Pbk. – 0 416 58270 2
Methuen, 1977, 80p. – 0 416 83220 2
illustrated by Dennis Ranston

In the same series:

MOUTH OPEN, STORY JUMP OUT
Methuen, 1987, 112p. – Pbk. – 0 416 07542 8
Methuen, 1984, 128p. – 0 416 23550 6
illustrated by Art Derry

A WEB OF STORIES
Methuen, 1990, 109p. – 0 416 09432 5
illustrated by Avril Turner

Three books of short stories, including an Anansi story, from the Caribbean. They are all traditional, and imbued with a special magic which only a master storyteller can contribute. Better read aloud, but older children will still enjoy reading them for themselves.
Age range: 7–10

HAMILTON, Virginia (Esther)

American. Born Yellow Springs, Ohio, 1936. Educated Antioch College, Yellow Springs; Ohio State University, Columbia; New School for Social Research, New York. Married Arnold Adolff (poet), 1960, one daughter, one son. Lecturer and Visiting Professor.

Awards:	Boston Globe Horn Book Award: *M. C. Higgins the Great*, 1974
	American Library Association Newbery Award: *M. C. Higgins the Great*, 1975
	Boston Globe Horn Book Award: *Sweet Whispers, Brother Rush*, 1983
	Children's Rights Workshop Other Award: *The People Could Fly*, 1986
Address:	BOX 293, Yellow Springs, Ohio 45387, USA
Agent:	Dorothy Markinko, McIntosh & Otis Inc., 310 Madison Avenue, New York City, New York 10017, USA

Virginia Hamilton's background enables her to tackle the issue of racial problems. Superb use of language and an honest attitude to the problems of youth ensure each book offers readers a life-enriching experience.

ARILLA SUN DOWN
Heinemann, 1977, 252p. – O/P. – 0 241 89548 0

Arilla, the narrator, is 12 years old, and struggling to come to terms with approaching adulthood. She is the product of a mixed marriage which causes anguish to her older brother, who feels himself to be a full Indian, and dresses accordingly. A book of emotions rather than actions, but compelling reading just the same. There are no easy or glib answers, but at least there is the promise of future happiness at the end of the book.
Age range: 12–14

JUSTICE AND HER BROTHERS
Hamish Hamilton, 1979, 256p. – O/P. – 0 241 10152 2

In the same series:

DUSTLAND
J. MacRae Books, 1980, 192p. – O/P. – 0 86203 080 3

THE GATHERING
J. MacRae books, 1981, 192p. – O/P. – 0 86203 037 4

A truly unusual trilogy about a little girl, her twin brothers and a friend. Together they form *The Unit* using super-sensory powers. In each book, they embark on a weird journey which draws the reader into its very heart. Each book is totally original and compelling, each with an outstanding conclusion. Not for the faint-hearted reader.
Age range: 13–15

M. C. HIGGINS THE GREAT
Cornerstone Books, 1989, 304p. – L/P. – 1 55736 075 8
Armada Books, 1976, 220p. – Pbk, O/P. – 0 00 671172 3
Hamish Hamilton, 1975, 278p. – O/P. – 0 241 89214 7

Although first published in 1974, this book still has a valid message for young people today. The Higgins family live in the shadow of an huge slag heap which threatens to engulf their home. M.C. daydreams about a better home until Lurhetta wanders into his life, causing him to start actively thinking about the situation. As always, there is a highly dramatic conclusion.
Age range: 12–15

THE PEOPLE COULD FLY: AMERICAN BLACK FOLK TALES
Walker Books, 1986, 180p. – O/P. – 0 7445 0524 0
illustrated by Leo and Diane Dillon

A collection of folk tales from American black history, which Virginia Hamilton has studied for many years. These re-tellings reflect her own love of folklore and are highly readable. The language is rhythmic and the stories flow easily. The print is large and clear, while the illustrations provide the perfect complement. A highly attractive book. *Age range:* 9–12

HAMLEY, Dennis

Married, two children. Lives in Hertfordshire. Education Advisor in English and drama.

Dennis Hamley has written several books for children over the years, but none have stood the test of time. Recent books, however, deserve mention.

DANGLEBOOTS

Collins, 1989, 140p. – Pbk. – 0 00 673246 1
Deutsch, 1987, 160p. – 0 233 98075 X
illustrated by Tony Ross

Andy is so useless at football that he is nicknamed 'Dangleboots'. One day he buys a little pair of football boots as a mascot and his life is changed. The plot positively races along, with lots of humourous happenings, perfectly illustrated by Tony Ross.
Age range: 8–10

HARE'S CHOICE

Collins, 1990, 112p. – Pbk. – 0 00 673503 7
Deutsch, 1988, 96p. – 0 233 98298 1
illustrated by Meg Rutherford

A most unusual and memorable book. It begins with a poetic and powerful description of a hare running to her death. The rest of the book concerns two children who find the body and take it to show at school. The class decides to write a story about her, and thus she is immortalized, while the whole school benefits from the original sad event.
Age range: 10–12

HARDCASTLE, Michael

Also writes as David Clark. British, born Huddersfield, Yorkshire, 1933. Educated, Huddersfield. Royal Army Educational Corps. Newspaper reporter, literary editor, feature writer.

Awards: M.B.E.

Address: 17 Molescroft Park, Beverley,
              North Humberside
              HU17 7EB, England

A very experienced and prolific writer for children. He specializes in fictional sports books, including football, cricket, motorbike racing, snooker and horse-riding. They are packed with action, not too demanding, and fill a definite need. A selection of his non-sporting novels is given below.

JAMES AND THE TV STAR

Penguin, 1990, 96p. – Pbk. – 0 14 032736 3
Blackie, 1986, 48p. – 0 216 91894 4
illustrated by Pat McCarthy

A simple and easy to read story in which James contrives to meet his television hero.
Age range: 10–12

MAGIC PARTY

Blackie, 1988, 48p. – 0 216 92108 2
illustrated by Vanessa Julian-Ottie

Katie is dismayed to find her party is on the same day as her friend's. The problem requires an imaginative solution.
Age range: 10–12

QUAKE

Faber, 1990, 160p. – Pbk. – 0 571 14281 8
Faber, 1988, 176p. – 0 571 14698 8

Absorbed in her thoughts of what it would be like to meet her new family, Tarrian had no idea why the train was swaying so alarmingly, until it fell into the hole created by an earthquake. A graphic description of a terrible disaster, and the bravery of those who survived.
Age range: 10–12

HILL, Douglas (Arthur)

Also writes as Martin Hillman. Canadian. Born Brandon, Manitoba, 1935. Educated in Prince Albert, Saskatchewan; University of Saskatchewan, B.A. (Hons); English University of Toronto. Married Gail Robinson, 1958 (divorced 1978), one son. Editor, science fiction advisor.

Address: 3 Hillfield Avenue, London N8 7DU, England

Agent: Sheila Watson, Watson Little Ltd, Suite 8, Charing Cross Road, London WC2H 0DG, England

A highly acclaimed writer of science fiction, with a great ability to make the reader believe in his alien worlds, while telling exciting stories.

BLADE OF THE POISONER
Pan Books, 1989. – Pbk. – 0 330 30692 8
Gollancz, 1987, 160p. – 0 575 03954 X

In the same series:

MASTER OF FIENDS
Pan Books, 1989, 192p. – Pbk. –
0 330 30691 X
Gollancz, 1987, 160p. – 0 575 04095 5

A world full of monsters and demons is the setting for these two novels. Powerful descriptions and excellent characterization bring this story of good versus evil vividly to life.
Age range: 12–14

EXILES OF COLSEC
Penguin, 1985, 128p. – Pbk, O/P. –
0 14 031767 8
Gollancz, 1984, 128p. – 0 575 03348 7

In the same series:

THE CAVES OF KLYDOR
Penguin, 1986, 128p. – Pbk. – 0 14 031768 6
Gollancz, 1984, 128p. – 0 575 03413 0

The first novel describes the harsh life on Earth ruled by the tyrannical ColSec, which causes a group of young people to face untold dangers in search of a better life. They hope that the planet Klydor is the answer. In the sequel, they are dismayed to learn that the dreaded ColSec has followed them. Finding out why proves to be dangerous and frightening.
Age range: 12–14

GALACTIC WARLORD
Pan Books, 1980, 128p. – Pbk. – 0 330 26186 X
Gollancz, 1979, 160p. – 0 575 02663 4

In the same series:

DEATHWING OVER VEYNAA
Pan Books, 1981, 128p. – Pbk. –
0 330 26446 X
Gollancz, 1980, 128p. – 0 575 02779 7

DAY OF THE STARWIND
Pan Books, 1982, 128p. – Pbk. –
0 330 26652 7
Gollancz, 1980, 128p. – 0 575 02917 X

PLANET OF THE WARLORD
Pan Books, 1982, 128p. – Pbk. –
0 330 26713 2
Gollancz, 1981, 128p. – 0 575 03009 7

YOUNG LEGIONARY
Pan Books, 1983, 128p. – Pbk. –
0 330 28104 6
Gollancz, 1982, 128p. – 0 575 03201 4

LAST LEGIONARY QUARTET: 'GALACTIC WARLORD', 'DEATHWING OVER VEYNAA', 'DAY OF THE STARWIND' and 'PLANET OF THE WARLORD'
Pan Books, 1985, 460p. – Pbk. –
0 330 28954 3

The customary recipe involving a young man of noble character who vows revenge on those who wrecked his home. A space adventure story.
Age range: 12–14

THE HUNTSMAN
Pan Books, 1984, 144p. – Pbk. – 0 330 26956 9
Heinemann, 1982, 128p. – O/P. – 0 434 33601 7

In the same series:

WARRIORS OF THE WASTELAND
*Pan Books, 1984, 128p. – Pbk. –
0 330 28452 5*

Finn Ferral is the hero in these stories. His task is to rescue the family who adopted him as an abandoned baby. They have been kidnapped by huge metal beings, and the task is fraught with terrible dangers.
Age range: 12–14

HOBAN, Russell (Conwell)

American. Born Lansdale, Pennsylvania, 1925. Educated Lansdale High School; Philadelphia Museum School of Industrial Art. US Army Infantry, WW II. Married: 1) Lillian Aberman (i.e. Lillian Hoban, illustrator), 1944 (divorced 1975), one son, three daughters; 2) Gundula Ahl, 1975, three sons. Artist, illustrator, copywriter, full-time writer since 1967.

Agent: David Higham Assoc. Ltd,
5–8 Lower John Street,
London W1R 4HA, England

THE MOUSE AND HIS CHILD
Chivers Press, 1990, 312p. – L/P. –
0 7451 1104 1
Penguin, 1976, 192p. – Pbk. – 0 14 030841 5
Faber, 1969, 200p. – 0 571 08844 9
illustrated by Lillian Hoban

Now considered a modern children's classic, this story has much to offer at a variety of levels. The plot is an exciting adventure story as the clockwork mice journey through life searching for their lost home. They suffer many hardships and are always pursued by their arch-enemy, the rat. There are jokes which lighten the sadness of their plight, and man's eternal pursuit of happiness will never be better described.
Age range: 10–12

HOLIDAY, Jane

British. Born Oxfordshire. Educated Banbury Grammar School; Winchester College of Art; Edinburgh University. Married, two daughters by first marriage. Teacher. Lives in Nelson, Lancashire.

For sheer light-hearted, entertaining reading, the books by Jane Holiday are hard to beat.

FLOELLA HITS THE ROOF
Armada Books, 1989, 128p. – Pbk. – 0 00 673375 1
illustrated by Kate Simpson

To the horror of the town dignitaries, there is a dragon on the Town Hall roof, and the Queen's visit is only a few days away. Floella decides to help.
Age range: 7–9

GRUESOME AND BLOODSOCKS
Granada, 1985, 96p. – Pbk. – 0 583 30734 5
Granada, 1984, 96p. – O/P. – 0 246 12545 4

In the same series:

GRUESOME AND BLOODSOCKS MOVE HOUSE
Armada Books, 1988, 128p. – Pbk. – 0 00 673047 7
Grafton Books, 1987, 96p. – Pbk, O/P. – 0 583 31141 5

GRUESOME ON WHEELS
Armada Books, 1988, 128p. – Pbk. – 0 00 673046 9
all illustrated by Steven Appleby

The best combination of all for ensuring popularity with children is horror and humour. Both are plentiful in these stories about a young vampire who cannot stand blood. Thoroughly enjoyable.
Age range: 8–10

VICTOR THE VULTURE
Penguin, 1981, 80p. – Pbk. – 0 14 031255 2
Hamish Hamilton, 1978, 96p. – O/P. – 0 241 89959 1
illustrated by Jo Worth

Like many children, Garth would like a pet, and is pleased when his father wins a small vulture in a raffle. His problems begin at once, to the amusement of the reader. A jolly read.
Age range: 7–9

HOOVER, Helen Mary

American. Born Stark County, Ohio, 1935. Educated Louisville High School; Mount Union College, Alliance, Ohio; Los Angeles School of Nursing.

Address: 9405 Ulysses Court, Burke, Virginia 22015, USA

Agent: Russell and Volkening, 50 West 29th Street, New York, New York 100001, USA

A prolific writer of imaginative and thought-provoking science fiction. Truths about present society are highlighted by comparison with other worlds, other sets of values.

ANOTHER HEAVEN, ANOTHER EARTH
Methuen, 1983, 174p. – O/P. – 0 416 23040 7

A choice has to be made between a simple life on the doomed planet Xilan, and a new technological life on Earth. This is not, by any means, a straightforward choice, as it involves a completely different set of values.
Age range: 12–14

CHILDREN OF MORROW
Penguin, 1987, 240p. – Pbk. – 0 14 031873 9
Methuen, 1975, 240p. – O/P. – 0 416 81540 5

Tra's life is unbearably hard; because she is different and can 'see' things, she is an outcast. Gradually she comes to realize she has full telepathic powers, which she uses to try to escape, but time is against her. Undemanding, but totally absorbing.
Age range: 11–13

THE DELIKON
Methuen, 1978, 240p. – 0 416 86220 9

Varina, about to leave Earth and return to her own people, the Delikon, is kidnapped along with her pupils. They succeed in escaping, but time is running out for her if she is to be able to return to the Delikon. A powerful story, and excellent characterization.
Age range: 12–14

THE LOST STAR
Penguin, 1987, 160p. – Pbk, O/P. – 0 14 032166 7

A moral tale of choices, movingly told. Lian, investigating the planet Balthor, discovers the gentle 'Lumpies'. (What an evocative name!) She must decide whether to reveal their existence, or to try to protect them.
Age range: 12–14

THE RAINS OF ERIDAN
Methuen, 1979, 292p. – O/P. – 0 416 87100 3

Eridan is a beautiful planet, which strongly contrasts with the stark horror of the drama played out in this novel. The whole population is overwhelmed by a fear for which there appears to be no cause. Only when it is almost too late and the rains have begun does it become obvious what the strange, huge, mummified mounds are.
Age range: 11–13

THE SHEPHERD MOON
Methuen, 1984, 144p. – O/P. – 0 416 45630 8

Set in the distant future on Earth, Merry watches the arrival of a young man who has come from an artificial moon, generally believed to be uninhabited. This sparks off an investigation which reveals as much about Earth as it does about the Shepherd Moon. An exciting plot with an underlying serious message.
Age range: 12–14

THIS TIME OF DARKNESS
Penguin, 1987, 176p. – Pbk, O/P. – 0 14 031872 0
Methuen, 1982, 160p. – O/P. – 0 416 21770 2

Amy's whole life has been spent in the underground city until she befriends Axel, who tells her the truth about Outside. They plan to escape, but survival is hazardous, even in the devastated landscape Outside. Pointing the finger at social structures based on class invites comparison with our own culture. The climax is cautiously optimistic.
Age range: 12–14

HOROWITZ, Anthony

British. Born London, 1955. Educated Rugby School; University of York. Married, one son.

Awards: Lancashire County Library Children's Book of the Year Award: *Groosham Grange,* 1989

Address: 32 Wandsworth Bridge Road, London SW6 2TH, England

DAY OF THE DRAGON
Methuen, 1989, 160p. – 0 416 11392 3

In the same series:

THE DEVIL'S DOORBELL
Magnet Books, 1985, 160p. – Pbk. –
0 416 45700 2
P. Hardy Books, 1983, 160p. – 0 7444 0007 4

THE NIGHT OF THE SCORPION
Magnet Books, 1986, 160p. – Pbk. –
0 416 54550 5
P. Hardy Books, 1985, 160p. – 0 7444 0053 8

THE SILVER CITADEL
Methuen, 1987, 160p. – Pbk. – 0 416 02572 2
Methuen, 1987, 150p. – O/P. – 0 416 97000 1

A series of thrillers about a group of children whose task is to defeat the Old Ones in order to break their power. Each one has a different setting, but all are full of action and excitement.
Age range: 12–14

THE FALCON'S MALTESER
Grafton Books, 1987, 160p. – Pbk. –
0 583 30887 2
Grafton Books, 1986, 160p. – 0 246 12863 1

An humorous thriller with an unusual beginning when a dwarf walks into a private detective's office and leaves a mysterious parcel. Eventually it is discovered that it contains Maltesers, not sufficient reason for murder. Tim tries to solve the mystery. It is fun to read, especially if readers are already familiar with Raymond Chandler's *The Maltese Falcon.*
Age range: 10–13

HOWE, James

American. Born Oneida, New York, 1946. Educated Boston University, B.F.A.; Hunter College, New York, M.A. Married: 1) Deborah Smith, 1969 (died 1978); 2) Betsy Imershein, 1981, one daughter. Freelance actor, director, literary agent.

Address: Hastings On Hudson, New York, USA

Agent: Amy Berkower, Writers' House Inc, 21 West 26th Street, New York City, New York 10010, USA

BUNNICULA
Windrush, 1989, 104p. – L/P. – 1 85089 998 3
Armada Books, 1989, 96p. – Pbk. –
0 00 673276 3
Grafton Books, 1986, 96p. – Pbk. –
0 583 30801 5
Hodder, 1984, 98p. – O/P. – 0 340 34758 9
illustrated by Alan Daniel

In the same series:

THE CELERY STALKS AT MIDNIGHT
Armada Books, 1989, 96p. – Pbk. –
0 00 673277 1
Grafton Books, 1987, 96p. – Pbk. –
0 583 30906 2
Hodder, 1986, 112p. – O/P. – 0 340 36190 5
illustrated by Leslie Merrell

HOWLIDAY INN
Armada Books, 1989, 176p. – Pbk. –
0 00 673048 5
Grafton Books, 1987, 160p. – Pbk. –
0 583 31104 0
illustrated by Lynn Munsinger

Mr and Mrs Monroe have an unusual collection of animals: a dog who is a passable detective, a super-intelligent cat, and, the latest addition, a vampire rabbit! Straightforward, really funny books with highly satisfactory endings.
Age range: 8–10

HUGHES, Shirley

British. Born Hoylake, Lancashire, 1929.
Educated West Kirby High School for
Girls; Liverpool Art School; Ruskin
College of Art, Oxford. Married John
Vulliamy, 1952, two sons, one daughter.
Freelance illustrator and writer.

Awards: Children's Rights Workshop
Other Award: *Helpers*, 1976
Eleanor Farjeon Award, 1984

Address: 63 Lansdowne Road,
London W11 2LG, England

One of the best known and most talented
names in the field of children's literature,
equally capable in writing and illustrating.
Most of her work is for pre-school
children, but some of her books are
suitable for older children.

ANOTHER HELPING OF CHIPS
*Armada Books, 1988, 64p. – Pbk. –
0 00 672745 X
Bodley Head, 1986, 64p. – 0 370 30751 8*

In the same series:

CHARLIE MOON AND THE BIG BONANZA BUST-UP
*Chivers Press, 1990, 184p. – L/P. –
0 7451 1151 3
Armada Books, 1983, 128p. – Pbk. –
0 00 672160 5
Bodley Head, 1982, 128p. – 0 370 30918 9*

CHIPS AND JESSIE
*Bodley Head, 1985, 64p. – 0 370 30666 X
Armada Books, 1987, 64p. – Pbk. –
0 00 672532 5*

HERE COMES CHARLIE MOON
*Red Fox, 1991, 32p. – Pbk. – 0 09 992230 4
Chivers Press, 1990, 184p. – L/P. –
0 7451 1067 3
Bodley Head, 1980, 144p. – 0 370 30335 0*

A wonderful combination of cartoons,
pictures and continuous text. Different
stories about two friends and their dog
and cat entice the reader on to the end.
Age range: 7–9

IT'S TOO FRIGHTENING FOR ME
*Penguin, 1986, 64p. – Pbk. – 0 14 032008 3
Hodder, 1977, 48p. – O/P. – 0 340 21656 5*

An amusing ghost story with lots of
illustrations. Together, they form an
irresistible combination for young
readers.
Age range: 7–9

HUGHES, Ted (i.e. Edward James)

British. Born Mytholmroyd, Yorkshire, 1930. Educated Mexborough Grammar School, Yorkshire; Pembroke College, Cambridge, B.A. Archaeology and Anthropology, M.A. RAF, 1948–50. Married: 1) Sylvia Plath, poet, 1956 (died 1963), one daughter, one son; 2) Carol Orchard, 1970. Gardener, night-watchman, zoo attendant, teacher and reader. Lived in the USA 1957–59. Now lives in North Tawton, Devon.

Awards: Signal Poetry Award 1979, 1983, 1985.
Guardian Children's Fiction award: *What is the Truth?*, 1985
Kurt Maschler Award: *The Iron Man*, 1985
Hon. Fellow, Pembroke College, Cambridge, 1986
O.B.E., 1977
Poet Laureate, 1984

Address: C/o Faber & Faber Ltd
3 Queen's Square, London
WC1N 3AU, England

Better known for his poetry, it is, therefore, logical that any book for children by Ted Hughes will be a powerful linguistic experience. At the same time, he creates stories so well that his linguistic excellence is no barrier to sheer enjoyment.

HOW THE WHALE BECAME, AND OTHER STORIES
Faber, 1989, 72p. – Pbk. – 0 571 14184 6
Faber, n.d., 72p. – O/P. – 0 571 05615 6
illustrated by George Adamson

Imaginative stories recounting how each of the animals became the way we know them.
Age range: 8–10

THE IRON MAN: A STORY IN FIVE NIGHTS
Faber, 1989, 64p. – Pbk. – 0 571 14149 8
Faber, 1985, 53p. – 0 571 13675 3
illustrated by Andrew Davidson

A modern fairy story or fable with an important message. It has a gripping beginning, and holds the reader, (or listener, as it is superb for reading aloud), spellbound to the very end.
Age range: 8–10

HUTCHINS, Pat (née Goundry)

British. Born Catterick Camp, Yorkshire, 1942. Educated Darlington School of Art; Leeds College of Art. Married Laurence Hutchins, 1966, two children. Art Director, illustrator, writer.

Awards: Library Association Kate Greenaway Medal: *The Wind Blew*, 1974

Address: 75 Flask Walk, London NW3 1ET, England

Well known for her admirable picture books, Pat Hutchins shows that her talents easily stretch to writing humourous mystery stories with enormous appeal to young readers who need encouragement.

THE CURSE OF THE EGYPTIAN MUMMY
Armada Books, 1985, 160p. – Pbk. – 0 00 672463 9
Bodley Head, 1983, 160p. – O/P. – 0 370 30983 9

In the same series:

FOLLOW THAT BUS!
Armada Books, 1979, 112p. – Pbk. – 0 00 671480 3
Bodley Head, 1977, 112p. – O/P. – 0 370 30055 6

THE MONA LISA MYSTERY
Armada Books, 1987, 192p. – Pbk. – 0 00 672589 9
Bodley Head, 1981, 192p. – 0 370 30310 5
all illustrated by Laurence Hutchins

Amusing plots, packed with action and told in large, clear print: these books are excellent for readers gaining confidence. *Age range: 7–9*

RATS!
Bodley Head, 1989, 96p. – 0 370 31305 4
illustrated by Laurence Hutchins

Sam loves rats and would like one for a pet. Not surprisingly, Mum says no, but he buys one to prove to her that they are lovable. That is when the fun begins. *Age range: 7–9*

I

IRESON, Barbara

Married. Lives in France. Teacher, writer.

Barbara Ireson is an experienced and knowledgeable contributor to the field of children's books and reading. She can always be relied on to provide excellent material (not necessarily written by her), for a variety of age groups. The various collections of poems and stories serve the dual purpose of being suitable for reading aloud and for giving to children to enjoy reading for themselves.

CREEPY-CRAWLY STORIES
Beaver Books, 1987, 96p. – Pbk. –
0 09 951230 0
Hutchinson, 1986, 112p. – 0 09 165080 1
illustrated by Lesley Smith

Delightful, amusing stories by different authors about a variety of insects and mini-beasts.
Age range: 8–10

FANTASY TALES
Hamlyn, 1981, 192p. – Pbk, O/P. –
0 600 20056 6
Faber, 1977, 218p. – 0 571 10922 5

An excellent collection of weird and wonderful stories by first-class authors. Some are chilling, some are exciting – all are gripping.
Age range: 12–14

FIGHTING IN BREAK, AND OTHER STORIES
Penguin, 1989, 128p. – Pbk. – 0 14 032741 X
Faber, 1987, 124p. – 0 571 14623 6
illustrated by Susan Hellard

In the same series:

IN A CLASS OF THEIR OWN: SCHOOL STORIES
Penguin, 1987, 160p. – Pbk. – 0 14 032024 5
Faber, 1985, 149p. – O/P. – 0 571 13474 2

School stories are always popular, being within the experience of every child, and a wide range of themes and styles is included in these collections. Some stories are complete, some are excerpts; undoubtedly something for everyone.
Age range: 9–12

GHOSTLY LAUGHTER
Hamlyn, 1981, 160p. – Pbk, O/P. –
0 600 20322 0

Although some of the ghosts in these stories are frightening, most provoke laughter. A thoroughly enjoyable collection of stories.
Age range: 10–12

NAUGHTY STORIES: TALES OF TERRIBLE CHILDREN
Red Fox, 1990, 96p. – Pbk. – 0 09 969920 6
Hutchinson, 1989, 96p. – 0 09 173893 8

In the same series:

EVEN NAUGHTIER STORIES
Red Fox, 1991, 96p. – Pbk. – 0 09 980890 0
Hutchinson, 1990, 96p. – 0 09 174388 5
both illustrated by Tony Ross

An irresistible combination with Barbara Ireson choosing stories about naughty children who won't brush their teeth, or tidy their room, or eat their meals, and Tony Ross providing the perfect illustrations. Large clear print makes this a really attractive book.
Age range: 7–9

NEVER MEDDLE WITH MAGIC
Penguin, 1988, 288p. – Pbk. – 0 14 032269 8

In the same series:

THE RUNAWAY SHOES: PUFFIN BEDTIME STORY CHEST
Penguin, 1989, 304p. – Pbk. – 0 14 032270 1
both illustrated by Glenys Ambrus and Caroline Shaw

Two collections of varied stories, chosen by Barbara Ireson as being particularly suitable for bedtime.
Age range: 5–7

J

JONES, Diana Wynne

British. Born London, 1934. Educated
Friends' School, Saffron Walden;
St Anne's College, Oxford, B.A. Married
J. A. Burrow, 1956, three sons. Writer.

Awards: Guardian Children's Fiction
        Award: *The Spellcoats*, 1977
        Guardian Children's Fiction
        Award: *A Charmed Life*, 1978

Address: 9 The Polygon, Clifton,
        Bristol BS8 4PW, England

Agent: Laura Cecil, 17 Alwyne Villas,
        London N1 2HG, England

An unusually gifted fantasy writer who is
able to inject humour even into really
grim stories. She makes magic acceptable
to sceptics and provides reading that is
powerful, moving and thought-
provoking. Her stories are products of the
imagination, and therefore do not lend
themselves easily to illustration. This
makes attractive book-jackets hard to
provide, thus lessening the immediate
appeal to children, and the lack of
illustration also makes them less
accessible to the many children who
require visual appeal in order to be
persuaded to read. Children who can
overcome this barrier are rewarded with
enjoyable and unusual stories.

ARCHER'S GOON

*Magnet Books, 1986, 256p. – Pbk. –
0 416 62280 1
Methuen, 1984, 144p. – 0 416 49260 6*

Read at face value, this story is a superb
mystery, full of surprises which keep the
reader's attention. There is, however,
much more to it. It is a masterly fantasy
told with such literary expertise that
reading it provides an enriching
experience.
Age range: 12–14

CART AND CWIDDER

*Penguin, 1978, 176p. – Pbk, O/P. –
0 14 031018 5
Macmillan, 1975, 208p. – O/P. – 0 333 17939 0*

Set in the imaginary kingdom of
Dalemark, the story concerns a family of
wandering singers. The political climate is
unsteady, with the North now free while
the South is still oppressed. The situation
affects the members of the family in
different ways. Intrigues develop as terror
mounts when the magic begins its work.
Age range: 12–14

CHARMED LIFE

*Chivers Press, 1987, 360p. – L/P. –
0 7451 0490 8
Penguin, 1979, 208p. – Pbk. – 0 14 031075 4
Macmillan, 1977, 216p. – O/P. – 0 333 21426 9*

Gwendolen shows such promise that she
is being tutored in witchcraft free of
charge. Cat, her brother, is worried about
the whole situation and becomes more so
when they are transported to a castle
splendidly named Chrestomanci. It has
been prophesied that Gwendolen will
rule the world – discovering the truth of
this provides a fantasy read of the highest
quality, imbued with characteristic
humour.
Age range: 12–14

DROWNED AMMET

Macmillan, 1977, 262p. – O/P – 0 333 22620 8

Also set in Dalemark at the time of the
Sea Festival, which focuses attention on
the wicked Earl and his cruel band of
secret police. The Freedom Fighters
continue with their struggle, but are in
dire need of help which only magic can
provide.
Age range: 12–14

EIGHT DAYS OF LUKE
Chivers Press, 1988, 176p. – L/P. –
0 8599 7893 1
Penguin, 1977, 176p. – Pbk, O/P. –
0 14 030969 1
Macmillan, 1975, 176p. – O/P. – 0 333 17141 1

David's homecoming after school is a dismal affair. No–one wants him or feels pleased to see him. In his misery he curses the family, resulting in an earthquake, followed by a fire, a snake attack, and, finally, the appearance of Luke. David's loneliness and misery disappear until sinister events make him wonder who Luke really is and just where he came from. An excellent mixture of realism and magic told with warmth and humour.
Age range: 10–13

THE HOMEWARD BOUNDERS
Mammoth, 1990, 224p. – Pbk. – 0 7497 0281 8
Magnet Books, 1984, 224p. – Pbk, O/P. –
0 416 22940 9
Macmillan, 1981, 192p. – O/P. – 0 333 30979 0

Curiosity causes Jamie's downfall. He is banished to another world from which he must try to find his way home. Eventually he finds himself in the company of fellow wanderers all trying to get home.
Together they try to defy the mysterious and powerful 'They'. An unusual and absorbing story.
Age range: 10–13

THE LIVES OF CHRISTOPHER CHANT
Mammoth, 1989, 256p. – Pbk. – 0 7497 0033 5
Methuen, 1988, 240p. – 0 416 10742 7

Christopher has magic powers, and therefore has nine lives, like a cat. Nevertheless, his enemies seem remarkably successful in using up his lives, so he journeys to Chrestomanci Castle to study magic in the hope of defeating the forces of evil. Characteristic flashes of humour enliven this story of good versus evil, which requires a certain level of fluency to be appreciated.
Age range: 10–13

THE MAGICIANS OF CAPRONA
Beaver Books, 1987, 192p. – Pbk. –
0 09 954280 3
Macmillan, 1980, 224p. – O/P. – 0 333 27891 7

Spells are an essential part of this story. Although Tonino cannot manage them, he can understand cats, who are good with spells. Once again the forces of evil are at work. An unusual and amusing story.
Age range: 10–13

THE OGRE DOWNSTAIRS
Penguin, 1977, 192p. – Pbk. – 0 14 030898 9
Macmillan, 1974, 191p. – O/P. – 0 333 15917 9

The Ogre is the step-father of Johnny and Caspar, and not much loved! However, one day he presents them with a chemistry set, which sets them off on an exciting adventure from which they would never fully recover. Magic can seem very real.
Age range: 10–13

POWER OF THREE
Beaver Books, 1989, 272p. – Pbk. –
0 09 963620 4
Macmillan, 1976, 256p. – O/P. – 0 333 18643 5

To read this story is to enter a fantasy world that all too quickly becomes as real as the reader's own. It is peopled by giants and the sinister, shadowy Dorig. The curse that binds the place is exceptionally strong, and Gair feels he is not equal to the task of freeing them. An intriguing plot told, as always, with warmth and humour.
Age range: 10–13

THE SPELLCOATS
Macmillan, 1979, 256p. – O/P. – 0 333 25351 5

Tanaqui has the task of weaving coats that will tell the story and the meaning of the journey the children have to undertake when their father dies. It is a grim journey, beset by dangers, but courage wins through and finally the weaving is complete.
Age range: 10–13

THE TIME OF THE GHOST

Beaver Books, 1984, 192p. – Pbk. –
0 09 935950 2
Macmillan, 1981, 160p. – O/P. – 0 333 32012 3

An unusual ghost story in which the ghost is the central character trying to communicate. At first, it only succeeds with the dog, and no–one takes any notice of his alarms. The tension builds as a life is put at risk, but in the midst of high drama there is a welcome thread of humour.
Age range: 10–13

WARLOCK AT THE WHEEL AND OTHER STORIES

Arrow Books, 1989, 192p. – Pbk. –
0 09 965090 8
Macmillan, 1984, 156p. – O/P. – 0 333 37613 7

A volume of excellent short stories of a type similar to her full length novels. It is very welcome, as it means that readers who are reluctant to tackle her long novels may be able to partake of Diana Wynne Jones's enjoyable writing.
Age range: 10–12

WILD ROBERT

Methuen, 1989, 96p. – 0 416 15192 2
illustrated by Emma Chichester Clark

Less substantial than most of her novels, this story is still of a high literary and imaginative standard. Heather leads a lonely life in the Stately Home where her parents are curators. She is pleased to find a companion, until she realizes who it is.
Age range: 10–12

WILKIN'S TOOTH

Penguin, 1975, 176p. – Pbk. – 0 14 030765 6
Macmillan, 1973, 176p. – O/P. – 0 333 14548 8

Desperate to make some extra money when a misdeed causes their father to stop their pocket money, Jess and Frank found their own company, designed to help people who desire revenge. How it all gets out of hand is described in an amusing, lively style.
Age range: 10–13

WITCH WEEK

Mammoth, 1989, 224p. – Pbk. – 0 7497 0174 9
Macmillan, 1982, 192p. – O/P. – 0 333 33189 3

Another story woven around Chrestomanci Castle. Witchcraft is an offence punished by burning. One of the pupils in Mr Crossley's class is a witch. Trying to discover who it is in a race against time provides a dramatic story.
Age range: 10–13

K

KAYE, Geraldine (née Hughesdon)

British. Born Watford, Hertfordshire, 1925. Educated Felixstowe College, Suffolk; Watford Grammar School; London School of Economics, B.Sc. (Hons). WRNS WW II. Married Barrington Kaye, 1948 (divorced 1975), two daughters, one son. Scriptwriter, teacher.

Awards: Children's Rights Workshop
            Other Award: *Comfort
            Herself*, 1985

A perceptive author who can sympathize with the problems facing children who have to live in a different country from the one they were born in, or where their relatives are.

THE BEAUTIFUL TAKE-AWAY PALACE
*Magnet Books, 1988, 96p. – Pbk. –
0 416 06462 0*
Heinemann, 1987, 68p. – O/P. – 0 434 94571 4
illustrated by Glenys Ambrus

Adjusting to the difference between Hong Kong and his new home in England is hard for a young boy. Finding a sympathetic friend is the first step towards improving his new life.
Age range: 9–11

COMFORT HERSELF
*Mammoth, 1990, 160p. – Pbk. – 0 7497 0196 X
Deutsch, 1984, 192p. – 0 233 97614 0
illustrated by Jennifer Northway*

In the same series:

GREAT COMFORT
*Mammoth, 1990, 192p. – Pbk. –
0 7497 0193 5
Deutsch, 1988, 192p. – Pbk. – 0 233 98300 7*

Comfort is devastated by her Mum's death, but quickly realizes that she must now learn to make her own decisions. The first one is whether to stay with her grandparents in England, or to go and live with her father in Ghana. Having decided to share her time, she is devastated for a second time when she arrives in Ghana to find her step-family gone. Moving but enjoyable stories which give an insight into the structure of society in both Africa and England.
Age range: 12–14

KEMP, Gene (née Rushton)

British. Born Wigginton, Staffordshire, 1926. Educated Wigginton Church Primary School; Tamworth Girls' High School; University of Exeter, B.A. (Hons), English, M.A. Married: 1) Norman Pattison, 1949 (divorced 1958), one daughter; 2) Allan Kemp, 1958, one daughter, one son. Teacher, now freelance writer.

Awards: Children's Rights Workshop Other Award: *The Turbulent Term of Tyke Tiler*, 1977 Library Association Carnegie Medal: *The Turbulent Term of Tyke Tiler*, 1977

Address: 6 West Avenue, Exeter, Devon EX4 4SD, England

Agent: Gerald Pollinger, Laurence Pollinger Ltd, 18 Maddox Street, London W1R 0EU, England

As an ex-teacher, Gene Kemp is particularly able to portray school life realistically. Cricklepit Primary is the setting for her books, but the stories are varied. She understands children and can give convincing portrayals which allow the reader to empathize fully while enjoying the humour of the situation.

CHARLIE LEWIS PLAYS FOR TIME
Chivers Press, 1987, 168p. – L/P. –
0 7451 0548 3
Collins, 1986, 128p. – 0 00 330025 0
Penguin, 1986, 128p. – Pbk. – 0 14 031864 X
illustrated by Vanessa Julian-Ottie

Charlie is musical, but lives in the shadow of his mother, a famous concert pianist. When his favourite teacher is absent, old 'Garters' takes over, both at school and at home. Charlie finds his own solution to these problems. The characters are amusing, and the various episodes described with a liberal sprinkling of jokes, making the book an easy read.
Age range: 9–11

CHRISTMAS WITH TAMWORTH PIG
Faber, 1990, 96p. – Pbk. – 0 571 14445 4
Faber, 1977, 93p. – O/P. – 0 571 11117 3

In the same series:

THE PRIME OF TAMWORTH PIG
Faber, 1989, 112p. – Pbk. – 0 571 15345 3
Faber, 1972, 112p. – O/P. – 0 571 09780 4

TAMWORTH PIG AND THE LITTER
Faber, 1990, 128p. – Pbk. – 0 571 14290 7
Faber, 1975, 94p. – O/P. – 0 571 10743 5

TAMWORTH PIG SAVES THE TREES
Faber, 1989, 104p. – Pbk. – 0 571 14186 2
Faber, 1973, 104p. – O/P. – 0 571 10115 1

TAMWORTH PIG STORIES
Faber, 1987, 212p. – 0 571 14931 6
all illustrated by Carolyn Dinan

Just as much a delight to read today as when first published; these books never lose their appeal. Tamworth is a pig with extraordinary talents, whose encounters with life are described with such humour and fun that the reader is really sorry to reach the end.
Age range: 9–11

THE CLOCK TOWER GHOST
Penguin, 1984, 96p. – Pbk. – 0 14 031554 3
Faber, 1981, 89p. – O/P. – 0 571 11767 8
illustrated by Carolyn Dinan

An unusual story about a mean ghost who meets his match when an equally mean child comes to live in the tower. The resulting clash of personalities provides many amusing situations as they battle for supremacy.
Age range: 9–11

DOG DAYS AND CAT NAPS
Penguin, 1983, 112p. – Pbk. – 0 14 031419 9
Faber, 1980, 110p. – 0 571 11595 0
illustrated by Carolyn Dinan

A collection of ten short stories about a variety of pets and their equally varied owners. Fun to read.
Age range: 9–11

GOWIE CORBY PLAYS CHICKEN
Penguin, 1981, 144p. – Pbk. – 0 14 031322 2
Faber, 1979, 136p. – 0 571 11405 9

An unusual choice for a 'hero', as Gowie is mean, friendless and tough. This is the story of how such a boy becomes integrated into the life of the school he hates so much. It is a realistic yet optimistic portrayal of school life.
Age range: 11–14

JASON BODGER AND THE PRIORY GHOST
Chivers Press, 1988, 192p. – L/P. –
0 7451 0656 0
Penguin, 1987, 144p. – Pbk. – 0 14 032088 1
Faber, 1985, 144p. – O/P. – 0 571 13645 1
illustrated by Elaine McGregor Turney

A particular speciality of Gene Kemp is the unpleasant child who is changed by a supernatural experience, hence Jason Bodger. He is the despair of his teacher and classmates, and looks certain to disrupt the class outing to a priory. Mathilda, prowling the priory for seven hundred years, decides he is just the person she has been waiting for. Fast-paced and hilarious, this book is a thoroughly enjoyable read.
Age range: 10–12

JUNIPER
Penguin, 1988, 112p. – Pbk. – 0 14 032410 0
Faber, 1986, 112p. – 0 571 13902 7

A serious and haunting tale of a girl who has more than her fair share of problems. She has a physical disability, a criminal father, and a mother who cannot cope. There is a dramatic climax to a situation which is skilfully built up as the story progresses.
Age range: 10–12

MR MAGUS IS WAITING FOR YOU
Faber, 1986, 170p. – O/P. – 0 571 14686 4
Faber, 1986, 92p. – Pbk. – 0 571 14687 2
illustrated by Alan Baker

Four children, disgruntled and bored, find themselves in an enchanted garden. Each child reacts differently, but the appearance of the sinister Mr Magus signals the beginning of a frightening adventure. The book became a thrilling television serial.
Age range: 9–12

THE TURBULENT TERM OF TYKE TILER
Penguin, 1979, 128p. – Pbk. – 0 14 031135 1
Faber, 1977, 118p. – 0 571 10966 7
illustrated by Carolyn Dinan

The last term at junior school is often difficult for both teachers and pupils. When the class concerned tends to be difficult anyway, the result is a recipe for disaster. An excellent book.
Age range: 9–11

KING, (David) Clive

British. Born Richmond, Surrey, 1924.
Educated King's School, Rochester,
Kent; Downing College, Cambridge, B.A.
English; School of Oriental and African
Studies, London. Sub-Lieutenant,
RNVR, WW II. Married: 1) Jane Tuke,
1949 (divorced 1974); 2) Penelope
Timmins, 1974, one daughter, one son.
British Council Officer 1948–71, acting
as lecturer and education advisor.

Agent: Murray Pollinger, 4 Garrick
           Street, London WC2E 9BH,
           England

Here is an author with extra-special
talents. He sees the world rather
differently to the average adult, and is,
therefore, able to communicate with
children on their terms. His use of
language is unparalleled, and his
descriptions are vigorous and
meaningful. The result of this
combination is lively stories which
capture the imagination of children and
at the same time enhance their linguistic
ability.

ME AND MY MILLION

Penguin, 1979, 144p. – Pbk. – 0 14 031128 9
Kestrel Books, 1976, 144p. – O/P. –
0 7226 5185 6

Realism and fantasy are combined in this
remarkable story. Ringo is an illiterate,
street-wise youth who is entrusted with
the delivery of a laundry bag, a simple
task which goes dramatically wrong. The
ensuing chaos becomes increasingly
amusing, and yet exciting, as he struggles
in vain to put things right.
Age range: 10–13

NINNY'S BOAT

Penguin, 1983, 272p. – Pbk, O/P. –
0 14 031424 5
Kestrel Books, 1980, 256p. – 0 7226 5617 3
illustrated by Ian Newsham

Abandoned to his fate during a flood,
Ninny has no-one to rely on but himself.
In order to keep his spirits up during his
search for his home, he makes jokes

about, and enjoys, his situation to the
best of his ability. The verbal wit makes
the reader laugh out loud, and Clive King
makes the reader view the world through
the fresh and wondering eyes of his Dark
Age hero. A special book.
Age range: 9–12

THE SOUND OF PROPELLERS

Penguin, 1988, 208p. – Pbk, O/P. –
0 14 032106 3
Viking Kestrel, 1986, 208p. – 0 670 81106 8
illustrated by David Parkins

The complex, rewarding story of
Morugan, sent from his home in India to
boarding school in England. His feelings
of bewilderment take second place to the
exciting discovery that the sound of
propellers heralds a spying raid on the
aircraft factory next to the school. The
boys cannot ignore the situation, and
must decide what action to take.
Age range: 10–13

STIG OF THE DUMP

Viking Kestrel, 1985, 160p. – 0 670 80027 9
Penguin, 1970. – Pbk. – 0 14 030196 8
illustrated by Edward Ardizzone

A modern classic, this book has
continued to capture the imagination of
children for many years. Barney, unable
to convince anyone that he has found a
Stone Age boy living on the dump, just
enjoys being friends with him, and
learning about his way of life. It has also
been translated to the stage.
Age range: 9–12

THE TOWN THAT WENT SOUTH

Penguin, 1970, 112p. – Pbk. – 0 14 030442 8
Hamish Hamilton, 1969, 124p. – O/P. –
0 241 01717 3
illustrated by Maurice Bartlett

The inhabitants of Ramsly wake up one
morning to find their town has broken
away from the English coast and drifted
across to France – what a splendid idea!
Fun to read, it gives an entirely new slant
to the concept of twin towns.
Age range: 9–12

KING-SMITH, Dick

British. Born Bitton, Gloucestershire, 1922. Educated Marlborough College, Wiltshire; University of Bristol, B.Ed. 2nd Lieutenant, Grenadier Guards, WW II. Married Myrle England, 1943, two daughters, one son. Farmer, teacher, freelance writer.

Awards: Guardian Children's Fiction Award: *Sheep-pig*, 1984

Address: Diamond's Cottage, Queen Charlton, near Keynsham, Avon BS18 2SJ, England

Agent: A. P. Watt Ltd, 20 John Street, London WC1N 2DR, England

An endlessly inventive author whose intentions are plainly to entertain and amuse. His farming experience has given him detailed knowledge of animal characteristics which he uses, with a certain poetic licence, to good effect to produce original, unsentimental and amusing stories.

ACE

Gollancz, 1990, 128p. – 0 575 04725 9
illustrated by Liz Graham-Yooll

Descended from Sheep-pig (see below), Ace is bound to be above average. He catches the eye of Farmer Tubbs, who saves him from the market. Helped by his friends, he manages to oust the hitherto favourite Corgi, and take his place.
Age range: 8–10

DAGGIE DOGFOOT

Chivers Press, 1990, 192p. – L/P. –
0 7451 1229 3
Penguin, 1982, 160p. – Pbk. – 0 14 031391 5
Gollancz, 1980, 112p. – 0 575 02767 3
illustrated by Mary Rayner

A satisfying story in which the underdog (or 'underpig') triumphs over many difficulties to become a hero. Daggie is the runt of the litter and, with typical farming unsentimentality, would have been quickly disposed of in a manner likely to bring a lump to the throat of little pink pig lovers. However, the pigman's attention is diverted and Daggie is rescued, going from strength to strength.
Age range: 8–12

DODOS ARE FOREVER

Penguin, 1990, 80p. – Pbk. – 0 14 034044 0
Viking, 1989, 224p. – 0 670 82681 2
illustrated by David Parkins

Here is a book for everyone who regrets the demise of the dodo, as it convincingly puts forward the theory that a few may have survived, but their continued existence is threatened by a colony of rats. There is much to both laugh and cry at.
Age range: 8–12

EMILY'S LEGS

MacDonald, 1988, 48p. – O/P. – 0 356 13685 X
MacDonald, 1988, 48p. – Pbk. – 0 356 13686 8
illustrated by Katinka Kew

Ideal for children who can read but need stimulating yet simple reading material, with lots of illustrations. Emily is easily the fastest spider, but there is a reason for this.
Age range: 6–8

THE FOX-BUSTERS

Chivers Press, 1987, 160p. – L/P. –
0 7451 0492 4
Penguin, 1980, 120p. – Pbk. – 0 14 031175 0
Gollancz, 1978, 128p. – 0 575 02444 5
illustrated by Jon Miller

A band of chickens find a way to defeat the foxes who are determined to eat them. As always, it is highly original, exceptionally funny, and yet some readers will also shed a few tears.
Age range: 8–12

FRIENDS AND BROTHERS

Mammoth, 1989, 96p. – Pbk. – 0 7497 0048 3
Heinemann, 1987, 96p. – O/P. – 0 434 94581 1
illustrated by Susan Hellard

William often feels he would like Charlie, his little nuisance of a brother, to disappear. When Charlie is in trouble,

however, William finds himself rushing to his rescue.
Age range: 7–9

GEORGE SPEAKS
Penguin, 1989, 96p. – Pbk. – 0 14 032397 X
Viking Kestrel, 1988, 96p. – 0 670 81798 8
illustrated by Judy Brown

George is a miracle baby. At four weeks he can speak in whole sentences, and this leads to many hilarious situations.
Age range: 7–9

HARRY'S MAD
Chivers Press, 1990, 136p. – L/P. –
0 7451 1101 7
Penguin, 1986, 128p. – Pbk. – 0 14 031897 6
Gollancz, 1984, 120p. – 0 575 03497 1
illustrated by Jill Bennett

Harry inherits a parrot called Madison when his great-uncle dies. The parrot has many exceptional talents which make him a welcome addition to the household. When he is lost, the family realize they cannot manage without him, and so begins a great hunt which ends in a most unusual way.
Age range: 8–12

THE HODGEHEG
Windrush, 1990, 96p. – L/P. – 1 85089 860 X
Penguin, 1989, 96p. – Pbk. – 0 14 032503 4
Hamish Hamilton, 1987, 88p. – 0 241 11980 4

Easy to read and completely absorbing, it tells how Max sets out to solve the problem of how hedgehogs can cross the road in safety.
Age range: 6–9

MAGNUS POWERMOUSE
Chivers Press, 1991, 168p. – L/P. –
0 7451 1296 X
Penguin, 1984, 128p. – Pbk. – 0 14 031602 7
Gollancz, 1982, 128p. – 0 575 03116 6

Magnus is a giant among mice, and causes his mother endless problems. The bigger he grows, the worse the problems, and the more entertaining the child finds it. A wonderfully happy ending.
Age range: 8–10

MARTIN'S MICE
Penguin, 1989, 128p. – Pbk. – 0 14 034026 2
Chivers Press, 1989, 152p. – L/P. –
0 7451 0956 X
Gollancz, 1988, 128p. – 0 575 04264 8
illustrated by Jez Alborough

Martin is an embarrassment. As a farm cat, he is supposed to catch mice, but he prefers tinned food and keeps a mouse as a pet! Extremely funny and quite believable.
Age range: 8–12

THE MOUSE BUTCHER
Penguin, 1983, 128p. – Pbk. – 0 14 031457 1
Gollancz, 1981, 128p. – 0 575 02899 8
illustrated by Wendy Smith

Definitely not a book for the faint-hearted. The description of Great Mog, the cat whose experiences caused him to hate everyone and everything, is detailed and gruesome, leaving nothing to the imagination. Tom Plug, the butcher's cat, volunteers to rid them of this fearful menace, an arrangement culminating in a battle to the death. Hard-hitting and realistic, but with a lighter side too, it will appeal to readers already acquainted with books by this author, but is not a good one to start with. Cat lovers will find it hard to decide whose side they are on.
Age range: 10–12

NOAH'S BROTHER
Windrush, 1989, 76p. – L/P. – 1 85089 947 9
Penguin, 1988, 80p. – Pbk. – 0 14 032354 6
Gollancz, 1986, 72p. – 0 575 03876 4
illustrated by Ian Newsham

A short story with lots of illustrations and a highly entertaining plot concerning the truth about the building of the Ark.
Age range: 8–10

PADDY'S POT OF GOLD
Windrush, 1991, 122p. – L/P. – 1 85089 811 1
Viking, 1990, 96p. – 0 670 82903 X
illustrated by David Parkins

Brigid is pleased when the little leprechaun chooses her to show himself to. She and Paddy have many amusing

adventures together before the pot of gold is found.
Age range: 8–10

THE QUEEN'S NOSE
Penguin, 1985, 128p. – Pbk. – 0 14 031838 0
Gollancz, 1983, 128p. – 0 575 03228 6
illustrated by Jill Bennett

An immensely exciting story containing all the ingredients of a first-rate book. It has an unusual plot, a hint of mystery, lots of humour, and a wonderful ending. Harmony has to solve a set of cryptic clues in order to reach her uncle's present. When she finds it, she is a little disappointed, until she realizes its potential.
Age range: 9–12

SADDLEBOTTOM
Chivers Press, 1987, 112p. – L/P. –
0 7451 0629 3
Penguin, 1987, 128p. – Pbk. – 0 14 032177 2
Gollancz, 1985, 128p. – 0 575 03715 6
illustrated by Alice Englander

The hero is a saddleback pig whose 'saddle' has slipped, and who is, therefore, an outcast. Needless to say, he makes good, winning fame and fortune in the end. An entertaining story.
Age range: 8–12

THE SHEEP-PIG
Penguin, 1985, 128p. – Pbk. – 0 14 031839 9
Gollancz, 1983, 128p. – 0 575 03375 4
illustrated by Mary Rayner

Babe, the piglet, is fostered by Fly, the sheepdog. It is not surprising, therefore, that he grows up wanting to learn how to herd sheep. Excellent animal characterization, as always, makes this a memorable book.
Age range: 8–12

SOPHIE'S SNAIL
Walker Books, 1989, 96p. – Pbk. –
0 7445 0829 0
Walker Books, 1988, 96p. – O/P. –
0 7445 0820 7
illustrated by Claire Minter-Kemp

Six stories about a four year old girl called Sophie. She has a mind of her own, and everyone knows it. Lovely to read aloud.
Age range: 4–6

THE TOBY MAN
Windrush, 1990, 120p. – L/P. – 1 85089 880 4
Gollancz, 1989, 128p. – 0 575 04485 3
illustrated by Ian Newsham

Dick King-Smith's wonderful but zany sense of humour produces a book to enjoy. Tod sets off with a donkey, a mastiff, a ferret and a magpie to make his fortune as a highwayman.
Age range: 8–10

TUMBLEWEED
Penguin, 1988, 144p. – Pbk. – 0 14 032547 6
Windrush, 1988, 149p. – L/P. – 1 85089 939 8
Gollancz, 1987, 96p. – 0 575 03975 2
illustrated by Ian Newsham

It is surprising what a little magic can achieve for a shy knight always in trouble. An unusual theme for this author, but just as enjoyable.
Age range: 8–10

L

LAVELLE, Sheila

British. Born Gateshead, County Durham. Married, two sons. Lives at Bourne End, Buckinghamshire. Writer.

A writer of lively, popular books which are not too demanding, and fun to read.

DISASTER WITH THE FIEND
Armada Books, 1983, 112p. – Pbk. –
0 00 672082 X
Hamish Hamilton, 1982, 180p. – O/P. –
0 241 10774 1
illustrated by Margaret Chamberlain

In the same series:

FIEND NEXT DOOR
Armada Books, 1983, 112p. – Pbk. –
0 00 672082 X
Hamish Hamilton, 1982, 180p. – O/P. –
0 241 10774 1

HOLIDAY WITH THE FIEND
Armada Books, 1988, 128p. – Pbk. –
0 00 672787 5
Hamish Hamilton, 1986, 128p. –
0 241 11857 3
illustrated by Margaret Chamberlain

MY BEST FIEND
Armada Books, 1980, 128p. – Pbk. –
0 00 671661 X
illustrated by Linda Birch

TROUBLE WITH THE FIEND
Armada Books, 1985, 128p. – Pbk. –
0 00 672433 7
Hamish Hamilton, 1984. – 0 241 11305 9

A series of books about Charlie Ellis and Angela Mitchell who live next door to each other. Life is never dull, for Angela is always full of bright ideas and tricks. Sometimes Charlie gets fed up of being the victim, and plans revenges. Each book is similar – only the tricks are different.
Age range: 7–9

LEE, Tanith

British. Born London, 1947. Educated Prendergaste Grammar School; Calford Grammar School; Art College.

Address: C/o Macmillan Ltd, 4 Little Essex Street, London WC2R 3LF, England

To be successful at writing fantasy, it is essential to be able to create other worlds that readers can whole-heartedly believe in. To this ability, Tanith Lee adds a wonderful sense of humour and an originality of plot that makes her books both intriguing and thought-provoking, and able to stand the test of time.

THE DRAGON HOARD
Beaver Books, 1989, 176p. – Pbk. –
0 09 957160 9
Macmillan, 1971, 176p. – O/P. – 0 333 12850 8
illustrated by Graham Oakley

Prince Jasleth must seek his fortune in the traditional way of princes. The trouble is, he is cursed, and he turns into a raven when it is most inconvenient. Very amusing.
Age range: 10–12

PRINCE ON A WHITE HORSE
Beaver Books, 1989, 160p. – Pbk, O/P. –
0 09 957150 1
Macmillan, 1982, 160p. – O/P. – 0 333 32929 5

The prince riding along talks to himself, as people on their own do. He is surprised when the horse answers him, and puzzled when the horse stoutly denies being able to talk. How he discovers his identity makes an amusing and enjoyable read.
Age range: 10–12

SHON THE TAKEN
Beaver Books, 1989, 144p. – Pbk. –
0 09 963130 X
Macmillan, 1979, 160p. – O/P. – 0 333 27036 3

In Shon's world, if you were touched by one of Crow's people, you had to die. Shon convinces himself he has not been touched, and dismisses the tiny sense of foreboding. Intent on settling a score with his brother, it is too late when the full realization of events is made plain.
Age range: 10–12

THE WINTER PLAYERS
Beaver Books, 1988, 112p. – Pbk. –
0 09 957140 4
Macmillan, 1976, 112p. – O/P. – 0 333 19840 9

The exciting first chapter plunges the reader directly into a scene of powerful conflict, between Oaive, the young priestess guarding the shrine, and the young man intent on stealing. Which of them is the ultimate victor makes a superb story.
Age range: 10–12

LEESON, Robert (Arthur)

British. Born Barnton, Cheshire, 1928. Educated Sir John Deane's Grammar School; University of London, external B.A. (Hons). British Army, Middle East, 1946–48. Married Gunvor Hagen, 1954, one son, one daughter. Journalist, Parliamentary correspondent, editor.

Awards: Eleanor Farjeon Award, 1985.

Address: 18 McKenzie Road, Broxbourne, Hertfordshire, England

Although associated by many children with the popular television series *Grange Hill*, Robert Leeson has written several books on various themes for different age groups, some with a specific appeal to boys.

BEYOND THE DRAGON PROW
Collins, 1973, 160p. – O/P. – 0 00 184061 4
illustrated by Ian Robbins

Set in Viking times, this stirring adventure story is a useful book to read to a class studying the Vikings. Once the reader has mastered the strange names, it is an easy and exciting story to read, whilst also conveying a realistic impression of everyday life of the period.
Age range: 10–12

CHALLENGE IN THE DARK
Armada Books, 1979, 98p. – Pbk. –
0 00 671648 2
Collins, 1978, 112p. – O/P. – 0 00 184065 7
illustrated by Jim Russell

Young readers will appreciate the skilful combination of realism and humour in this story about Steven, the class bully, and Mike, his victim. When the two of them are challenged to see who can stay in the old air-raid shelter without light, Mike rises to the occasion. Easy, entertaining and exciting.
Age range: 9–11

THE DEMON BIKE RIDER
Armada Books, 1977, 94p. – Pbk. –
0 00 671320 3
Collins, 1976, 96p. – O/P. – 0 00 184163 7
illustrated by Jim Russell

A mixture of mystery and ghosts, this has proved one of Robert Leeson's most popular books. The idea of a ghost on a motorbike appeals to boys. Not very long or demanding, but lots of action.
Age range: 9–11

GENIE ON THE LOOSE
Armada Books, 1984, 128p. – Pbk. –
0 00 672294 6
Hamish Hamilton, 1984, 128p. – O/P. –
0 241 11177 3

In the same series:

THIRD CLASS GENIE
Hamish Hamilton, 1981, 128p. –
0 241 10623 0
Collins, 1975, 128p. – Pbk, O/P. –
0 00 670930 3

If you have ever wondered how a genie manages to work miracles, these books have the answer. Alec is lucky enough to own a beer can which houses a genie who is learning the job, and does not yet merit a lamp. His 'miracles' often go wrong, sometimes quite disastrously, leading to many hilarious situations. The stories are full of action, but quite dense in appearance, although competent readers will have no problems.
Age range: 10–12

HAROLD AND BELLA, JAMMY AND ME
Hamish Hamilton, 1982, 128p. – O/P. –
0 241 10722 9
Armada Books, 1980, 128p. – Pbk. –
0 00 671606 7

An uninspiring title for a collection of comical stories about four children and their adventures in an unspecified town in the north. There is enough dialect for authenticity, but not too much to spoil the sense of the story. The flavour of bygone days pervades throughout.
Age range: 8–10

SILVER'S REVENGE
Armada Books, 1985, 208p. – Pbk. –
0 00 672466 3
Collins, 1978, 196p. – O/P. – 0 00 184783 X

Cleverly contrived, this sequel to *Treasure Island* is written in a similar style with the same sense of humour. This book will not have universal appeal, but is rewarding for those who do persevere. *Age range:* 10–12

WHEEL OF DANGER

Armada Books, 1987, 96p. – Pbk. –
0 00 672803 0
Collins, 1986, 96p. – 0 00 184790 2
Collins, 1986, 96p. – Pbk. – 0 00 184791 0
illustrated by Anthony Kervins

Mike and his friends are pleased with themselves when they succeed in turning the huge water wheel. Their pleasure is, unfortunately, short-lived, as it floods the mill with the children trapped inside. Tense to read, but with amusing moments, it is an excellent story for children who require coaxing. *Age range:* 9–11

LINDGREN, Astrid

Swedish. Born Vimmerby, 1907. Married Sture Lindgren, 1931, one son, one daughter. Children's book editor.

Awards: Hans Christian Andersen
International Medal, 1958
Welsh Arts Council
International Writers' Prize
German Booksellers' Peace
Prize for the International Year
of the Child
Hon. Doctorate of Letters,
Leicester University
Leo Tolstoy Gold Medal

An author with the rare quality of having both international appeal and a popularity that survives the passage of time. Her books portray a strong feeling for the security and happiness to be found in a family circle, something many children are deprived of.

CHERRY TIME AT BULLERBY
Methuen, 1965. – O/P. – 0 416 23100 4

In the same series:

CHRISTMAS AT BULLERBY
Methuen, 1970, 96p. – 0 416 22250 1

DAY AT BULLERBY
Methuen, 1967, 24p. – 0 416 94500 7

HAPPY DAYS AT BULLERBY
Methuen, 1965. – O/P. – 0 416 23100 4

THE SIX BULLERBY CHILDREN
*Magnet Books, 1980, 96p. – Pbk. –
0 416 89500 X
Methuen, n.d., 92p. – O/P. – 0 416 26180 9*

SPRINGTIME AT BULLERBY
*Methuen, 1981, 32p. – 0 416 88710 4
all illustrated by Ilon Wikland*

Warm, humorous stories about the families living on farms in the Swedish village of Bullerby. Far from being sentimental, they take an honest look at the difficulties as well as the joys of relationships.
Age range: 7–9

ALL ABOUT THE BULLERBY CHILDREN
*Penguin, 1974, 192p. – Pbk, O/P. –
0 14 030705 2
Methuen, 1970, 224p. – 0 416 15280 5
illustrated by Ilon Wikland*

Combines the stories of the above books; the hardback edition is published with exceptionally clear print, making it accessible to younger children.
Age range: 7–9

EMIL AND HIS CLEVER PIG
*Beaver Books, 1984, 144p. – Pbk, O/P. –
0 09 937600 8
Hodder, 1975, 160p. – O/P. – 0 340 18971 1
illustrated by Bjorn Berg*

In the same series:

EMIL AND THE BAD TOOTH
Hodder, 1976, 32p. – O/P. – 0 340 20923 2

EMIL GETS INTO MISCHIEF
*Beaver Books, 1985, 126p. – Pbk, O/P. –
0 09 942222 0
Hamlyn, 1979, 126p. – Pbk, O/P. –
0 600 33164 4*

EMIL IN THE SOUP TUREEN
*Beaver Books, 1985, 96p. – Pbk, O/P. –
0 09 942210 7
Hodder, 1970, 90p. – O/P. – 0 340 10404 X*

EMIL'S LITTLE SISTER
*Hodder, 1985, 64p. – O/P. – 0 340 38114 0
illustrated by Bjorn Berg*

EMIL'S PRANKS
Hodder, 1973, 128p. – O/P. – 0 340 16944 3

EMIL'S STICKY PROBLEM
*Hodder, 1986, 60p. – O/P. – 0 340 39842 6
illustrated by Bjorn Berg*

THAT EMIL
Hodder, 1973, 32p. – O/P. – 0 340 17213 4

Emil is a naughty child, but his antics delight young readers. Enjoyable when read aloud.
Age range: 6–8

KARLSON FLIES AGAIN
*Methuen, 1978, 144p. – Pbk. – 0 416 86540 2
Methuen, 1977, 144p. – 0 416 58390 3*

In the same series:

KARLSON ON THE ROOF
Methuen, 1977, 128p. – Pbk, O/P. –
0 416 58010 6
Methuen, 1975, 128p. – 0 416 80240 0

THE WORLD'S BEST KARLSON
Methuen, 1980, 160p. – 0 416 88020 7
all illustrated by Ilon Wikland

Karlson is amazing. He is very small and lives on a roof with a propeller fastened to his back. He cheers Midge up when he flies into his life with his mischievous ideas. Escapism at its amusing best.
Age range: 7–9

LOTTA
Methuen, 1982, 160p. – 0 416 26840 4
Methuen, 1979, 160p. – Pbk, O/P. –
0 416 86510 0

In the same series:

LOTTA LEAVES HOME
Magnet Books, 1983, 64p. – Pbk. –
0 416 27430 7
Methuen, 1969, 64p. – O/P. – 0 416 48170 1

LOTTA'S BIKE
Methuen, 1973, 32p. – 0 416 76600 5

LOTTA'S CHRISTMAS SURPRISE
Magnet Books, 1980, 36p. – Pbk. –
0 416 88600 0
Methuen, 1978, 32p. – O/P. – 0 416 86690 5

THE MISCHIEVOUS MARTENS
Magnet Books, 1983, 96p. – Pbk, O/P. –
0 416 25610 4
Methuen, 1969, 96p. – O/P. – 0 416 48160 4
illustrated by Ilon Wikland

Ordinary family stories, told with love and humour. Very easy to read.
Age range: 7–9

MARDIE
Magnet Books, 1979, 156p. – Pbk, O/P. –
0 416 87610 2
Methuen, 1979, 160p. – O/P. – 0 416 57640 0

In the same series:

MARDIE TO THE RESCUE
Methuen, 1981, 196p. – 0 416 20650 6
both illustrated by Ilon Wikland

Endearing stories about a Swedish family in the 1920s. They are poor, but Mardie's rascally adventures take place against the secure family background that Astrid Lindgren portrays so well. The usual mixture of warmth, humour and mischief.
Age range: 7–9

PIPPI LONGSTOCKING
Penguin, 1976, 176p. – Pbk. – 0 14 030894 6
OUP, 1954, 128p. – 0 19 271097 4
illustrated by Richard Kennedy

The exception to warm family stories. Pippi has to live alone as her mother is dead and her father marooned. However, she is very strong, both physically and emotionally, and, instead of feeling sorry for herself, she gets on with life, defying all conventions. It is this successful defiance and energetic, imaginative ideas which children find so easy to identify with. It has to be said that, because her father is a Cannibal King on the island, and tongue-in-cheek references are made to cannibal language and customs, the book is considered by some to be racist. It is, however, all part of the unreal life Pippi leads, a fact children will accept purely at face value, without delving beneath for hidden and unintended meanings.
Age range: 9–11

LISTER, Mary
(married name Walker)

British. Born Wiltshire, 1950. Educated St Mary's School, Wantage; Nottingham University, B.A. (Hons), English. Married 1971, one son, one daughter. Teacher, writer, performer.

CREEPO MACABRE AND THE BEAST OF LOCH HORAR
Methuen, 1990, 96p. – 0 416 13612 5
illustrated by Kathryn Lamb

Thrilled at first to have an American relative on a visit, Creepo soon learns that Hiram is not all that he seems. Very amusing.
Age range: 7–9

CREEPO'S BIRTHDAY HONOURS
Methuen, 1986, 93p. – 0 416 61490 6
illustrated by John Mansbridge

Easy to read, this humourous tale proves that it is not easy to do a good deed if you are a monster who has spent 21 years doing bad deeds.
Age range: 7–9

PRINCESS POLLY TO THE RESCUE
Magnet Books, 1986, 96p. – Pbk. –
0 416 00572 1
Methuen, 1984, 96p. – O/P. – 0 416 49890 6

In the same series:

PRINCESS POLLY AND THE MAGIC MEGA-PLOT
Methuen, 1989, 96p. – 0 416 13302 9
illustrated by Ron Hanna

Lively, amusing stories by an author whose own puppet shows have thrilled countless children. Princess Polly is a modern, no nonsense young woman who is quite prepared to do her share of rescuing if necessary.
Age range: 7–9

LITTLE, (Flora) Jean

Canadian. Born Tainon, Formosa, now Taiwan, 1932. Educated in Guelph, Ontario; Victoria College, University of Toronto, B.A. English; Institute of Special Education. Teacher.

Awards: Canadian Children's Book Award: *Mine for Keeps*, 1961 Canadian Library Association Book of the Year Award: *Mama's Going to Buy you a Mocking Bird*, 1985 Ruth Schwartz Award: *Mama's Going to Buy you a Mocking Bird*, 1985

Address: 198 Glasgow Street North, Guelph, Ontario, Canada

Jean Little has an understanding of children and their problems which enables her to write simply and directly for them. As a result, her books deal honestly with different emotional problems and are meaningful in every way.

DIFFERENT DRAGONS
Penguin, 1988, 144p. – Pbk. – 0 14 031998 0
Viking Kestrel, 1987, 124p. – O/P. –
0 670 80836 9
illustrated by Laura Fernandez

Ben is timid, and feels he will not manage to cope with staying with Aunt Rose, whom he does not know very well. He is sure he cannot cope when she presents him with a big dog, for he is terrified. How this problem is resolved makes a warm, satisfying story.
Age range: 7–9

LOST AND FOUND
Penguin, 1987, 96p. – Pbk. – 0 14 031997 2
Viking Kestrel, 1986, 82p. – 0 670 80835 0
illustrated by Leoung O'Young

A moving story about a little girl, feeling strange in a new town, who finds a stray dog. She is allowed to keep him while a search is made for his owner. Eventually she has to make a difficult decision.
Age range: 9–11

MAMA'S GOING TO BUY YOU A MOCKING BIRD
Penguin, 1986, 224p. – Pbk. – 0 14 031737 6
Viking Kestrel, 1985, 212p. – O/P. –
0 670 80346 4

A brave and successful attempt to face a problem which is real, and which many children have to come to terms with. Jeremy's father has cancer and will die. Dealing with grief is personal, but sometimes books can provide a stimulus which allows both children and adults to express their feelings.
Age range: 10–14

LIVELY, Penelope
(Margaret, née Low)

British. Born Cairo, Egypt, 1933, came to England 1945. Educated boarding school, Sussex; St Anne's College, Oxford, B.A. (Hons), Modern History. Married Jack Lively, 1957, one daughter, one son. Radio presenter, reviewer.

Awards: Fellow of the Royal Society of Literature
Library Association Carnegie Medal: *The Ghost of Thomas Kempe*, 1973
Whitbread Award: *A Stitch in Time*, 1976

Address: Duck End, Great Rollright, Chipping Norton, Oxfordshire OX7 5SB, England

Agent: Murray Pollinger, 4 Garrick Street, London WC2E 9BH, England

A distinguished writer with a fascination for time-slips and a sense of history and the way it can affect the present. Children need to be fluent readers as her style is rather adult and makes no compromise. The originality of the plots and the ever-present air of expectation tempered by verbal humour, however, engage the reader's interest to the end.

ASTERCOTE
Penguin, 1987, 160p. – Pbk. – 0 14 031973 5
Heinemann, 1970, 160p. – 0 434 94890 X
illustrated by Antony Maitland

Peter and Mair discover the ruins of an old village called Astercote. They become fascinated, and delve deeper into the history of the village, gradually bringing it back to life.
Age range: 11–14

THE DRIFTWAY
Penguin, 1985, 160p. – Pbk. – 0 14 031497 0
Heinemann, 1972, 144p. – 0 434 94893 4

The Driftway is an old road with a long memory. While hitching a lift to go and visit Gran, Paul and his sister see the ghosts of long dead travellers. A slow-moving but atmospheric story which is strangely compelling.
Age range: 12–14

FANNY AND THE MONSTERS
Heinemann, 1983, 128p. – O/P. – 0 434 94888 8
Penguin, 1982, 128p. – Pbk. – 0 14 031501 2
illustrated by John Lawrence

A collection of stories about a Victorian girl who longs to be a boy so that she can have adventures.
Age range: 9–11

THE GHOST OF THOMAS KEMPE
Chivers Press, 1986, 256p. – L/P. –
0 7451 0303 0
Penguin, 1984, 160p. – Pbk. – 0 14 031496 2
Heinemann, 1973, 160p. – 0 434 94894 2
illustrated by Antony Maitland

Once James realizes that there is a ghost in the house, he spends all his time trying to ascertain who he is. The humour in this story verges on slapstick at times. Quite riveting, with a highly satisfactory ending.
Age range: 11–14

GOING BACK
Penguin, 1991, 128p. – Pbk. – 0 14 014509 5
Heinemann, 1975, 96p. – 0 434 94896 9

Jane returns to Medleycott where she grew up. She relives her childhood during the Second World War. Excellent period detail and atmosphere, making absorbing reading, but likely to remain a minority choice.
Age range: 11–14

THE HOUSE IN NORHAM GARDENS
Penguin, 1986, 176p. – Pbk. – 0 14 031976 X
Heinemann, 1974, 160p. – 0 434 94895 0

A strange mixture of reality and fantasy. The house is Victorian, and the spirit of the previous owner, an explorer, lives on to disturb the present occupants.
Age range: 11–14

THE REVENGE OF SAMUEL STOKES

Penguin, 1983, 144p. – Pbk. – 0 14 031504 7
Heinemann, 1981, 160p. – 0 434 94889 6
illustrated by Martin J. Cottam

Strange happenings abound on the new housing estate. Washing machines go wrong, televisions won't work, and a greenhouse becomes a Greek Temple. Tim and Jane are convinced a ghost is at work and set out to find out the reason. Amusing and enjoyable.
Age range: 11–14

A STITCH IN TIME

Chivers Press, 1988, 264p. – L/P. –
0 7451 0726 5
Penguin, 1986, 160p. – Pbk. – 0 14 031975 1
Heinemann, 1976, 128p. – 0 434 94897 7

A haunting story about Maria, staying in a cottage while on holiday, who feels the presence of a long dead child. She slowly unravels the mystery of why the child cries. Not very eventful, the book successfully relies on its intriguing atmosphere to hold the reader's interest.
Age range: 11–14

THE VOYAGE OF QV66

Mammoth, 1990, 192p. – Pbk. – 0 7497 0360 1
Heinemann, 1978, 192p. – 0 434 94898 5
illustrated by Harold Jones

An unusual book for Penelope Lively in that it is completely light-hearted and funny. A group of animals are travelling to a zoo in a country where there are no people. Their efforts to discover who

Stanley is are both amusing and intriguing.
Age range: 11–14

THE WHISPERING KNIGHTS

Chivers Press, 1990, 248p. – L/P. –
0 7451 1153 X
Heinemann, 1989, 160p. – 0 434 94884 5
Penguin, 1987, 160p. – Pbk. – 0 14 031977 8
illustrated by Neil Reed

William and Susie were having fun cooking up a witch's brew and chanting spells in the barn. Martha, knowing about the witch who reputedly lived there, many years ago, was worried that things may go wrong – rightly so as it turned out. A malevolent spirit is summoned that is beyond the children to control. An engrossing fantasy in which past and present merge in a realistic way.
Age range: 10–12

THE WILD HUNT OF HAGWORTHY

Heinemann, 1989, 144p. – 0 434 94886 1
Chivers Press, 1987, 256p. – L/P. –
0 7451 0491 6
Penguin, 1984, 144p. – Pbk. – 0 14 031495 4
illustrated by Robert Payne

The whole village of Hagworthy is helping in some way to prepare for the fete, but only a few are chosen to take part in the Horn Dance. The happy annual event gradually turns into a sinister, evil hunt where danger is a reality. Readers are enthralled.
Age range: 11–14

LOWRY, Lois
(née Hammersberg)

American. Born Honolulu, 1937.
Educated Brown University, Providence,
Rhode Island; University of South Maine,
Portland, B.A. English. Married Donald
Lowry 1956 (divorced 1977), two
daughters, two sons.

Awards: Boston Globe-Horn Book
Award: *Rabble Starkey*, 1987
American Library Association
Newbery Medal: *Number the
Stars*, 1989

Address: 34 Hancock Street, Boston,
Massachusetts 02114, USA

ALL ABOUT SAM
Collins, 1990, 128p. – Pbk. – 0 00 673436 7

Sam is the younger brother of Anastasia
(see below), and has his own story to tell.
Written in the same style, this book is also
enjoyable, but if the Anastasia theme has
been written to the full, and the author
wished to address a different age group,
a complete change would have been
better.
Age range: 9–11

ANASTASIA AGAIN!
*Cornerstone Books, 1989, – L/P. –
1 557 36074 X
Armada Books, 1986, 128p. – Pbk. –
0 00 672636 4*

In the same series:

ANASTASIA, ASK YOUR ANALYST
*Armada Books, 1988, 128p. – Pbk. –
0 00 672870 7*

ANASTASIA AT YOUR SERVICE
*Cornerstone Books, 1989, 224p. – L/P. –
1 557 36101 0
Armada Books, 1987, 160p. – Pbk. –
0 00 672867 7*

ANASTASIA HAS THE ANSWERS
*Chivers Press, 1991, 176p. – L/P. –
0 7451 1292 7
Armada Books, 1989, 128p. – Pbk. –
0 00 673011 6*

ANASTASIA KRUPNIK
*Cornerstone Books, 1988, 176p. – L/P. –
1 557 36073 1
Armada Books, 1986, 128p. – Pbk. –
0 00 672635 6*

ANASTASIA ON HER OWN
*Cornerstone Books, 1989, 184p. – L/P. –
1 557 36135 5
Armada Books, 1988, 144p. – Pbk. –
0 00 672871 5*

ANASTASIA'S CHOSEN CAREER
Collins, 1989, 160p. – Pbk. – 0 00 673012 4

A series of stories about a young lady
with a terrific sense of humour, which she
badly needs to see her through the
various pitfalls that life seems to save just
for her. There is an obvious American
slant, but this is no barrier. For sheer fun
reading, they are excellent.
Age range: 11–13

M

McBRATNEY, Sam

British. Born Belfast, Northern Ireland. Educated Trinity College, Dublin. Married, three children. Teacher.

A writer of down-to-earth, enjoyable and accessible stories which boys as well as girls can and do read for pleasure. He has an off-beat sense of humour which ensures a lot of laughs.

CLAUDIUS BALD EAGLE
Methuen, 1987, 96p. – O/P. – 0 416 96860 0
illustrated by Joanne Carey

Edward Moose is unhappy and his friend, Claudius, is fed up with him. When Harry arrives, determined to get moose antlers for his mantelpiece, Edward has good reason to feel unhappy.
Age range: 8–10

COLVIN AND THE SNAKE BASKET
Magnet Books, 1987, 96p. – Pbk. – 0 416 04492 1
Methuen, 1985, 96p. – O/P. – 0 416 52770 1
illustrated by Carol Holmes

Colvin hates being the middle child and feels nothing ever goes right for him. He finds that hiding himself away in the laundry basket is very helpful. Extremely funny.
Age range: 9–11

THE GHOSTS OF HUNGRYHOUSE LANE
Chivers Press, 1989, 112p.   0 85997 994 6
Hippo Books, 1988, 112p. – Pbk. – 0 590 70972 0
illustrated by David Farris

An unusual ghost story in which the resident ghosts are terrorized by the children when a family move in.
Age range. 9–11

JIMMY ZEST
Magnet Books, 1984, 128p. – Pbk, O/P. – 0 416 50130 3
Hamish Hamilton, 1982, 151p. – O/P. – 0 241 10807 1

In the same series:

THE JIMMY ZEST ALL-STARS
Hamish Hamilton, 1985, 128p. – O/P. – 0 241 11699 6
illustrated by Thelma Lambert

ZESTY
Magnet Books, 1985, 160p. – Pbk, O/P. – 0 416 52480 X
Hamish Hamilton, 1984, 148p. – 0 241 11254 0
illustrated by Susan Hellard

Collections of stories about Jimmy Zest and his cronies. The characters are remarkably true to life and the schemes they dream up are told with humour.
Age range: 9–11

UNCLE CHARLIE WEASEL AND THE CUCKOO BIRD
Magnet Books, 1988, 80p. – Pbk. – 0 416 07492 8
Methuen, 1986, 96p. – O/P. – 0 416 59710 6

In the same series:

UNCLE CHARLIE WEASEL'S WINTER
Methuen, 1988, 96p. – 0 416 05192 8
illustrated by Mike Daley

Two stories about a wily weasel whose antics provide amusing reading.
Age range: 8–10

McCAUGHREAN, Geraldine (née Jones)

British. Born Enfield, Middlesex, 1951. Educated Enfield Grammar School for Girls; Southgate Technical College, Middlesex; Christchurch College of Education, Canterbury, Kent, B.Ed. (Hons). Married John McCaughrean, 1988. Editor, writer.

Awards: Whitbread Award: *A Little Lower than the Angels*, 1987 Library Association Carnegie Medal: *Pack of Lies*, 1988 Guardian Children's Fiction Award: *Pack of Lies*, 1989

Address: 3 Melton Drive, Didcot, Oxfordshire OX11 7JP, England

Agent: Giles Gordon, Anthony Shiel Assoc., 43 Doughty Street, London WC1N 2LF, England

A comparative newcomer to the field of children's books, but very welcome. Her two books to date have been greeted with much praise as being extremely well written and innovative.

A LITTLE LOWER THAN THE ANGELS
Penguin, 1989, 144p. – Pbk. – 0 14 032818 1
OUP, 1987, 144p. – 0 19 271561 5

Gabriel is apprenticed to a stonemason who is a hard man. His cruelty forces Gabriel to flee; he escapes by jumping into the middle of a play, and decides to stay. Set in the Middle Ages, and told with compassion and humour, this story is an absorbing read.
Age range: 12–14

A PACK OF LIES
Penguin, 1990, 176p. – Pbk. – 0 14 034276 1
Chivers Press, 1990, 320p. – L/P. – 0 7451 1154 8
OUP, 1988, 192p. – 0 19 271612 3

Ailsa's mum is not doing very well at selling antiques, but when MCC arrives (rather like a stray cat), everything changes. He makes up stories to suit the customers' needs, thus persuading them to buy. The stories seem very like lies to Ailsa, who is shocked by them, but the reader is engrossed.
Age range: 12–14

McGOUGH, Roger

British. Born Liverpool, 1937. Educated Star of the Sea Junior School; St Mary's College, Crosby; Hull University. Married: 1) Thelma Monaghan, 1970 (dissolved 1980), two sons; 2) Hilary Clough, 1986, one son. Teacher, lecturer, poet, performer.

Awards: Signal Award: *Sky in the Pie*, 1984

Agent: A. D. Peters, 5th Floor, The Chambers, Chelsea Harbour, Lots Road, London SW10 0XF, England

Better known for his rather zany poetry, he nevertheless has written two highly amusing stories which have special appeal to reluctant readers as they are so obviously funny.

THE GREAT SMILE ROBBERY

Viking Kestrel, 1985, 80p. – 0 670 80021 X
Penguin, 1984, 80p. – Pbk. – 0 14 031437 7
illustrated by Tony Blundell

An original idea to have as a hero a boy who has his smiles stolen. The book describes his adventures as he tries to retrieve them. Rather silly, but very enjoyable; loved by children.
Age range: 8–10

THE STOWAWAYS

Penguin, 1988, 96p. – Pbk. – 0 14 031649 3
Viking Kestrel, 1986, 96p. – O/P. – 0 670 80135 6
illustrated by Tony Blundell

Four stories about two Liverpool lads who stow away to have an adventure, only to discover the Mersey Ferry doesn't go very far! Lots of laughs.
Age range: 8–10

MAHY, Margaret

New Zealander. Born Whakatane, 1936. Educated University of Auckland, B.A., Diploma of Librarianship. Two daughters. Librarian.

Awards: New Zealand Library Association Esther Glen Award: *Lion in the Meadow*, 1970
New Zealand Library Association Esther Glen Award: *First Margaret Mahy Story Book*, 1973
Library Association Carnegie Medal: *The Haunting*, 1982
New Zealand Library Association Esther Glen Award: *The Haunting*, 1983
Library Association Carnegie Medal: *The Changeover*, 1984
New Zealand Library Association Esther Glen Award: *The Changeover*, 1985
Young Observer Fiction Prize: *Memory*, 1987

Address: R.D.I., Lyttelton, New Zealand

There are many admirable qualities attributable to this extremely gifted author. She has written many books, all of a high standard; she is able to write for all age groups equally successfully. Original and inventive, she successfully marries fantasy, magic and everyday reality, and her use of language is superb. Readers require fluency to be able to reap the full benefit. Simply superb at every level.

THE BLOOD AND THUNDER ADVENTURE ON HURRICANE PEAK
Penguin, 1991, 144p. – Pbk. – 0 14 034282 6
Chivers Press, 1990, 192p. – L/P. – 0 7451 1230 7
Dent, 1989, 144p. – 0 460 07031 2
illustrated by Wendy Smith

A school story with a difference, or, rather, several differences, among them a cat as head prefect and a teacher who is a magician. Very funny in a slapstick way; short chapters make it an easy read.
Age range: 8–10

THE BUS UNDER THE LEAVES
Penguin, 1976, 80p. – Pbk, O/P. – 0 14 030721 4
Dent, 1975, 72p. – O/P. – 0 460 05899 1
illustrated by Margery Gill

Adam and David, thrilled at finding an old bus hidden on the dump for years, make it their den in which to escape from the girls. Only Anne is a match for them. Funny and imaginative.
Age range: 7–10

CLANCY'S CABIN
Penguin, 1987, 128p. – Pbk. – 0 14 032175 6
Dent, 1974, 96p. – O/P. – 0 460 05900 9
illustrated by Trevor Stubley

Set in her native New Zealand, this is the story of a camping holiday which turns into a treasure hunt when Skip finds the 'pattern for the finding of the treasure'. An enjoyable, straightforward read with lots of gentle humour.
Age range: 9–11

THE PIRATE UNCLE
Penguin, 1987. – Pbk. – 0 14 032250 7
Dent, 1977, 128p. – O/P. – 0 460 06795 8
illustrated by Mary Dinsdale

Uncle Ludovic is an unusual pirate, for he is trying to stop, but needs help. Caroline is just the person to do so.
Age range: 8–10

THE PIRATES' MIXED-UP VOYAGE: DARK DOINGS IN THE THOUSAND ISLANDS
Magnet Books, 1985, 160p. – Pbk, O/P. – 0 416 51150 3
Dent, 1983, 160p. – 0 460 06132 1
illustrated by Margaret Chamberlain

The crew of the pirate ship 'The Sinful Sausage' are a motley bunch whose escapades on the high seas provide excellent reading.
Age range: 9–11

RAGING ROBOTS AND UNRULY UNCLES

Dent, 1990, 93p. – 0 460 88042 X
Penguin, 1985, 96p. – Pbk. – 0 14 031817 8
illustrated by Peter Stevenson

'A linguistic romp' best describes this tale in which the vocabulary is as imaginative as the plot. Evil Jasper and saintly Julian, both less than pleased with their children, get a nasty shock when the robots arrive.
Age range: 10–12

THE BIRTHDAY BURGLAR AND THE VERY WICKED HEADMISTRESS

Dent, 1990, 144p. – 0 460 88041 1
Mammoth, 1990, 144p. – Pbk. – 0 7497 0249 4
illustrated by Margaret Chamberlain
Age range: 5–7

THE BOY WHO BOUNCED AND OTHER MAGIC TALES

Penguin, 1988, 160p. – Pbk. – 0 14 032468 2
illustrated by Shirley Hughes
Age range: 7–10

THE CHEWING-GUM RESCUE AND OTHER STORIES

Dent, 1990, 140p. – 0 460 88043 8
Mammoth, 1990, 160p. – Pbk. – 0 7497 0250 8
illustrated by Jan Ormerod
Age range: 7–9

CHOCOLATE PORRIDGE AND OTHER STORIES

Penguin, 1989, 176p. – Pbk. – 0 14 032906 4
illustrated by Shirley Hughes
Age range: 8–10

THE DOOR IN THE AIR AND OTHER STORIES

Penguin, 1990, 112p.   Pbk – 0 14 034283 4
Chivers Press, 1989, 176p. – L/P. – 0 7451 1046 0
Dent, 1988, 128p. – 0 460 06285 9
illustrated by Diana Catchpole
Age range: 10–12

THE DOWNHILL CROCODILE WHIZZ AND OTHER STORIES

Windrush, 1990, 162p. – L/P. – 1 85089 983 5
Penguin, 1987, 112p. – Pbk. – 0 14 032362 7
Dent, 1986, 136p. – Pbk. – 0 460 06237 9
illustrated by Ian Newsham
Age range: 5–7

THE FIRST MARGARET MAHY STORY-BOOK

Dent, 1976, 120p. – Pbk, O/P. – 0 460 02713 1
Dent, 1972, 118p. – O/P. – 0 460 05856 8
illustrated by Shirley Hughes
Age range: 6–10

THE GREAT PIRATICAL RUMBUSTIFICATION, and THE LIBRARIAN AND THE ROBBERS

Windrush, 1990, 76p. – L/P. – 1 85089 810 3
Penguin, 1981, 80p. – Pbk. – 0 14 031261 7
Dent, 1978, 64p. – 0 460 06871 7
illustrated by Quentin Blake
Age range: 6–8

LEAF MAGIC AND FIVE OTHER FAVOURITES

Magnet Books, 1986, 64p. – Pbk, O/P. – 0 416 63780 9
Dent, 1984, 64p. – 0 460 06151 8
illustrated by Margaret Chamberlain
Age range: 5–7

MAHY MAGIC

Windrush, 1991, 186p. – L/P. – 1 85089 816 2
Dent, 1986, 160p. – 0 460 06184 4
illustrated by Shirley Hughes
Age range: 6–10

NONSTOP NONSENSE

Mammoth, 1990, 128p. – Pbk. – 0 7497 0278 8
Dent, 1977, 128p. – 0 460 06806 7
illustrated by Quentin Blake
Age range: 8–10

THE SECOND MARGARET MAHY STORY-BOOK

Dent, 1977, 124p. – Pbk, O/P. – 0 460 02761 1
Dent, 1973, 124p. – O/P. – 0 460 05887 8
illustrated by Shirley Hughes
Age range: 6–10

THE THIRD MARGARET MAHY STORY-BOOK

Dent, 1975, 116p. – 0 460 06625 0
illustrated by Shirley Hughes
Age range: 6–10

Collections of stories and poems published in various anthologies. All are of excellent quality, covering a variety of themes, providing hours of storytelling material.

MARK, Jan
(Marjorie, née Busland)

British. Born Welwyn, Hertfordshire, 1943. Educated Ashford Grammar School; Canterbury College of Art, National Diploma of Design. Married Neil Mark, 1969, one son, one daughter. Teacher.

Awards: Library Association Carnegie Medal: *Thunder and Lightnings*, 1976
Library Association Carnegie Medal: *Handles*, 1983

Address: 98 Howard Street, Oxford OX4 3BY, England

Agent: Murray Pollinger, 4 Garrick Street, London WC2E 9BH, England

The quality that makes Jan Mark's books so successful is her understanding of children and her ability to portray them sympathetically. The plots are interesting, but often it is the interplay between characters which makes them above average.

DREAM HOUSE
Penguin, 1989, 144p. – Pbk. – 0 14 031589 6
Viking Kestrel, 1987, 128p. – 0 670 80189 5
illustrated by Joan Riley

Hannah loves the manor for its memories, Dina for its glamorous guests. Julia complicates life with her constant plotting, but when Tom enters the drama, the recipe for chaos is complete. An excellent plot with more than a hint of comedy.
Age range: 12–14

FEET, AND OTHER STORIES
Penguin, 1984, 160p. – Pbk. – 0 14 031586 1
Viking, 1983, 160p. – 0 670 82510 7
illustrated by Bert Kitchen

A collection of stories with lots of appeal for older readers. Varied in subject matter, they all have something of value to say.
Age range: 12–14

HANDLES
Chivers Press, 1988, 288p. – L/P. – 0 7451 0760 5
Penguin, 1985, 160p. – Pbk. – 0 14 031587 X
Viking Kestrel, 1985, 160p. – 0 670 80536 X
illustrated by David Parkins

A potentially boring holiday is rescued by providential happenings – not a very original idea. What saves this story from banality is the characters, who are larger than life, including a cat with false teeth. Not especially easy, but very enjoyable to read.
Age range: 12–14

NOTHING TO BE AFRAID OF
Chivers Press, 1985, 176p. – L/P. – 0 7451 0132 1
Viking Kestrel, 1985, 120p. – O/P. – 0 670 80018 X
Penguin, 1982, 128p. – Pbk. – 0 14 031392 3
illustrated by David Parkins

A book of scary yet funny stories. As always, even in short stories, Jan Mark's characterization is excellent.
Age range: 11–13

SCHOOL STORIES
Kingfisher Books, 1989, 256p. – 0 86272 418 X
illustrated by David Parkins

An excellent collection of school stories chosen by Jan Mark. The authors range from Enid Blyton to Charlotte Bronte. A pleasure to read.
Age range: 10–14

THE SHORT VOYAGE OF THE 'ALBERT ROSS'
Mayflower, 1981, 80p. – Pbk, O/P. – 0 583 30373 0
Granada, 1980, 72p. – O/P. – 0 246 11241 7
illustrated by Gavin Rowe

An excellent portrait of a bully and his victim who eventually finds the strength of character to stand up to him. At the same time it is an amusing adventure about Stephen's raft and his accidental journey down river.
Age range: 8–10

THUNDER AND LIGHTNINGS

Chivers Press, 1987, 248p. – L/P. – 0 7451 0496 7
Viking Kestrel, 1985, 176p. – 0 670 80116 X
Penguin, 1978, 176p. – Pbk. – 0 14 031063 0

Superficially the story of aircraft, and the demise of the old jets in particular, this novel is really concerned with the friendship between Victor and Andrew, which grows in spite of their many differences. Sensitive and gently amusing, it is a worthy prize-winner.
Age range: 10–12

TROUBLE HALF-WAY

Chivers Press, 1989, 200p. – L/P. – 0 7451 0958 6
Penguin, 1986, 128p. – Pbk. – 0 14 031588 8
Viking Kestrel, 1985, 128p. – 0 670 80188 7
illustrated by David Parkins

There are now many books about step-parents, but this is a particularly sensitive and perceptive story. Amy is forced, by circumstances, to spend time with her step-father, with whom she does not feel at ease. Among the everyday happenings, their relationship begins to develop – very well handled.
Age range: 11–13

UNDER THE AUTUMN GARDEN

Penguin, 1980, 160p. – Pbk. – 0 14 031248 X
Kestrel Books, 1977, 160p. – O/P. –
0 7226 5347 6

As part of his local history project for school, Matthew decides to dig up his garden in search of relics from the old priory. In reality, it turns out rather differently from the way he planned.
Age range: 10–12

MAYNE, William
(James Carter)

Also writes as Martin Cobalt, Dynely James, Charles Molin. British. Born Hull, Yorkshire, 1928. Educated Cathedral Choir School, Canterbury. Lecturer, writer.

Awards: Library Association Carnegie Medal: *A Grass Rope*, 1957

Agent: David Higham Assoc., 5–8 Lower John Street, London W1R 4HA, England

A brilliant but enigmatic writer with a distinctive style. His books do not have universal popular appeal, but there are children who fall under his spell as the result of a sensitive introduction by a knowledgeable adult. He has been writing for many years and some of his earlier works are out of print, although reprinting is currently under consideration. Some of his books are for older readers.

ALL THE KING'S MEN
Penguin, 1984, 192p. – Pbk, O/P. –
0 14 031682 5
Cape, 1982, 182p. – 0 224 02026 9

Three stories, completely different, but all compelling in their own way.
Age range: 12–14

ANTAR AND THE EAGLES
Walker Books, 1990, 216p. – Pbk. –
0 7445 1464 9
Walker Books, 1989, 224p. – 0 7445 0838 X

A most memorable book, but difficult to classify. Part fairy–tale, part adventure, reminiscent of classical stories where overwhelming tasks are accomplished after much stoical suffering. Antar is far too young to be entrusted with the rescue of the eagle's precious egg, but he manfully faces up to his destiny and tries his best. Powerfully described, it holds the reader to the very satisfying conclusion.
Age range: 9–12

THE FARM THAT RAN OUT OF NAMES
Cape, 1990, 88p. – 0 224 02757 3

The best fantasy books are those with a firm base in reality, which this one has. Owen is happy on his Welsh farm and becomes extremely upset when he is told that the Birmingham Water Authority want to build a reservoir on it. Not a man to take things lying down, he dreams up a scheme and carries it through. Superb storytelling, funny, touching and a wonderful climax.
Age range: 10–12

THE LAST BUS
Red Fox, 1990, 64p. – Pbk. – 0 09 975050 3
Hamish Hamilton, 1962, 96p. – O/P. –
0 241 90320 3
illustrated by Helen Parsley

Time has no meaning when you are young and busy, and Peter misses the last bus home. He believes he can catch up with it if he cuts across country. The terrain is difficult, and he needs a variety of help to make it across.
Age range: 7–9

RAVENSGILL
Red Fox, 1990, 171p. – Pbk. – 0 09 975270 0
Hamish Hamilton, 1970, 174p. – O/P. –
0 241 01746 7

Bob and Judith are cousins attending the same school, but they only accidentally discover that they are related. Then they set about finding out what caused the rift. Excellent storytelling, keeping the reader's interest to the last page.
Age range: 12–14

SALT RIVER TIMES
Penguin, 1982, 190p. – Pbk, O/P. –
0 14 031499 7
Hamish Hamilton, 1980, 178p. – O/P. –
0 241 10196 4
illustrated by Elizabeth Honey

Having lived in Australia for a time, William Mayne wrote this collection of stories, which are interwoven, to reveal the solution to a murder mystery in a

small Australian community. Evocative and full of atmosphere.
Age range: 11–13

SKIFFY
Penguin, 1980, 96p. – Pbk, O/P. –
0 14 031173 4
Hamish Hamilton, 1977, 120p. – O/P. –
0 241 89670 3

In the same series:

SKIFFY AND THE TWIN PLANETS
Hamish Hamilton, 1982, 144p. – O/P. –
0 241 10835 7

A trip into the realm of science fiction, an unusual theme for this author. Easy to read and very entertaining.
Age range: 8–10

WINTER QUARTERS
Penguin, 1984, 144p. – Pbk, O/P. –
0 14 031681 7
Cape, 1982, 144p. – 0 224 02035 8

Most readers will be unfamiliar with the lore of the travelling people, but William Mayne's skilful storytelling makes such a lack unimportant. Issy has been brought up in a house, but his birth made him the best person to seek out the old chief who alone could tell them where to stay for the winter. An absorbing and compelling story which gives some understanding of a group of people who are virtual outcasts from society.
Age range: 11–13

MORPURGO, Michael

British. Born St Albans, 1943. Educated King's School, Canterbury; King's College, London. Married Clare Allen, 1963 (the daughter of Allen Lane), two sons, one daughter. Teacher, writer, runs a farm for city children.

Address: Langlands, Iddesleigh, Winkleigh, Devon EX19 8SN, England

Agent: Gina Pollinger, 4 Garrick Street, London WC2E 9BH, England

Undoubtedly a leading figure in the field of children's books, Michael Morpurgo has quite a following. He writes for a wide age range, and there is a real sincerity in his writing which gives added weight to what he has to say.

JO-JO, THE MELON DONKEY
Deutsch, 1987, 32p. – 0 233 97945 X
illustrated by Chris Molan

A picture book for older children, as there is a detailed description of the grim life Jo-Jo has to endure. He is finally rescued to live a life of ease. A predictable story rescued by the marvellous illustrations.
Age range: 5–7

LITTLE FOXES
Mammoth, 1990, 129p. – Pbk. – 0 7497 0203 6
Kaye & Ward, 1984, 128p. – O/P. –
0 7182 3972 5
illustrated by Gareth Floyd

Billy feels an affinity with the wildlife living on some spare ground by the ruined church. Such things cannot remain private for long, and Billy makes his choice. Some very touching scenes.
Age range: 10–12

MY FRIEND WALTER
Mammoth, 1989, 160p. – Pbk. – 0 7497 0034 3
Heinemann, 1988, 160p. – 0 434 95203 6

The ghost of Walter Raleigh is really the hero of this light-hearted, amusing story. He and Bess work well together to restore Walter's stolen property to his descendants.
Age range: 10–12

TOM'S SAUSAGE LION
Corgi, 1987, 80p. – Pbk. – 0 552 52418 2
Black, 1986. – O/P. – 0 7136 2757 3
illustrated by Robina Green

Lacking originality, the story tells how Tom sees a lion but fails to convince anyone he is telling the truth. A slight story, told in a matter-of-fact style, the story proceeds at a brisk pace to the highly satisfactory ending. Useful for reluctant readers.
Age range: 8–10

WAITING FOR ANYA
Heinemann, 1990, 176p. – 0 434 95205 2

Jo is unaware that his chance meeting with the stranger will have such far-reaching consequences. Gradually he is drawn into helping with the hazardous task of assisting Jewish children to escape over the French border into Spain. A heart-warming, compelling story which is quite easy to read.
Age range: 11–13

WAR HORSE
Mammoth, 1990, 144p. – Pbk. – 0 7497 0445 4
Windrush, 1989. – L/P. – 1 85089 943 6
Kaye & Ward, 1982, 128p. – 0 7182 3970 9

A very moving story based on reality, which makes it even more poignant. Albert is heartbroken when his father sends his beloved horse to war, and believes he will never see him again. The horrors of war which the young horse has to face are graphically described.
Age range: 12–14

WHY THE WHALES CAME
Chivers Press, 1989, 224p. – L/P. – 0 7451 0925 X
Magnet Books, 1987, 144p. – Pbk, O/P. –
0 416 97090 7
Heinemann, 1985, 160p. – 0 434 95200 1

Set on the Isles of Scilly, this is also a story full of compassion. Gracie and

Daniel defy their parents and befriend the deaf Birdman. Life is hard for everyone, including the children, but, undaunted, they force the islanders to re-consider when a stranded whale is about to be butchered. The popularity of this book increased after the release of the film.
Age range: 10–12

MURPHY, Jill (Francis)

British. Born London, 1949. Educated
Ursuline Grammar School, Wimbledon;
Chelsea, Croydon and Camberwell
Schools of Art. Married, husband Roger,
step-children Chloe and Alice. Worked in
children's homes, now a freelance writer
and illustrator. Lives in Wadebridge,
Cornwall.

Agent: A. P. Watt Ltd, 20 John
           Street, London WC1N 2DL,
           England

A BAD SPELL FOR THE WORST
WITCH
Viking Kestrel, 1984, 128p. – 0 670 80030 9
Penguin, 1983, 128p. – Pbk. – 0 14 031446 6

In the same series:

THE WORST WITCH
Penguin, 1978, 112p. – Pbk. – 0 14 031108 4
Allison & Busby, 1975, 76p. – O/P. –
0 85031 142 X

THE WORST WITCH STRIKES
AGAIN
Viking Kestrel, 1988, 96p. – 0 670 82189 6
Penguin, 1981, 96p. – Pbk. – 0 14 031348 6
all illustrated by the author

This is one of the most popular 'witch'
series, becoming even more so after
being televised. Mildred, studying at the
Academy, seems to do everything wrong,
to the delight of the reader.
Age range: 7–9

WORLD'S APART
Walker Books, 1990, 112p. – Pbk. –
0 7445 1332 4
Walker Books, 1988, 128p. – O/P. –
0 7445 0803 7
illustrated by Tudor Humphries

Totally different from the 'Worst Witch'
stories, this book is more serious. Susan's
mother left her father when she was a
baby. Not until she is eleven does her
mother tell her anything about him.
Susan then determines to find him, a
quest which leads to an unexpected
ending, though one which is unlikely to
happen in real life.
Age range: 9–11

N

NEEDLE, Jan

British. Born Holybourne, Hampshire, 1943. Educated Church Street School, Portsmouth; Portsmouth Grammar School; University of Manchester, B.A. (Hons), Drama. Reporter, sub-editor, writer.

Agents: David Higham Assoc., 5–8 Lower John Street, London W1R 4HA, England

Rochelle Stevens Co., 15–17 Islington High Street, London N1 1LQ, England

An author who has original ideas, and who does not fight shy of dealing with serious issues.

ANOTHER FINE MESS
Armada Books, 1982, 192p. – Pbk, O/P. –
0 00 671978 3
Deutsch, 1981, 192p. – O/P. – 0 233 97370 2
illustrated by Roy Bentley

When the Professor invents the Cheap Day Return Transferer, Cynthia and George volunteer to test it. Off-beat, funny time-travel adventure.
Age range: 11–13

THE BEE RUSTLERS
Magnet Books, 1983, 80p. – Pbk, O/P. –
0 416 29310 7
Collins, 1980, 80p. – O/P. – 0 00 184043 6
illustrated by Paul Wright

An original storyline, describing Tony and Carol's attempt to save the hives which mean so much to their mother.
Age range. 9–11

BEHIND THE BIKE SHEDS
Methuen, 1985, 128p. – O/P. – 0 416 54990 X
Magnet Books, 1985, 128p. – Pbk, O/P. –
0 416 51840 0

An up-to-date school story in which both the events and the vocabulary reflect life in comprehensive schools today. The chapters are very short and may appeal to young people who believe that books are irrelevant. Successfully televised.
Age range: 11–14

A GAME OF SOLDIERS
Deutsch, 1985, 94p. – 0 233 97744 9
Armada Books, 1985, 96p. – Pbk. –
0 00 672460 4

First written for television, then published as a novel, this is a chilling account of a children's game suddenly turned into a nightmarish reality. It leaves the reader in no doubt about the horror of war.
Age range: 12–14

IN THE DOGHOUSE
Heinemann, 1988, 96p. – 0 434 95329 6
illustrated by Robert Bartelt

In the same series:

SKELETON AT SCHOOL
Heinemann, 1988, 96p. – 0 434 95328 8

THE SLEEPING PARTY
Heinemann, 1988, 96p. – 0 434 95331 8

UNCLE IN THE ATTIC
Heinemann, 1988, 96p. – 0 434 95327 X

A series of books aimed at younger readers. Sam and Springy are twins, and their exploits provide entertaining reading.
Age range: 8–10

LOSERS WEEPERS
Magnet Books, 1983, 128p. – Pbk, O/P. –
0 416 30170 3
Methuen, 1981, 128p. – 0 416 21510 6

Tony is delighted when he finds the ancient sword. He is unaware of the strong emotions and totally unsuspected reactions it evokes. The book deals realistically with the problem of treasure

trove, but is not without its lighter moments.
Age range: 9–11

MY MATE SHOFIQ
*Armada Books, 1979, 164p. – Pbk. –
0 00 671518 4
Deutsch, 1978, 144p. – O/P. – 0 233 96987 X*

Because his conscience will not allow him to keep silent, Bernard is forced into defending Shofiq. As a result, they gradually become friends, and Bernard learns the hard way what it means to be 'different'. A refreshing look at racism without dwelling too much on it. Remarkably realistic characterization and dialogue. Made into an enjoyable television drama.
Age range: 11–14

THE THIEF
Penguin, 1989, 108p. – Pbk. – 0 14 032905 6

Kevin feels very bitter when he is accused of stealing. Convinced it is because his father is in prison, and because he has often been in trouble before, he takes himself off, but becomes involved with thieves. An exciting read which was later made into a gripping television film.
Age range: 10–12

WAGSTAFF THE WIND-UP BOY
*Collins, 1989, 176p. – Pbk. – 0 00 672976 2
Deutsch, 1987, 118p. – 0 233 97715 5
illustrated by Roy Bentley*

Black humour, in which a horrible accident is described in detail. Lots of amusing illustrations ensure popularity.
Age range: 10–12

WILD WOOD
*J. Murray, 1989, 192p. – 0 7195 4651 6
Magnet Books, 1982, 192p. – Pbk, O/P. –
0 416 21520 3
illustrated by William Rushton*

Although it is not absolutely essential to have read *The Wind in the Willows*, it is easier to relate to the characters if there is some knowledge of the original story. It is not by any means easy to read, but it is extremely funny.
Age range: 11–14

NIMMO, Jenny

British. Born Windsor, Berkshire, 1944. Educated private boarding schools. Married David Wynn Millward, 1974, two daughters, one son. Actress, photographic researcher, floor manager, director, writer of children's television programmes; now a full-time writer.

Awards: Smarties Prize: *The Snow Spider*, 1986
Welsh Arts Council Tir na n'Og Award, 1987

Address: Henllan Llangynyw, Welshpool, Powys SY21 9EN, Wales

A writer of exceptional quality. All her books maintain a high literary standard, yet remain accessible to young readers. Her strong characterization of the children enables the reader to identify easily with them, and her love of Wales and Welsh mythology helps her to weave stories with a fine balance of magic and realism; stories which are both exciting and amusing.

THE SNOW SPIDER
Mammoth, 1989, 144p. – Pbk, O/P. – 0 7497 0139 0
Chivers Press, 1987, 208p. – L/P. – 0 7451 0590 4
Methuen, 1986, 144p. – 0 416 54530 0

In the same series:

EMLYN'S MOON
Chivers Press, 1989, 248p. – L/P. – 0 7451 1047 9
Mammoth, 1989, 144p. – Pbk, O/P. – 0 7497 0140 4
Methuen, 1987, 128p. – 0 416 02392 4

THE CHESTNUT SOLDIER
Mammoth, 1990, 176p. – Pbk. – 0 7497 0150 1
Chivers Press, 1990, 312p. – L/P. – 0 7451 1178 5
Methuen, 1989, 192p. – 0 416 11402 4
all illustrated by Joanna Carey

Gwyn gradually realizes that he has magical powers. Reassured by his Gran, he begins to accustom himself to using his gift, aided by the little white spider. Eventually he decides he can try to get in touch with his sister, who went missing when he was small, an event which has cast a shadow over the lives of all the family ever since. In the two sequels, the magical atmosphere is equally strong, which, coupled with intriguing plots, makes the whole trilogy totally compelling. *The Snow Spider* became an excellent television serial.
Age range: 10–12

TATTY APPLE
Magnet Books, 1986, 96p. – Pbk, O/P. – 0 416 52500 8
Methuen, 1984, 96p. – 0 416 50280 6
illustrated by Priscilla Lamont

Owen-Owen finds a golden rabbit which he takes home. Somehow, life begins to improve for the little family, which has had more than its fair share of problems.
Age range: 7–9

ULTRAMARINE
Methuen, 1990, 160p. – 0 416 15932 X

The legend of the kelpie, a water sprite which causes people to drown, is the basis for this spell-binding novel. In this version of the legend, the sprite's role is reversed, and it fights to protect the sea. Ned and Nell feel a great affinity with the sea, but at first cannot understand. Only when they discover Ultramarine is the puzzle clarified.
Age range: 10–12

O

O'BRIEN, Robert C.

Pseudonym for Robert Leslie Conly. American. Born Brooklyn, New York, 1918 (died 5 March 1973). Educated Amityville, Long Island, New York; Williams College, Williamstown, Massachusetts; Juilliard School of Music, New York; Columbia University, New York; University of Rochester, New York, B.A. English. Married Sally McCaslin, 1943, one son, three daughters. Advertising agent, researcher, writer, reporter.

Awards: American Library Association Newbery Medal: *Mrs Frisby and the Rats of Nimh*, 1972

MRS FRISBY AND THE RATS OF NIMH
Penguin, 1975, 197p. – Pbk. – 0 14 030725 7
Gollancz, 1972, 192p. – 0 575 01552 7

Mrs Frisby enlists the aid of a group of rats when she has to move her young son, who is ill. An excellent story, convincing and enjoyable.
Age range: 10–12

THE SILVER CROWN
Collins, 1975, 192p. – Pbk. – 0 00 671005 0
Gollancz, 1973, 256p. – 0 575 01608 6

The novel's opening chapter grabs the reader's attention at once by the juxtaposition of the innocence of a little girl out playing at being a queen, and her return to find her house burned to the ground and her family all dead. She bravely sets off to find her aunt, but becomes aware that she is being chased. Full of menacing atmosphere, it promises a gripping read.
Age range: 11–13

Z FOR ZACHARIAH
Windrush, 1989, 234p. – L/P. – 1 85089 955 X
Gollancz, 1984, 192p. – O/P. – 0 575 03378 9
Armada Books, 1976, 192p. – Pbk. –
0 00 671081 6

Compulsive and exciting reading, describing life after a nuclear holocaust. Ann's initial fear when Zachariah turns up is well described. The whole book is full of atmosphere, giving a convincingly frightening vision of a devastated land.
Age range: 12–14

P

PARK, (Rosina) Ruth (Lucia)

Australian. Born Auckland, New Zealand. Educated St Benedict's College, University of Auckland. Married D'Arcy Niland, 1942, five children. Proof-reader, editor.

Awards: Australian Children's Book Council Book of the Year Award: *Playing Beatie Bow*, 1982
Boston Globe-Horn Book Award: *Playing Beatie Bow*, 1982

Agent: Curtis Brown, PO Box 19, Paddington, New South Wales 2021, Australia

An experienced writer who has achieved success with both younger and older readers. She has an affinity with children which is reflected in her writing.

MY SISTER SIF
Penguin, 1988, 192p. – Pbk, O/P. – 0 14 032342 2
Viking Kestrel, 1987, 192p. – O/P. – 0 670 815241

A most unusual story about a family whose love for the creatures living in the sea originates with their mother. It is a story full of mystery and romance.
Age range: 13–15

PLAYING BEATIE BOW
Penguin, 1982, 196p. – Pbk. – 0 14 031460 1

A time slip book, extraordinarily well handled, in which Abigail is drawn into Beatie's world. She has to learn to cope with the poverty and hardships of Victorian slum life in Sydney. As she learns, her character changes. Enthralling to such a degree that readers almost hold their breath while trying to guess the outcome which proves highly satisfactory.
Age range: 12–15

THINGS IN CORNERS
Penguin, 1991, 240p. – Pbk. – 0 14 032713 4
Viking, 1989, 184p. – O/P. – 0 670 82225 6

Five superb stories with an unexpected twist to send a shiver down the spine.
Age range: 12–14

PATERSON, Katherine
(née Womeldorf)

American. Born Qing Jiang, China, 1932, moved to the USA 1940. Educated King College, Bristol, Tennessee, A.B. (summa cum laude); Presbyterian School of Christian Education, Richmond, Virginia, M.A.; Kobe School of Japanese Language, Japan; Union Theological Seminary, New York, M.R.E. Married John Barstow Paterson, 1962, two sons and two adopted daughters. Missionary, teacher.

Awards: National Book Award: *Master Puppeteer*, 1977
American Library Association Newbery Medal: *Bridge to Terabithia*, 1978
Christopher Award: *The Great Gilly Hopkins*, 1979
National Book Award: *The Great Gilly Hopkins*, 1979
American Library Association Newbery Medal: *Jacob Have I Loved*, 1981
Catholic Library Association Regina Medal, 1988

Address: C/o E. P. Dutton, 2 Park Avenue, New York City, New York 10016, USA

A widely acclaimed writer whose skill in storytelling and whose sensitivity towards children and their deepest feelings makes her popular with older children.

BRIDGE TO TERABITHIA
Cornerstone Books, 1987, 168p. – L/P. –
1 557 36010 3
Penguin, 1980, 144p. – Pbk. – 0 14 031260 9
Gollancz, 1978, 144p. – 0 575 02550 6

An extremely sad book, but one which gives courage to timid children. Jess's life is very harsh, but with Leslie he learns to create a fantasy world to escape to. The relief from reality together with Leslie's influence gradually build up his courage, so that he is able to cope with the concluding drama.
Age range: 10–12

COME SING, JIMMY JO
J. Murray, 1989, 176p. – 0 7195 4649 4
Penguin, 1987, 208p. – Pbk. – 0 14 032176 4
Gollancz, 1986, 198p. – 0 575 03737 7

Jimmy Jo attains fame as a country singing star, but does not know how to deal with the attendant problems. His grandmother is the only person who can help. Told with understanding and humour.
Age range: 10–12

THE GREAT GILLY HOPKINS
Cornerstone Books, 1987, 184p. – L/P. –
1 557 36011 1
Penguin, 1981, 144p. – Pbk. – 0 14 031302 8
Gollancz, 1979, 160p. – O/P. – 0 575 02587 5

Abandoned as a baby, Gilly has had to learn to be tough, to avoid further hurt. She scornfully rejects her latest foster-parents, only to realize she may have made a mistake. Sad without being sentimental.
Age range: 10–12

PARK'S QUEST
Penguin, 1990, 144p. – Pbk. – 0 14 034076 9
Gollancz, 1989, 160p. – 0 575 04487 X

Not an original story, telling how Park slowly uncovers the skeletons in the cupboard, learning about the father he never knew. As always, Katherine Paterson's skill and understanding have created in Park a memorable and sympathetic character, whose story will be read with interest.
Age range: 10–12

PEARCE, (Ann) Philippa

British. Born Great Shelford, Cambridgeshire. Educated Perse Girls' School, Cambridge; Girton College, Cambridge, B.A. (Hons) English, M.A. History. Married Martin Christie, 1963 (died 1965), one daughter. Scriptwriter, producer, editor, reviewer and lecturer.

Awards: Library Association Carnegie Medal: *Tom's Midnight Garden*, 1959
Whitbread Award: *The Battle of Bubble and Squeak*, 1978

Agent: Laura Cecil, 17 Alwyne Villas, London N1 2HG, England

Undoubtedly one of the best writers for children, Philippa Pearce succeeds with all age groups. She is a compelling storyteller, able to create memorable characters, and she allows the reader to escape into a completely satisfying 'created' world, and still be able to leave that world feeling all the better for the brief sojourn. Well written, all the books require a certain degree of fluency.

THE BATTLE OF BUBBLE AND SQUEAK
Chivers Press, 1985, 112p. – L/P. – 0 7451 0134 8
Penguin, 1980, 96p. – Pbk. – 0 14 031183 1
Deutsch, 1978, 112p. – 0 233 96986 1
illustrated by Alan Baker

A drama that has been enacted in countless homes over the years is the setting for this entertaining story. The children want to keep gerbils, Mum says 'No!', loudly, clearly and often. Sensitively written in Philippa Pearce's inimitable style, in which humour is mixed with sadness, this book will be read with pleasure.
Age range: 9–11

A DOG SO SMALL
Chivers Press, 1987, 232p. – L/P. – 0 7451 0497 5
Kestrel Books, 1975, 142p. – O/P. –
0 7226 5261 5
Penguin, 1970. – Pbk. – 0 14 030206 9
illustrated by Antony Maitland

Many children will sympathize with Ben who longs for a dog. He is bitterly disappointed when his birthday present turns out to be a picture of a dog. The strength of his feelings actually creates a dog in his mind's eye; imagination and reality become blurred. Both heart-rending and heart-warming to the very last page.
Age range: 10–12

MINNOW ON THE SAY
Penguin, 1978, 256p. – Pbk. – 0 14 031022 3
OUP, 1974, 241p. – 0 19 277064 0
illustrated by Edward Ardizzone

David is delighted when, on holiday, he finds first a canoe, and then the owner who becomes a friend. Together they decide to look for the lost treasure, which, unknown to them, others are also searching for. A classic adventure story for committed readers.
Age range: 10–12

THE SHADOW-CAGE
Penguin, 1978, 160p. – Pbk. – 0 14 031073 8
Kestrel Books, 1977. – Pbk, O/P. – 0 7226 5243 7
illustrated by Chris Molan

Stories with a supernatural flavour – mysterious and thoroughly enjoyable.
Age range: 11–14

TOM'S MIDNIGHT GARDEN
Windrush, 1987, 261p. – L/P. – 1 85089 914 2
Penguin, 1976, 224p. – Pbk, O/P. –
0 14 030893 8
OUP, 1958, 232p. – 0 19 271128 8
illustrated by Susan Einzig

A wonderful, evocative story full of mystery and atmosphere. Tom, feeling bitter at being banished from home, finds solace in the garden which comes to life at midnight. As his friendship with Hetty develops, so does the reader's interest. It has an excellent climax.
Age range: 10–12

THE WAY TO SATTIN SHORE

Chivers Press, 1986, 312p. – L/P. – 0 7451 0332 4
Viking Kestrel, 1985, 176p. – O/P. –
0 670 80616 1
Penguin, 1985, 192p. – Pbk. – 0 14 031644 2
illustrated by Charlotte Voake

Kate gradually comes to realize that there is a mystery involving her family, but no-one will enlighten her. A moving and compelling story, not without its lighter moments, which can be read again and again, with each reading offering something new.
Age range: 11–14

WHAT THE NEIGHBOURS DID AND OTHER STORIES

Chivers Press, 1990, 160p. – L/P. – 0 7451 1246 3

Penguin, 1975, 144p. – Pbk. – 0 14 030710 9
Kestrel Books, 1975, 120p. – O/P. –
0 7226 5262 3
illustrated by Faith Jacques

In the same series:

WHO'S AFRAID?: AND OTHER STRANGE STORIES

Viking Kestrel, 1986, 128p. – 0 670 80907 1
Penguin, 1988, 128p. – Pbk. – 0 14 032057 1
illustrated by Peter Melnyczuk

Two collections of stories, one about every-day happenings, the other ghost stories. Well written and with interesting illustrations.
Age range: 9–11

PERRY, Ritchie (John Allen)

Pseudonym for John Allen. British. Born King's Lynn, Norfolk, 1942. Educated King Edward VII Grammar School, King's Lynn; St John's College, Oxford, B.A. Modern History. Wife: Lynne Mary Charlotte Allen, two daughters.

Agent: Michael Sissons, A. D. Peters & Co., 10 Buckingham Street, London WC2N 6BU, England

Rather lightweight but with the gift of writing thoroughly entertaining stories which encourage the enjoyment of reading.

THE CREEPY TALE
Red Fox, 1990, 111p. – Pbk. – 0 09 966890 4
Hutchinson, 1989, 111p. – 0 09 173943 8

Tom, determined not to be outdone by his sister, agrees to go to the Monson House, looking for conkers. It is against his better judgement, for it is a house to avoid since the violent deaths which occurred there.
Age range: 10–12

FENELLA FANG
Beaver Books, 1988. – Pbk. – 0 09 951270 X
Hutchinson, 1986, 96p. – O/P. – 0 09 165820 9

In the same series:

FENELLA FANG AND THE GREAT ESCAPE
Beaver Books, 1988, 112p. – Pbk. –
0 09 955460 7
Hutchinson, 1987, 144p. – O/P. –
0 09 171910 0

FENELLA FANG AND THE TIME MACHINE
Hutchinson, 1991, 160p. – 0 09 176367 3

FENELLA FANG AND THE WICKED WITCH
Beaver Books, 1990, 144p. – Pbk, O/P. –
0 09 962260 2
Hutchinson, 1989, 144p. – 0 09 173710 9
all illustrated by Jean Baylis

Very popular, these gruesome tales tell how Fenella's friends need rescuing from the hairy situations they find themselves in. Easy reading.
Age range: 9–11

GEORGE H. GHASTLY
Beaver Books, 1987, 80p. – Pbk. – 0 09 952020 6
Hutchinson, 1981, 77p. – O/P. – 0 09 143590 0

In the same series:

GEORGE H. GHASTLY AND THE LITTLE HORROR
Beaver Books, 1987, 144p. – Pbk. –
0 09 952040 0
Hutchinson, 1985, 96p. – O/P. –
0 09 162460 6

GEORGE H. GHASTLY TO THE RESCUE
Beaver Books, 1987. – Pbk. – 0 09 952030 3
Hutchinson, 1983, 103p. – O/P. –
0 09 152100 9
all illustrated by Chris Winn

Excellent combinations of the humorous and the spooky. Failure as a ghost drives George to desperate measures.
Age range: 9–11

PEYTON, K. M.

Pseudonym for Kathleen Wendy Peyton, also writing as Kathleen Herald. British. Born Birmingham, Warwickshire, 1929. Educated Wimbledon High School; Manchester Art School, Art Teacher's Diploma. Married Michael Peyton, two daughters. Art teacher.

Awards: Library Association Carnegie Medal: *Edge of the Cloud*, 1969
           Guardian Children's Fiction Award: *Flambards*, 1970

Address: Rookery Cottage, North Fambridge, Chelmsford, Essex CM3 6LP, England

A writer with a deep understanding and sympathy for teenagers and their problems, and the ability to translate this into enjoyable books. Her books for younger readers are also well written and enjoyable. She has remained a popular author over many years.

FLY-BY-NIGHT
Sparrow Books, 1981, 176p. – Pbk. – 0 09 926390 4
OUP, 1979, 172p. – 0 19 277091 8

In the same series:

THE TEAM
Sparrow Books, 1982. – Pbk. – 0 09 927680 1
OUP, 1975, 177p. – O/P. – 0 19 271372 8
both illustrated by the author

Horse and pony stories continue to be popular with girls. These two are particularly good quality novels. The character of Ruth is well developed over the two books. The problems and expense of keeping a horse are honestly described, but there is still a heart-warming storyline for horse lovers.
Age range: 9–11

FROGGETT'S REVENGE
Penguin, 1987, 96p. – Pbk. – 0 14 032115 2
OUP, 1985, 80p. – 0 19 271513 5
illustrated by Maureen Bradley

A child's delight, in which justice prevails. Wayne, the school bully, finds himself on the receiving end of his own medicine. A very satisfying story.
Age range: 8–10

GOING HOME
Magnet Books, 1985, 96p. – Pbk. – 0 416 50290 3
OUP, 1982, 104p. – 0 19 271459 7
illustrated by Chris Molan

An unusual story about two children on holiday in France. They do not always see eye to eye with the relatives they are staying with, so they decide to make their own way home.
Age range: 8–10

THUNDER IN THE SKY
Red Fox, 1990, 159p. – Pbk. – 0 09 975150 X
Bodley Head, 1985, 168p. – Pbk. – 0 370 30885 9
illustrated by Victor Ambrus

When war breaks out in 1914, Sam cannot understand why Gil refuses to go to fight, yet is willing to work on the barges taking ammunition to France. Sam's gradual understanding of this apparent conflict provides an excellent plot.
Age range: 12–14

PILLING, Ann

Also writes as Ann Cheetham. British. Born Warrington, Lancashire, 1944. Educated King's College, University of London, B.A. (Hons), M.Phil., English. Married Joe Pilling, 1968, two sons. English teacher.

Awards: Guardian Children's Fiction Award: *Henry's Leg*, 1986

Address: 57 St. John Street, Oxford OX1 2LQ, England

Agent: Gina Pollinger, 4 Garrick Street, London WC2E 9BH, England

Best known for her originality of plot, Ann Pilling is also able to share her sense of humour in a variety of ways. Sometimes verbal, sometimes slapstick, there is much to laugh at in between the mounting tension which she realistically creates.

THE BIG PINK
Chivers Press, 1989, 328p. – L/P. – 0 7451 0959 4
Penguin, 1988, 160p. – Pbk. – 0 14 032319 8
Viking Kestrel, 1987, 156p. – 0 670 81156 4

Although at times very funny, this book is essentially a moving and painful story. Angela has to struggle to carve out a niche for herself in an alien environment. It will strike a chord with many young readers who also feel out on a limb.
Age range: 11–14

HENRY'S LEG
Chivers Press, 1987, 280p. – L/P. – 0 7451 0550 5
Penguin, 1986, 160p. – Pbk, O/P. –
0 14 032016 4
Viking Kestrel, 1985, 176p. – 0 670 80720 6
illustrated by Rowan Clifford

An original and amusing story. Henry finds a discarded leg from a tailor's dummy. Taking a fancy to it, he lugs it home, where it proves to be a catalyst for some hair-raising events.
Age range: 10–12

ON THE LION'S SIDE
Pan Books, 1990, 192p. – Pbk. – 0 330 31046 1
Heinemann, 1988, 160p. – 0 434 95671 6

The story of a friendship between two boys which begins with open hostility, and cautiously develops throughout the solving of the mystery of the wall. Mutual understanding is achieved at the same time as the final tragedy is unearthed. Simultaneously sensitive and exciting.
Age range: 10–12

OUR KID
Penguin, 1991, 208p. – Pbk. – 0 14 032974 9
Chivers Press, 1991, 368p. – L/P. – 0 7451 1295 1
Viking, 1989, 160p. – 0 670 82584 0

Acquiring a paper round gives Frank an opportunity to get to know the posh part of his home town. The people he gets to know broaden his horizons, and set him on the trail of a mystery. An excellent plot.
Age range: 12–14

STAN
Penguin, 1989, 192p. – Pbk. – 0 14 032388 0
Viking, 1988. – 0 670 81770 8

Stan's foster home is intolerable, so he runs away, hoping to find his brother, with whom he can make the real home he has never experienced. His difficult journey becomes a nightmare as he is relentlessly pursued. Totally gripping.
Age range: 12–14

THE YEAR OF THE WORM
Chivers Press, 1988, 248p. – L/P. – 0 7451 0825 3
Penguin, 1985, 144p. – Pbk. – 0 14 031821 6
Kestrel Books, 1984, 144p. – 0 7226 5868 0
illustrated by Ian Newsham

Peter is a timid boy, hence the nickname 'Worm'. He is bullied and made fun of until the holiday proves to him and others that he has more than enough courage.
Age range: 10–12

POWLING, Chris

British. Born London, 1943. Educated Bromley Grammar School; St Catherine's College, Oxford, M.A.; King's College, University of London, Postgraduate Certificate in Education; Royal Academy of Music, Diploma in Speech and Drama; Institute of Education, London, Advanced Diploma in Education, 1970; University of Sussex, M.A. Married Janet Smith, two daughters. Teacher, lecturer, contributor and presenter, BBC radio.

Address: The Old Chapel, Easton, near Winchester, Hampshire SO21 1EG, England

A writer whose ideas are firmly based on today's society, making the stories relevant and meaningful. He has particular appeal to boys.

DAREDEVILS OR SCAREDYCATS

Fontana, 1981, 128p. – Pbk. – 0 00 671897 3
Abelard-Schuman, 1979, 128p. – O/P. –
0 200 72623 4
illustrated by Stephen Levis

A collection of stories demonstrating the various ways people can show courage. It includes bullying, coping with an emergency, and other situations children sometimes have to face alone.
Age range: 11–13

FINGERS CROSSED: STORIES FOR NINE-YEAR-OLDS

Hodder, 1988, 128p. – Pbk. – 0 340 48566 3
Blackie, 1987, 112p. – O/P. – 0 216 92113 9
illustrated by Jean Baylis

An excellent collection of stories and poems to suit every mood and taste.
Age range: 8–10

MOG AND THE RECTIFIER

Hodder, 1982, 144p. – Pbk. – 0 340 28046 8
Abelard–Schuman, 1980, 134p. – O/P. –
0 200 72697 8
illustrated by Stephen Levis

The narrator of this story is a nameless child, nameless because he feels too ashamed to 'reveal' his name. He belongs to a gang with Mog as leader. Mog hero-worships the Rectifier, a modern-day Robin Hood. There comes a point when a choice has to be made, Mog or the scholarship and a future.
Age range: 11–13

THE MUSTANG MACHINE

Hodder, 1983, 128p. – Pbk, O/P. – 0 340 32101 6
Abelard–Schuman, 1981, 128p. – O/P. –
0 200 72764 8

A book with an unusual hero – an extraordinary bicycle. Becca and the gang do so want to enter the competition, but without a bike they cannot. Mr Amos introduces them to the Mustang machine and everything changes. An enjoyable adventure story.
Age range: 11–13

STUNTKID

Hodder, 1987, 128p. – Pbk. – 0 340 40437 X
Blackie, 1985, 128p. – O/P. – 0 216 91778 6

An exciting mystery in which Andy has to discover the identity of 'Stuntkid' in order to find out why Vic Hogan's film was never finished.
Age range: 11–13

PRATCHETT, Terry

British. Born 1948. Married.

Address: C/o Colin Smythe, PO Box 6,
Gerrards Cross,
Buckinghamshire SL9 8XA,
England

TRUCKERS
Corgi, 1990, 208p. – Pbk. – 0 552 52595 2
Doubleday, 1989, 169p. – 0 385 26961 7

In the same series:

DIGGERS
Doubleday, 1990. – 0 385 26979 X

WINGS
Doubleday, n.d., 199p. – 0 385 40018 7

A powerful fantasy about a tribe of gnomes who live under the floorboards of a large department store about to be demolished. They make their plans to escape and face the dangers of Outside. The story of their hazardous journey, so courageously faced, comes to a satisfactory climax.
Age range: 10–12

PRICE, Susan

British. Born Rounds Green, Staffordshire, 1955. Educated Tividale Comprehensive School. Writer.

Awards: Children's Rights Other Award: *Twopence a Tub*, 1975
          Library Association Carnegie Medal: *The Ghost Drum*, 1987

Address: C/o Faber & Faber Ltd, 3 Queen Square, London WC1N 3AU, England

Agent: Michael Thomas, A. M. Heath, 79 St Martin's Lane, London WC2N 4AA England

THE GHOST DRUM
Faber, 1989, 167p. – Pbk. – 0 571 15340 2
Faber, 1987, 167p. – 0 571 14613 9

A grim tale of a power struggle with a life at stake. Czar Guidon rules by terror, and keeps his son imprisoned in terrible circumstances. Out in the frozen wastes is a witch, who listens to messages from the ghost drum, and hears the cries of the imprisoned son. An excellent story, but the names are difficult and form a barrier which prevents some children tackling the book.
Age range: 12–14

GHOSTS AT LARGE
Penguin, 1986, 96p. – Pbk. – 0 14 032021 0
Faber, 1984, 96p. – O/P. – 0 571 13282 0
illustrated by Allison Price

Lesser known traditional stories re-told by a master storyteller. Weird ghostly happenings in each story ensure the reader will be kept enthralled.
Age range: 11–13

HOME FROM HOME
Faber, 1990, 178p. – Pbk. – 0 571 14316 4
Faber, 1977, 123p. – O/P. – 0 571 11022 3

Paul's home life is not ideal, and has turned him into a trouble maker, the bane of his teachers. He certainly doesn't want to be roped in to doing 'good works' by helping old Mrs Maxwell. In her turn, she is apprehensive about him being in her house, but somehow it all works out. Realistic and down-to-earth, the story can be successfully read to a class, and appeals to children who feel they have a lot in common with Paul.
Age range: 11–13

IN A NUTSHELL
Faber, 1983, 120p. – O/P. – 0 571 13075 5
illustrated by Alison Price

A delightful tale of Thumb and Thumbling banished in nutshells to live with human beings. Being so tiny means that every problem seems so huge as to be insurmountable. Eventually they resolve the problem and achieve happiness.
Age range: 8–10

R

RANSOME, Arthur (Michell)

British. Born Leeds, Yorkshire, 1884 (died 3 June 1967). Educated Old College, Windermere; Rugley College, Warwickshire; Yorkshire College (now Leeds University). Married: 1) Ivy Walker, 1909 (divorced 1924), one daughter; 2) Eugenia Shelepin, 1924. Correspondent, writer.

Awards: Library Association Carnegie Medal: *Pigeon Post*, 1936
University of Leeds: Litt.D.
University of Durham: M.A.
O.B.E.

In a sense, it can be said that Arthur Ransome is the father of children's literature as we know it today. Of course, there were children's books before his, but they were restricted to moralizing and improving. In the midst of this, Arthur Ransome's stirring tales of adventure shine like a beacon. The children in the stories, albeit middle class, are independent, resourceful and imaginative. Their characters are well rounded, and, therefore, memorable, and the books have their share of humorous incidents. They continue to give discerning readers hours of pleasure. Ransome drew all the maps, diagrams and illustrations himself. The new paperback editions have colourful jackets which make them more immediately attractive to today's child, used to seeing everything in colour. The books are listed below in reading order.
Age range for all titles: 10–12

SWALLOWS AND AMAZONS
Penguin, 1970, 368p. – Pbk. – 0 14 030171 2
Cape, 1930, 352p. – 0 224 60631 X

The first book which introduces readers to the two families, the Walkers and the Blacketts, who are the heroes of most of the other books. Each has a small dinghy, and they spend the summer camping on an island in the lake, playing pirates, sailing, and generally having a wonderful time. The book has been made into a delightful film.

SWALLOWDALE
Penguin, 1968, 448p. – Pbk. – 0 14 030339 1
Cape, 1931, 454p. – 0 224 60632 8

In a moment of carelessness, Captain John runs *Swallow* onto a rock, and sinks her. With only one boat for the rest of the holiday, they are forced ashore, and find a secret valley complete with a hidden cave. Their spirits rise as they start to explore, and the climax is the ascent of a local mountain, called Kanchenjunga by the children.

PETER DUCK
Cape, 1983, 416p. – 0 224 02125 7
Penguin, 1968, 448p. – Pbk. – 0 14 030340 5

Actually a story 'written' by the children themselves during the winter holiday when they are unable to sail. They create a pirate story in which Black Jake pursues Peter Duck, who is sailing with the Swallows and Amazons to find the treasure that Peter Duck once saw being buried.

WINTER HOLIDAY
Penguin, 1968, 336p. – Pbk. – 0 14 030341 3
Cape, 1933, 360p. – 0 224 60634 4

With their boats laid up for the winter, the children find other roles to adopt. They become Arctic explorers, and a great expedition is planned for the Swallows and Amazons, also joined for the first time by the two Ds. When the lake freezes over, they decide to journey to the 'North Pole'. Fate also takes a hand, in the form of mumps.

COOT CLUB
Penguin, 1969, 349p. – Pbk. – 0 14 030392 8
Cape, 1934, 352p. – 0 224 60635 2

Tom throws caution to the winds and casts a motor launch adrift so that the noise of the engine cannot disturb a coot nesting nearby. The owners are angry and plot revenge. A different set of children from most of his books.

PIGEON POST
Cape, 1983, 384p. – 0 224 02124 9
Penguin, 1969, 382p. – Pbk. – 0 14 030393 6

On this holiday, the Swallows and Amazons, always ready to be helpful, decide to go prospecting for gold to help Uncle Jim, whose own expedition to South America has ended in failure. Serious as they are in their quest, there are others who are more so, and they spend much time outwitting a possible 'claim jumper'.

WE DIDN'T MEAN TO GO TO SEA
Cape, 1983, 344p. – 0 224 02123 0
Penguin, 1969, 336p. – Pbk. – 0 14 030414 2

Perhaps the best of the series, but featuring only the Walker children. When the boat they are spending the night on drags her anchor, they are subjected to a very frightening experience as they drift out to sea, in thick fog. Helpless at first, their confidence and courage increase as the story progresses, and they cross the North Sea successfully.

SECRET WATER
Penguin, 1969, 376p. – Pbk. – 0 14 030413 4
Cape, 1939, 384p. – 0 224 60638 7

Excited, and a little apprehensive, the children are put ashore on an island, charged with the holiday task of making a map, fending for themselves while they do so. While exploring, they find mysterious tracks which they identify as those of a Mastodon, and also meet up with another group of children whose home ground the island is.

BIG SIX
Penguin, 1970, 368p. – Pbk. – 0 14 030449 5
Cape, 1940, 400p. – 0 224 60639 5

The children from *Coot Club* are wrongly suspected of setting boats adrift. Proving their innocence is difficult, as evidence is piling up against them. They are joined in this adventure by the two Ds.

MISSEE LEE
Penguin, 1971. – Pbk. – 0 14 030450 9
Cape, 1941, 340p. – 0 224 60640 9

A rather more melodramatic plot, dreamed up by the children like *Peter Duck* to while away the winter holiday. Captain Flint (Uncle Jim) accidentally sets his boat on fire, so they abandon ship and sail off in the two boats *Swallow* and *Amazon*, and are subsequently shipwrecked on the coast of China in a storm. They meet Missee Lee, a pirate, who holds them against their will. Their escape makes a lively adventure.

THE PICTS AND THE MARTYRS
Penguin, 1971. – Pbk. – 0 14 030479 7
Cape, 1943, 304p. – 0 224 60641 7

The Martyrs are the Amazons, who have to stay indoors and be good, tidy, clean children during the visit of a fearsome Great Aunt. The Picts are the two Ds, who camp out in a hut on the hillside like the Picts of old used to do during raids. When the Great Aunt disappears, their holiday plans take a turn for the better.

GREAT NORTHERN?
Penguin, 1971, 368p. – Pbk. – 0 14 030492 4
Cape, 1947, 352p. – 0 224 60642 5

Mooring their boat in an isolated cove to get her cleaned up, the children see what turns out to be a pair of rare birds nesting. To their horror, they soon realize that a ruthless egg-collector is about to kill the birds to steal the eggs. They must somehow form a rescue plan.

OLD PETER'S RUSSIAN TALES
Cape, 1984, 256p. – 0 224 02959 2
Penguin, 1974, 272p. – Pbk, O/P. –
0 14 030696 X

Arthur Ransome travelled a great deal in Russia when he was a war correspondent. He learnt Russian in order to study the folk-lore, and these stories are his version of the tales Old Peter told his grandchildren during the long winter evenings.

S

SAMPSON, Fay

British. Born South Devon. Educated University of Exeter, B.A. (Maths). Married, two children. Teacher, author.

This author deserves to be more widely read, but as some of her books have a historical flavour, they tend to be overlooked by some children. She creates individual and memorable children in dramatic situations which can sometimes shock the reader, but justifiably so.

FINNGLAS AND THE STONES OF CHOOSING
Lion Publishing, 1986, 128p. – Pbk. – 0 7459 1124 2

In the same series:

FINNGLAS OF THE HORSES
Lion Publishing, 1985, 128p. – Pbk. – 0 8564 8899 2

PANGUR BAN: THE WHITE CAT
Lion Publishing, 1983, 128p. – Pbk. – 0 8564 8580 2

THE SERPENT OF SENARGAD
Lion Publishing, 1989, 128p. – Pbk. – 0 7459 1520 5

SHAPE-SHIFTER: THE NAMING OF PANGUR BAN
Lion Publishing, 1988, 128p. – Pbk. – 0 7459 1347 4

THE WHITE HORSE IS RUNNING
Lion Publishing, 1990, 176p. – Pbk. – 0 7459 1915 4

A series of books set in the kingdom of Senargad where evil triumphs over good.

Great battles are waged to try to redress the balance. Exciting fantasy stories.
Age range: 12–15

A FREE MAN ON SUNDAY
Collins, 1990, 160p. – Pbk. – 0 00 673501 0
Gollancz, 1987, 128p. – 0 575 04114 5

Clifford Ramsden is a serious rambler who spends much of his time on and around Kinder Scout. He and his fellow ramblers feel strongly about the right of common people to be able to wander freely. Edie, his daughter, loves to accompany him and desperately wants to show her support for him on the day of the trespass. The outcome of her decision to defy him is unexpected. A very enjoyable fictional account of the Mass Trespass on Kinder Scout in 1932. It echoes the present situation where many public footpaths and rights of way are being eroded and obstructed, and individuals still try to protect the public right.
Age range: 10–12

THE HUNGRY SNOW
Dobson, 1980, 184p. – 0 234 72262 2

A vivid and memorable tale of the days of poverty when baby boys were welcome because they could work and earn money, and baby girls were thought to be too much of a liability. Marie is filled with horror as she comes to realize that babies are deliberately left to die. She finally rebels against her fellow villagers and saves her baby sister.
Age range: 12–14

SEFTON, Catherine

For biographical details, see Martin WADDELL.

In general, the books by this author make fairly easy reading and the plots proceed at a good pace, maintaining the reader's interest. Not too demanding, they can be used to encourage reluctant readers.

BLUE MISTY MONSTERS

Magnet Books, 1986, 112p. – Pbk. –
0 416 61670 4
Faber, 1985, 106p. – O/P. – 0 571 13564 1
illustrated by Elaine McGregor-Turney

A fun science fiction story in which Mo lands her Pod in Spud's garden quite by mistake. Spud is delighted to have a spaceship until it shrinks to the size of a marble, and until Mo takes on human shape, but remains bright blue, which is inconvenient, to say the least.
Age range: 8–10

EMER'S GHOST

Mammoth, 1990, 128p. – Pbk. – 0 7497 0690 2
Hamish Hamilton, 1981, 137p. – O/P. –
0 241 10619 2

A wooden doll which sheds real tears is a portent not to be ignored, as Emer finds out. When she is finally convinced she has seen a ghost, trying to solve the mystery leads her into danger.
Age range: 9–11

THE EMMA DILEMMA

Magnet Books, 1984, 96p. – Pbk. – 0 416 46800 4
Faber, 1982, 96p. – O/P. – 0 571 11841
illustrated by Jill Bennett

After falling and bumping her head, Emma realizes that a second Emma has appeared, and looks set to stay. Unfortunately, she is full of tricks, which makes life difficult for Emma number one.
Age range: 8–10

THE FINN GANG

Hippo Books, 1985, 96p. – Pbk, O/P. –
0 590 70353 6
Hamish Hamilton, 1981, 96p. – O/P. –
0 241 10694 X
illustrated by Michael Charlton

The shed used by the gang as their HQ has been taken over. The children are angry and determined to expose the wrong-doers. An air of mystery is maintained to the end.
Age range: 9–11

THE GHOST AND BERTIE BOGGIN

Penguin, 1983, 96p. – Pbk. – 0 14 031363 X
Faber, 1980, 94p. – O/P. – 0 571 11524 1
illustrated by Jill Bennett

Amusing ghost stories are always popular. Bertie Boggin's best friend is a ghost who shows him where the best blackberries are and helps him to build winning sand castles. The ghost's fondness for Florence Nightingale leads to difficulties but there is a highly satisfying ending.
Age range: 9–11

THE GHOST GIRL

Magnet Books, 1986, 128p. – Pbk. –
0 416 61530 9
Hamish Hamilton, 1985, 160p. – 0 241 11428 4

A little bit of everything – ghost story, romance, family story and mystery, set in Ireland. Clare sees a ghost, but perhaps it is her imagination, as she is not enjoying her holiday. Following the clues, she begins to put together Lucie's story. Very light-hearted.
Age range: 11–13

ISLAND OF THE STRANGERS

Mammoth, 1990, 128p. – Pbk. – 0 7497 0182 X
Hamish Hamilton, 1983, 160p. – O/P. –
0 241 10914 0

A stirring tale of the residents against the Gobbers – a group of city kids complete with skin-head hair-dos and earrings who 'invade' Inishnagal, the island of strangers. Only Nora goes against the majority and almost pays with her life.

Written in a typical racy, undemanding style, there is, however, a more serious lesson to be learned.
Age range: 12–14

SLEEPERS ON THE HILL
Mammoth, 1990, 128p. – Pbk. – 0 7497 0691 0
Faber, 1973. – O/P. – 0 571 10305 7

When Miss Cooney broke her leg, a chain of events began that changed many lives. Tom had to see to her hens, and found the bangle. He could feel its power at once, especially in the vicinity of the graves. Then he discovers the girl hiding in the cottage. An exciting mystery with rather more substance.
Age range: 10–12

SEVERY, Richard

British. Born Nottingham, 1944.
Educated Guildford Royal Grammar
School; Bristol University, LLB (Hons);
Bath University, Certificate in Education.
Lives with Jann Howarth (illustrator), one
son, with three daughters by a marriage
dissolved in 1979. (Jann Howarth also
has two daughters.) Solicitor, teacher,
business man, writer.

Address: Lodge Farm, Hinton
Charterhouse, near Bath,
Avon BA3 6BG, England

Agent: Jon Thurley, 213 Linen Hall,
156–170 Regent Street,
London W1R 5TA, England

Superb plots laced with humour are
Richard Severy's strong point. Some of
the stories are written about his own
family, which may account for the
excellent characterization.

ANGEL
Mammoth, 1989, 144p. – Pbk. – 0 7497 0014 9
Methuen, 1988, 128p. – 0 416 09552 6
illustrated by Jann Haworth

This can best be described as a 'gem'.
Angie, a wonderfully drawn character,
and her twin brother, travel to school on
a steam train because their father is a
signalman. Times are changing, and
rumours about the projected closure of
the railway line are making life at home
unhappy. At school, the new
headmistress is making life difficult for
Angie, who feels she has nowhere to
turn. She does, however, fight on to win
in a most spectacular way.
Age range: 10–12

BATTLEFIELDS
Methuen, 1987, 144p. – O/P. – 0 416 03882 4

Jerry had looked forward to his new
home in the country where he and his
dog could explore in safety. It was
completely ruined for him by Captain
Packham, who, being crippled, takes his
frustration with life out on those around
him, particularly Jerry and his dog. Each
time they meet, the unpleasantness and
near-violence escalate until the
unexpected climax.
Age range: 11–13

MYSTERY PIG
J. MacRae Books, 1983, 60p. – O/P. –
0 86203 125 7
illustrated by Karen Haworth

The pig arrived looking tired and damp.
Kay and Dee fell in love with him, but he
proved to be too much of a handful.
Absolutely hilarious.
Age range: 7–9

RAT'S CASTLE
J. MacRae, 1985, 96p. – 0 86203 193 1
illustrated by Karen Haworth

There is so much packed into this short
novel. Excellent atmospheric description
of the castle in the snow, plus the
mysterious footprints and the courage of
the children, together combine to make
an excellent book.
Age range: 7–9

UNICORN TRAP
J. MacRae, 1984, 82p. – O/P. – 0 86203 156 7
illustrated by Karen Haworth

One rainy day, the children make
plasticine models to pass the time. Kay
chooses to make a unicorn which she
stands on the windowsill in the
moonlight. Strange things happen after
that, but the children cannot decide if it
is proper magic, or man-made magic. A
lovely story with a magical ending.
Age range: 7–9

SOUTHALL, Ivan (Francis)

Australian. Born Canterbury, Victoria, 1921. Educated Chatham State School; Mont Albert Central School; Box Hill Grammar School. Australian Army, Royal Australian Air Force, WW II, Distinguished Flying Cross. Married: 1) Joyce Blackburn, 1945, one son, three daughters; 2) Susan Stanton, 1976. Lecturer, writer.

Awards: Australian Children's Book Council Book of the Year Award: *Ash Road*, 1966 Australian Children's Book Council Book of the Year Award: *To the Wild Sky*, 1968 Australian Children's Book Council Book of the Year Award: *Fly Old Wardrobe*, 1969 Australian Children's Book Council Book of the Year Award: *Bread and Honey*, 1971 Library Association Carnegie Medal: *Josh*, 1971 I.B.B.Y. Honour Award: *Josh*, 1974 Australian Children's Book Council Book of the Year Award: *Fly West*, 1976 Member: Order of Australia, 1981

Address: PO Box 25, Healesville, Victoria 3777, Australia

A writer of the highest quality who deals with emotions as well as events. He has a firm belief that, when necessary, children can and will rise to the occasion, however disastrous. His books are mostly not easy light reading, but for fluent readers they offer tense, exciting plots and characters they can sympathize with.

ASH ROAD

Penguin, 1970, 192p. – Pbk. – 0 14 030314 6
Angus & Robertson, 1966, 160p. – O/P. –
0 207 94629 9
illustrated by Clem Seale

Fire is very dangerous and destructive, so whenever it starts, everyone sets off to fight it, leaving the children of Ash Road alone. Then the impossible happens, and the children start a fire which gets out of control, threatening them within seconds. A moment's carelessness will affect them forever.
Age range: 12–14

CHINAMAN'S REEF IS OURS

Hodder, 1975, 192p. – Pbk, O/P. – 0 340 18744 1
Angus & Robertson, 1970, 160p. – O/P. –
0 207 95365 1

The story, powerfully told, of a group of children who fight to save the town in which they are growing up from the bulldozers.
Age range: 12–14

FLY WEST

Penguin, 1978, 192p. – Pbk, O/P. –
0 14 047118 9
Angus & Robertson, 1975, 176p. – O/P. –
0 207 13002 7

A fictional account of a personal experience, telling of the men who flew Sunderland flying boats during the war.
Age range: 12–14

THE FOX HOLE

Magnet Books, 1980, 128p. – Pbk, O/P. –
0 416 89440 2
Methuen, 1967, 126p. – 0 416 11100 9
illustrated by Ian Ribbons

Although this is one of Ivan Southall's easier books, it is nevertheless an excellent combination of an exciting story and a moving description of developing relationships. Ken feels strange with his cousins when he first comes to stay. The tension builds as the children go camping and Ken falls into a hole while chasing a thieving fox. He is genuinely afraid he won't be rescued.
Age range: 10–12

HILL'S END

Penguin, 1970, 224p. – Pbk. – 0 14 030245 X
Angus & Robertson, 1962, 174p. – O/P. –
0 207 94635 3
illustrated by Jim Phillips

A tribute to the sterling courage that children are capable of in times of adversity. While the children are away from home, a cyclonic storm destroys the whole area, so that when they struggle home, there is nothing left. They must somehow survive until help arrives, but the hazards are many, and they are not used to making their own decisions. The suspense is maintained to the very end.
Age range: 12–14

JOSH

Penguin, 1974, 225p. – Pbk, O/P. –
0 14 030598 X
Angus & Robertson, 1978, 179p. – O/P. –
0 207 13656 4

The book spans three days, and, at the same time, a whole lifetime. Josh goes to visit Aunt Clara as a sort of initiation ceremony – if he comes up to scratch there, he can be considered a Plowman. His visit starts badly as he treads in a cowclap and stands on her cat, but worse is to come when he meets the other children, and two worlds collide head-on. It is a different Josh who returns home.
Age range: 12–14

LET THE BALLOON GO

Penguin, 1972, 112p. – Pbk, O/P. –
0 14 030513 0
Methuen, 1968, 142p. – O/P. – 0 416 29420 0

When first published, this book was innovative as it was one of the few, at that time, to fictionalize the problems of disabled children. Since then, many books have tackled the subject, but this is still among the best. John is spastic, and often feels frustrated by his over-protective mother and the restrictions she puts on his life. One day, he is left alone at home, and, revelling in unaccustomed freedom, he seizes the opportunity to try many of the things he has not previously been allowed to do.
Age range: 10–12

TO THE WILD SKY

Penguin, 1971. – Pbk, O/P. – 0 14 030483 5
Angus & Robertson, 1967, 192p. – O/P. –
0 207 94634 5

In the same series:

A CITY OUT OF SIGHT

Angus & Robertson, 1985, 143p. – O/P. –
0 207 14943 7

A group of children, involved in an air crash, find themselves on an uninhabited island. Hoping for rescue, they must nevertheless set about surviving. Tense and absorbing, the story is realistically convincing.
Age range: 12–14

STRACHAN, Ian

British. Born Altrincham, 1938. Married, two children. BBC producer.

A capable author whose successive books are increasingly striking and absorbing. He chooses themes which may not immediately appeal to children, but once started, the books will not be put down until finished.

BANG! BANG! YOU'RE DEAD
Methuen, 1988, 96p. – 0 416 05182 0
illustrated by Paul Wright

Two children are held at gunpoint in their own home by a thief looking for the money he hid there some time ago. Very exciting, but believable at the same time.
Age range: 10–12

THE FLAWED GLASS
Mammoth, 1990, 288p. – Pbk. – 0 7497 0151 X

A remarkable story, told with extreme sensitivity. Shona, an islander, is severely disabled, and because she cannot easily communicate, is often disregarded. The arrival of the American businessman finally results in releasing the Shona who has been imprisoned within her for so many years. A very moving ending.
Age range: 12–14

JOURNEY OF 1000 MILES
Magnet Books, 1985, 144p. – Pbk, O/P. – 0 416 51880 X

The very human story that lies behind a news headline for a day or two, and is then mostly forgotten. Lee, together with the rest of his family, flee from Vietnam crammed into a rickety fishing boat, which is itself a hazard. If the patrols or the pirates don't get them, hunger and thirst will. Packed with incidents, exciting and yet sad, it is a book that lingers in the memory.
Age range: 10–12

SWINDELLS, Robert (Edward)

British. Born Bradford, Yorkshire, 1939. Educated Huddersfield Polytechnic, Teaching Certificate; University of Bradford, M.A., Peace Studies. Royal Air Force, 1957–60. Married Brenda, 1980, 2nd marriage: two daughters from first marriage. Copywriter, advertising clerk, engineer, teacher.

Awards: Children's Rights Workshop Other Award: *Brother in the Land*, 1984
Children's Book Award: *Brother in the Land*, 1984
Children's Book Award: *Room 13*, 1989

Address: 3 Upwood Park, Blackmoor Road, Oxenhope, West Yorkshire BD22 9SS, England

Agent: J. Luithcen, 88 Holmfirth Road, Leicester, England

A CANDLE IN THE DARK
Firecrest Publications, 1987, 136p. – 0 85997 698 X
Hodder, 1983, 144p. – Pbk, O/P. – 0 340 32098 2
illustrated by Gareth Floyd

Jimmy finds life in the pit hard, but when he discovers that a man is being kept a prisoner, his own life is also put at risk.
Age range: 10–12

DRACULA'S CASTLE
Doubleday, n.d., 62p. – 0 385 40023 3
illustrated by Jon Riley

When Marvin walks up the drive of the big, empty old house nicknamed 'Dracula's Castle', and fails to turn up at school, his classmates fear the worst. A slight story, published in extra large print with lots of bold illustrations to encourage children.
Age range: 7–9

THE GHOST MESSENGERS
Hodder, 1988, 96p. – Pbk. – 0 340 48668 6
Collins, 1988, 128p. – 0 00 330036 6

Meg finds her school work is suffering as her sleep is disturbed by the ghost of her grandfather who keeps trying to tell her something. Easy to read.
Age range: 10–12

THE ICE PALACE
Armada Books, 1980, 96p. – Pbk, O/P. – 0 00 671699 7
Hamish Hamilton, 1977, 96p. – O/P. – 0 241 89614 2
illustrated by June Jackson

Storjik the childtaker steals Ivan's brother, but Ivan is determined to be brave and to rescue him. Easy to read, with very large print, and quite short.
Age range: 7–9

THE SERPENT'S TOOTH
Penguin, 1990, 144p. – Pbk. – 0 14 034017 3
Hamish Hamilton, 1988, 160p. – 0 241 12207 4

Many issues are touched upon in this highly readable and enjoyable novel. Lucy, just entering her 'teens', is at odds with her parents and their views, but feels at ease with 'daft Alice'. She is pleased when heart-throb Tim Ogden asks her to a party, but is typically disappointed when she gets there. She can't decide just where she stands on the issue of a nuclear waste disposal site.
Age range: 12–14

THE THOUSAND EYES OF NIGHT
Hodder, 1986, 128p. – Pbk, O/P. – 0 340 39359 9
Hodder, 1985, 120p. – O/P. – 0 340 35389 9

Little out-of-the-ordinary events are one thing, but a big one, like finding a dead man, is quite a different matter. As the children slowly make the connections the tension builds up to reach a nail-biting climax.
Age range: 10–12

WHEN DARKNESS COMES
Hamlyn, 1976, 158p. – Pbk, O/P. – 0 600 38374 7
Hodder, 1973, 160p. – O/P. – 0 340 17506 0

A primitive tribe is torn apart by jealousy and thwarted ambition. The children are saddened at being separated from their friends, and plot together to re-unite

them. Only when an outside danger threatens are they able to forget their differences and work together. A surprising ending.
Age range: 11–13

WORLD-EATER
Hodder, 1983, 112p. – Pbk, O/P. – 0 340 32884 3
Hodder, 1981, 104p. – O/P. – 0 340 26576 0

Orville's overriding interest is his pigeons, but even they take second place as the discovery of a new planet is revealed. Slowly the reader realizes just how badly the planet's existence will affect the world. Quite compelling, yet not too demanding.
Age range: 10–12

T

THOMAS, Ruth

Awards: Guardian Children's Fiction
Award: *The Runaways*, 1988

A comparative newcomer to children's literature, Ruth Thomas appears to have found a recipe for success. Lots of action, realistic children, and events described in a direct way, that readers can relate to.

THE CLASS THAT WENT WILD
Beaver Books, 1989, 224p. – Pbk. –
0 09 963210 1
Hutchinson, 1988. – 0 09 173618 8

Class 4L are not best pleased when their teacher leaves to have a baby, and they refuse to behave for the constant supply of temporary teachers. Gillian is really worried about her brother, but his disappearance brings matters to a head.
Age range: 11–13

THE NEW BOY
Red Fox, 1990, 264p. – Pbk. – 0 09 973410 9
Hutchinson, 1989, 264p. – 0 09 173799 0

Donovan, newly arrived in class, is a disruptive influence. Fights begin, things are stolen, but Amy defends him and helps him until he needs to be hidden.

Then she must make her own decision.
Age range: 11–13

THE RUNAWAYS
Beaver Books, 1988, 256p. – Pbk. –
0 09 959660 1
Hutchinson, 1987, 252p. – 0 09 172633 6

Unpopular children always feel sure that money will buy popularity, so when Julia and Nathan find a substantial amount, they decide to use it for this purpose. But questions are asked, until they become afraid and run away.
Age range: 11–13

THE SECRET
Hutchinson, 1990, 246p. – 0 09 176341 X

Left at home on their own, and with time passing, Nicky and Roy become anxious when their mother fails to return. Afraid of what will happen if they betray her, they try to cope with the problems. Not very plausible, but young readers will undoubtedly overlook the faults in construction in their enjoyment of the plot.
Age range: 9–12

TOWNSEND, John Rowe

British. Born Leeds, West Yorkshire, 1922. Educated Leeds Grammar School; Emmanuel College, Cambridge, B.A., M.A. Royal Air Force, WW II. Married Vera Lancaster, 1948, two daughters, one son. Reporter, editor, lecturer.

Awards: Boston Globe–Horn Award: *The Intruder*, 1970

Address: 72 Water Lane, Cambridge CB4 4LR, England

Almost a household word in the realm of children's literature, John Rowe Townsend has not only written successfully for many years, but he has also made a substantial contribution to the reviewing of children's books. He is particularly successful in writing for teenagers, but his books for younger children are also popular. His male characters are always well drawn, giving them special appeal to boys.

DAN ALONE
Penguin, 1985, 192p. – Pbk, O/P. – 0 14 031626 4
Kestrel Books, 1983, 176p. – O/P. – 0 7226 5812 5

Dan's young life has been a nightmare; deserted by his alcoholic father, then by his mother who cannot cope alone, he has to go to relatives who do not want him. He decides to run away and live rough, which leads him to Leo who is not all he seems. Dan finds he can no longer hold on to his dream of belonging to a family. Realistic, with a finely constructed ending.
Age range: 12–14

GUMBLE'S YARD
Viking Kestrel, 1984, 128p. – 0 670 80081 3

In the same series:

GOOD-BYE TO GUMBLE'S YARD
Penguin, 1987, 158p. – Pbk. – 0 14 031403 2

When Sandra and Keith are left on their own, they realize the authorities will put them into care, so they move into Gumble's Yard. Unknown to them, it is used by a gang of thieves, who make life uncomfortable for them. Fast-paced and exciting adventure stories.
Age range: 10–12

THE PERSUADING STICK
Penguin, 1988, 96p. – Pbk, O/P. – 0 14 032131 4
Viking Kestrel, 1986, 96p. – O/P. – 0 670 81170 X
illustrated by Pat Fogarty

Sarah realizes she needs help in making Beth and Katherine listen to her. Convinced the special stick she has found has magical powers, she puts it to the test with astonishing success. The way the real magic of the stick is revealed makes an excellent conclusion.
Age range: 9–11

ROB'S PLACE
Penguin, 1988, 176p. – Pbk, O/P. – 0 14 032318 X
Viking Kestrel, 1987, 176p. – 0 670 80998 5

Like Dan in *Dan Alone*, Rob is deserted by everyone he cares about. Finding reality unbearable, he begins to live in a fantasy world which gradually takes over in a frightening way, and he begins to fear he is going insane. A very powerful and sensitive story of a boy under stress.
Age range: 12–14

TOM TIDDLER'S GROUND
Chivers Press, 1987, 168p. – L/P. – 0 7451 0591 2
Penguin, 1987, 112p. – Pbk, O/P. – 0 14 031914 X
Viking Kestrel, 1985, 144p. – 0 670 80689 7
illustrated by Mark Peppe

This book is a straightforward adventure story, with none of the emotional drama that John Rowe Townsend excels at. A group of children find an old barge which they adopt as their den. When they discover an old horse-brass, it sets them off on a mysterious trail.
Age range: 9–11

THE XANADU MANUSCRIPT
Red Fox, 1990, 176p. – Pbk. – 0 09 975180 1
OUP, 1977, 176p. – O/P. – 0 19 271406 6

A fantastic yet convincing story of people coming from the future into the present day. The difficulties they experience are sometimes funny, sometimes sad. A gentle story that is thoroughly enjoyable.
Age range: 12–14

TOWNSON, Hazel

British. Born Nelson, Lancashire, 1928.
Educated Leeds University, B.A.;
Associate of the Library Association.

For a good, light–hearted, entertaining
read, Hazel Townson is hard to beat.
There are lots of stories, all with original
plots, full of humour, with good
illustrations – fun to read. Many of her
books are illustrated by Tony Ross; they
make an excellent combination.

THE BARLEY SUGAR GHOSTS
Red Fox, 1990, 96p. – Pbk. – 0 09 975990 X
Hodder, 1976, 96p. – O/P. – 0 340 20291 2
illustrated by Val Biro

When Nell discovers she has sold her
Gran's tin containing her valuables to
Black Logan, she sets off to recover it. A
recipe for hilarious misadventure.
Age range: 8–10

THE CRIMSON CRESCENT
Beaver Books, 1987, 80p. – Pbk. – 0 09 952110 5
Andersen Press, 1986, 80p. – 0 86264 130 6

In the same series:

FIREWORKS GALORE
Beaver Books, 1989, 88p. – Pbk. –
0 09 965540 3
Andersen Press, 1988, 80p. – 0 86264 214 0

THE GREAT ICE-CREAM CRIME
Red Fox, 1990, 80p. – Pbk. – 0 09 976000 2
Beaver Books, 1986, 80p. – Pbk. –
0 09 948640 7
Andersen Press, 1981, 72p. – 0 86264 005 9

HAUNTED IVY
Beaver Books, 1986, 80p. – Pbk. –
0 09 941320 5
Andersen Press, 1984, 80p. – 0 86264 082 2

THE SIEGE OF COBB STREET SCHOOL
Red Fox, 1990, 80p. – Pbk. – 0 09 975980 2
Andersen Press, 1983, 64p. – 0 86264 041 5

THE STAGGERING SNOWMAN
Beaver Books, 1988, 80p. – Pbk. –
0 09 956820 9
Andersen Press, 1987, 80p. – 0 86264 181 0

THE VANISHING GRAN
Beaver Books, 1985, 80p. – Pbk. –
0 09 935480 2
Andersen Press, 1983, 72p. – 0 86264 058 X
all illustrated by Philippe Dupasquier

Adventure stories for younger readers.
Racy and humorous, these books feature
Lenny and Jake, amateur sleuths who
always solve their mysteries.
Age range: 8–10

DANNY – DON'T JUMP
Beaver Books, 1987, 80p. – Pbk. – 0 09 946290 7
Andersen Press, 1985, 80p. – 0 86264 112 8
illustrated by Amelia Rosato

There is a good reason for the accident-
prone Danny being on the roof.
Discovering what the reason is provides
the reader with the usual exciting and
funny story.
Age range: 8–10

THE MOVING STATUE
Beaver Books, 1990, 64p. – Pbk. – 0 09 973370 6
Andersen Press, 1989, 72p. – 0 86264 243 4
illustrated by Shelagh McNicholas

The issue at stake in this story is whether
or not the statue moved. Even those who
did not see it swear they did. An easy and
entertaining read.
Age range: 7–9

ONE GREEN BOTTLE
Andersen Press, 1987, 56p. – 0 86264 164 0
illustrated by David McKee

Tim hopes to make his fortune with his
new board-game. He cannot believe it
when it disappears. A most engaging
story.
Age range: 8–10

PILKIE'S PROGRESS
Beaver Books, 1988, 64p. – Pbk. – 0 09 956360 6
Andersen Press, 1986, 80p. – 0 86264 149 7
illustrated by Tony Ross

Benny Pilkington, alias Pilkie, explodes
the 'test your heart' machine. He
convinces himself he is dying.
Age range: 8–10

THE SHRIEKING FACE

Beaver Books, 1986, 90p. – Pbk. – 0 09 941310 8
Andersen Press, 1984, 94p. – 0 86264 065 2
illustrated by Tony Ross

An intriguing title for an unusual story. Angus wins a prize for his picture of a shrieking face, but the attendant publicity is not to his liking.
Age range: 8–10

THE SPECKLED PANIC

Beaver Books, 1985, 78p. – Pbk. – 0 09 935490 X
Andersen Press, 1982, 76p. – 0 86264 031 8

In the same series:

THE CHOKING PERIL

Beaver Books, 1987, 80p. – Pbk. –
0 09 950530 4
Andersen Press, 1985, 72p. – 0 86264 093 8
illustrated by David McKee

Both books feature Kip and Herbie and are fast and funny. The first involves their headmaster and some toothpaste, while the second addresses the problem of litter.
Age range: 8–10

VICTOR'S PARTY

Red Fox, 1991, 96p. – Pbk. – 0 09 973390 0
Andersen Press, 1990, 80p. – 0 86264 276 0
illustrated by Tony Ross

Victor hates parties, especially his own. First, not enough guests, then too many. One escapade swiftly follows another in this extremely funny book.
Age range: 8–10

U

URE, Jean

Also writes as Sarah McCulloch. British. Born Caterham, Surrey, 1943. Educated Croydon High School, Surrey; Webber-Douglas Academy of Dramatic Art. Married Leonard Gregory, 1967. Full-time writer.

Awards: Lancashire County Library Children's Book of the Year Award: *Plague 99*, 1990

Address: 88 Southbridge Road, Croydon, Surrey CR0 1AF, England

Agent: Maggie Noach Agency, 21 Redan Street, London W14 0AB, England

An excellent, sympathetic writer, often writing for teenagers, but equally successful for younger readers.

A BOTTLED CHERRY ANGEL
Beaver Books, 1987. – Pbk. – 0 09 951370 6
Hutchinson, 1986, 144p. – 0 09 165280 4

A story for the 'in-betweens'. It concerns three friends of the same age but with different priorities in life. Two of them have begun to go to discos and to shop for clothes. The third, Midge, still enjoys playing with her dolls, and, above all, she hates boys. One day, out sledging by herself, she feels left out and lonely. She meets a boy, who, to her surprise, feels just as she does. Slowly, they both begin to change.
Age range: 11–13

COOL SIMON
Orchard Books, 1990, 192p. – 1 85213 186 1
Orchard Books, 1990, 192p. – Pbk. –
1 85213 213 2

Simon is deaf, and therefore speaks with an impediment. When he moves to a new school where the children are not used to him, they find they cannot easily understand what he is saying, and will not make any effort. Only Sam tries, and that is because she is full of tricks, and the other children in the class don't want her as a friend. A good read.
Age range: 9–11

FRANKIE'S DAD
Beaver Books, 1989, 144p. – Pbk. –
0 09 959720 9
Hutchinson, 1988, 144p. – 0 09 173491 6

Frankie hates Billie Small, and is horrified to learn that her mother has agreed to marry him. Life becomes intolerable, for he is violent, and Jasper is too pathetic for words, so Frankie is on her own.
Age range: 11–13

THE FRIGHT
Orchard Books, 1987, 64p. – 1 85213 087 3

In the same series:

WHO'S TALKING
Orchard Books, 1987, 64p. – 1 85213 088 1
illustrated by Beverly Lees

Two well illustrated stories for younger children. They are fairly short and very attractive, but still require a degree of reading ability.
Age range: 7–9

HI THERE, SUPERMOUSE
Windrush, 1989, 150p. – L/P. – 1 85089 954 1
Penguin, 1985, 128p. – Pbk. – 0 14 031716 3
Hutchinson, 1983, 124p. – 0 09 152090 8
illustrated by Martin White

Sibling rivalry is the subject of this amusing story of family life. Rose is the talented one, who is expected to go far in the world of show business. Nicola, tall and gangly, has always rather resentfully taken a back seat, until the accident gives her a chance to shine.
Age range: 9–11

MEGASTAR
Hippo Books, 1986, 128p. – Pbk. – 0 590 70529 6
Blackie, 1985, 112p. – O/P. – 0 216 91700 X

Jason wants to be an actor, but his command of standard English leaves much to be desired. When the Community Arts Festival decides to make a local video, he seizes the chance to be in it, hoping it will lead to other opportunities.
Age range: 10–12

TEA-LEAF ON THE ROOF
Windrush, 1989, 158p. – L/P. – 1 85089 965 7
Blackie, 1987, 112p. – 0 216 92112 0
illustrated by Val Sassoon

William is sure he can track down the burglar who is stealing lead from the roofs of houses in his street. It proves less easy than he expected.
Age range: 9–11

WAR WITH OLD MOULDY
Methuen, 1987, 128p. – 0 416 00262 5
illustrated by Alice Englander

Jody leads the campaign to rid the school of Old Mouldy. The battle commences, with hilarious results.
Age range: 9–11

THE YOU TWO
Beaver Books, 1985, 176p. – Pbk. – 0 09 93810 1
Hutchinson, 1984, 150p. – 0 09 154810 1

Elizabeth cannot face having to attend Gladeside Comprehensive, which is huge, noisy and full of rude children making fun of her posh 'Lady Margaret' accent. Meeting Paddy and becoming inseparable friends (hence the 'You two'), makes life a lot better for a while. Sensitive and realistic character portrayal.
Age range: 10–12

W

WADDELL, Martin

Also writes as Catherine Sefton. Irish.
Born Belfast, Northern Ireland, 1941.
Married Rosaleen Canagher, 1969, three
sons.

Awards: Arts Council of Northern
Ireland Bursaries: 1971, 1974,
1981
Children's Rights Workshop
Other Award (as Catherine
Sefton): *Starry Night*, 1986
Smarties Prize: *Can't you
Sleep, Little Bear*, 1988
Emil/Kurt Maschler Award:
The Park in the Dark, 1989

Address: 139 Central Promenade,
Newcastle, County Down,
Northern Ireland

An able writer who appeals to a wide age
range. He has written fictional sports
stories for older readers, and many fine
picture books for the youngest.

FRED THE ANGEL
*Walker Books, 1990, 129p. – Pbk. –
0 7445 0832 0*
*Walker Books, 1989, 112p. – O/P. –
0 7445 0823 1*
illustrated by Patrick Benson

Five stories about an angel who is in the
process of learning his job, and who
encounters many problems. Amusing
and very easy to read.
Age range: 7–9

HARRIET AND THE CROCODILES
Blackie, 1986, 80p. – O/P. – 0 216 91886 3
*Abelard–Schuman, 1982, 80p. – O/P. –
0 200 72780 X*

In the same series:

HARRIET AND THE FLYING
TEACHERS
*Hippo Books, 1990, 156p. – Pbk. –
0 590 76345 8*
Blackie, 1987, 80p. – O/P. – 0 216 92239 9

HARRIET AND THE HAUNTED
SCHOOL
Blackie, 1988, 68p. – 0 216 92408 1
*Hippo Books, 1985, 78p. – Pbk. –
0 590 70441 9*

HARRIET AND THE ROBOT
*Hippo Books, 1988, 96p. – Pbk. –
0 590 70939 9*
Blackie, 1985, 80p. – O/P. – 0 216 91806 5
all illustrated by Mark Burgess

A series of amusing easy readers about a
little girl with a penchant for disaster.
Age range: 7–9

THE HOUSE UNDER THE STAIRS
Magnet Books, 1984, 96p. – Pbk. – 0 416 46170 0
Methuen, 1983, 96p. – O/P. – 0 416 25040 8
illustrated by Maggie Ling

This is an excellent book. Although fairly
short, it has a good story and endearing
characters, showing a deep
understanding of children and what
troubles them. The ending is marvellous.
Age range: 7–9

OWL AND BILLY
Methuen, 1986, 96p. – 0 416 54180 1

In the same series:

OWL AND BILLY AND THE SPACE
DAYS
Methuen, 1988, 96p. – O/P. – 0 416 07552 5
illustrated by Carolyn Dinan

Satisfying and amusing, these books are
excellent for reading aloud. They
describe incidents as seen through the
eyes of Billy and his companion, Owl.
Age range: 4–6

WALSH, Jill Paton
(Gillian Paton Walsh, née Bliss)

British. Born London, 1937. Educated St
Michael's Convent, London; St Anne's
College, Oxford, Dip.Ed., M.A. (Hons),
English. Married Anthony Edmund Paton
Walsh, 1961, one son, two daughters.
Teacher, co–founder (with John Rowe
Townsend) of Green Bay Publishers,
1986.

Awards: Whitbread Award: *The*
Emperor's Winding Sheet,
1974
Boston Globe–Horn Book
Award: *The Unleaving*, 1976
Arts Council Creative Writing
Fellowship, 1976
Smarties Prize: *Gaffer*
Samson's Luck, 1985

Address: 72 Water Lane, Histon,
Cambridge CB4 4LR,
England

A writer of exceptional quality who brings
history to life with her stories. Readers
undoubtedly require fluency to tackle
these stories which are linguistically rich,
with complex characters, but the plots are
riveting.

BABYLON
Beaver Books, 1988, 32p. – Pbk. – 0 09 938080 3
Deutsch, 1982, 32p. – O/P. – 0 233 97362 1
illustrated by Jennifer Northway

Beautifully illustrated, this story tells of
three children playing on an old railway
line. Many wise words are spoken in
between the poetical reminiscences.
Age range: 6–8

BIRDY AND THE GHOSTIE
Macdonald, 1989, 48p. – 0 356 16779 8
illustrated by Alan Marks

An unusual short story, well illustrated
with large print, making it a most
attractive book. Birdy learns that second
sight is a curse, not a blessing, but it
serves her well when the 'ghosties' arrive.
Age range: 7–9

THE BUTTY BOY
Penguin, 1986, 128p. – Pbk. – 0 14 031962 X
Macmillan, 1975, 128p. – O/P. – 0 333 18567 6
illustrated by Juliette Palmer

A wonderfully descriptive novel about life
on a narrow boat. Harriet, hating her new
home, glimpses a boat and investigates.
She is intrigued to discover children
managing the narrow boats and helps
them through the lock. She decides she
is too dirty to return home and stays on
the barge. It proves to be the most
exciting time of her life.
Age range: 9–11

THE CHANCE CHILD
Chivers Press, 1988, 232p. – L/P. – 0 7451 0659 5
Penguin, 1985, 160p. – Pbk. – 0 14 031816 X
Macmillan, 1978, 160p. – O/P. – 0 333 23833 8

Totally compelling, this book has many
facets. The beginning is quite gripping,
describing a poor ill-treated scrap of
humanity who emerges from a cardboard
box. There is a taut air of mystery as
Christopher, trying to find Creep, sees his
name carved in stone on a bridge, but it
is covered by the moss of many years. It
focuses on the horror of working
conditions in the mills, particularly for
children. Not a book for the faint-hearted,
but a moving interpretation of a bygone
age.
Age range: 12–14

THE DAWNSTONE
Pan Books, 1979, 96p. – Pbk, O/P. –
0 330 25735 8
Hamish Hamilton, 1973, 86p. – O/P. –
0 241 02397 1
illustrated by Mary Dinsdale

Easy to read with an intriguing story.
Adam finds a stone which he feels sure
belongs to the Stone Age. He sleeps with
it under his pillow and has frightening
dreams. Eventually it finds its true place
when he takes it to the zoo.
Age range: 7–9

THE DOLPHIN CROSSING
Penguin, 1970. – Pbk. – 0 14 030457 6
Macmillan, 1967, 144p. – O/P. – 0 333 09096 9

In spite of their differences, Pat and John become friends. John is an evacuee from London and finds life difficult. When news of Dunkirk is received, the two boys respond promptly in spite of the danger.
Age range: 11–13

FIREWEED
Penguin, 1972, 128p. – Pbk. – 0 14 030560 2
Macmillan, 1969, 144p. – O/P. – 0 333 10618 0

The setting is London during the blitz. Two young adolescents are hiding from officials because they want to stay in London. At first they enjoy the cat and mouse games, but as the relentless bombing continues they find the effort of surviving too much. Full of atmosphere, it sensitively portrays the youngsters and their friendship.
Age range: 12–15

GAFFER SAMSON'S LUCK
Penguin, 1987, 112p. – Pbk. – 0 14 031765 1
Chivers Press, 1987, 160p. – L/P. – 0 7451 0451 7
Viking Kestrel, 1985, 112p. – 0 670 80122 4

James doesn't like the flatness of the Fens; he is not happy at school, but he does like Gaffer Samson. He sees no harm in helping him find his good luck charm, but the school gang have other ideas. Excellent characterization, and a memorable story.
Age range: 11–13

GOLDENGROVE
Red Fox, 1990, 124p. – Pbk. – 0 09 975210 7
Bodley Head, 1985, 126p. – O/P. –
0 370 30630 9

Madge and Paul meet up every summer in spite of their parents' disapproval. This summer is somehow different. They are not quite at ease together, and Goldengrove also seems different. Growing up can be hard.
Age range: 12–14

THE GREEN BOOK
Macmillan, 1981, 128p. – O/P. – 0 333 31910 9
illustrated by Joanna Stubbs

Leaving doomed Earth forever seems exciting to the children who do not fully understand the implications. The journey is long, and the new planet needs exploring. With so much to do, it takes time to realize how badly they chose which books to take along. Only the children seem to realize the importance of stories.
Age range: 8–10

A PARCEL OF PATTERNS
Chivers Press, 1989, 264p. – L/P. – 0 7451 0926 8
Penguin, 1988. – Pbk. – 0 14 032627 8
Viking Kestrel, 1986, 144p. – 0 670 80861 X

Set in Eyam in Derbyshire at the time of the plague, this novel is quite compelling. The horror of the plague is well described, as is the courage of the villagers who decide they must contain the disease. There is the added dimension of the love between Emmot and Roland and the way the plague affects them.
Age range: 12–15

WESTALL, Robert (Atkinson)

British. Born Tynemouth, 1929.
Educated Tynemouth High School;
Durham University, B.A. (Hons), Fine Art;
Slade School, University of London,
D.F.A. Royal Corps of Signals, 1953–55.
Married Jean Underhill, 1958, one son
(deceased). Art master, antiques dealer,
art critic, writer.

Awards: Library Association Carnegie
Medal: *The Machine Gunners*,
1975
Library Association Carnegie
Medal: *The Scarecrows*, 1981

Address: 2 Dyar Terrace, Winnington,
Northwich, Cheshire CW8
4DN, England

A writer of enormously powerful stories
which are capable of stirring deep
feelings and, at times, a genuine sense of
dread. Many of his books are set during
the Second World War, bringing alive this
important period for a new generation of
children. His strength lies in the realism of
his characters and settings.

BLITZCAT

Pan Books, 1990, 240p. – Pbk. – 0 330 31040 2
Chivers Press, 1990, 352p. – L/P. – 0 7451 1177 7
Macmillan, 1990, 240p. – Pbk. – 0 333 47499 6
Macmillan, 1989, 240p. – O/P. – 0 333 47498 8

A haunting, heart-warming story of a cat
which survives an air-raid in Coventry,
and is determined not to rest until she is
united with the man she adores. It is a
hazardous journey of pain and fear, so
that the reader is almost afraid to reach
the end. Robert Westall gives no
guarantees of a happy ending.
Age range: 11–14

THE CREATURE IN THE DARK

Methuen, 1990, 176p. – 0 416 15662 2
Blackie, 1989, 112p. – 0 216 92760 9
Blackie, 1988, 144p. – 0 216 92472 8

An easy to read mystery, beginning with
a sheep being worried, then lambs
missing, then calves! It is impossible for a
dog to be responsible, but neither

Sammy nor his father can guess what sort
of creature it can be. An exciting, well
constructed story with a satisfying ending.
Age range: 9–11

THE KINGDOM BY THE SEA

Methuen, 1990, 176p. – 0 416 15662 2

The story of Harry, and how he copes
with the loss of his family in an air-raid
during the Second World War, makes
stirring reading. His journey along the
Tyneside coast, accompanied by a stray
dog he befriends equates with his journey
to independence. It is moving, exciting,
and utterly absorbing.
Age range: 11–13

OLD MAN ON A HORSE

Hippo Books, 1989, 196p. – Pbk. – 0 590 76082 3

Tobias is brought up by peace-loving
parents who have opted out of society
and joined a hippy following. Life is
suddenly turned upside-down when the
police arrest his father. Finding a statue of
a man on a horse causes a time-slip to the
time of Charles II, which helps to resolve
the problems faced by Tobias and his
family. Rather easier to read than many
of Westall's novels, it is an unusual and
accessible read for younger children.
Age range: 10–12

THE SCARECROWS

Penguin, 1989, 176p. – Pbk. – 0 14 032731 2
Windrush, 1989, 283p. – L/P. – 1 85089 973 8
Bodley Head, 1984, 160p. – O/P. –
0 370 30844 1

Being able to empathize with young boys
and their interests and fears is one of
Robert Westall's strong points. In this
novel he has created a memorable
character in Simon, who feels at odds
with his step-father, and therefore with
his mother too. Gradually, and chillingly,
the emphasis changes from his feelings of
self-pity to the fear that grows in him
when the scarecrows appear. A gripping
story in which many readers may learn

something about themselves, as well as enjoying the plot.
Age range: 11–13

A WALK ON THE WILD SIDE
Methuen, 1989, 128p. – 0 416 13592 7

Seven completely different stories about a variety of cats. The animal world is often violent and cruel, and there is no attempt to soften the reality in these stories, some of which are quite scary.
Age range: 12–14

WILDE, Nicholas

British. Born Cheltenham. Educated Cheltenham; King's College, Cambridge. Teacher.

A relative newcomer to children's fiction writing, this author is proving himself to be a first-rate mystery writer with an extraordinary ability to create a feeling of tension within a good, strong storyline. It is unusual to find an author whose next book is awaited with such anticipation.

DEATH KNELL
Collins, 1990, 224p. – 0 00 107217 X

An atmospheric mystery which Tim and Jamie are determined to solve. They cannot decide how much relevance the legend of the crypt has to the body found in the locked crypt. As the sense of danger mounts, they begin to wish they had kept out of it. The final solution is ingenious and plausible.
Age range: 12–14

INTO THE DARK
Collins, 1989, 176p. – Pbk. – 0 00 673517 7
Collins, 1987, 160p. – 0 00 184426 1

Matthew is excited at the prospect of a proper holiday for the first time. Set in Norfolk, the site of many holidays for the author, there is a strong feeling of mystery which is maintained to the end. A superb story which the reader is sorry to finish.
Age range: 11–13

WILDER, Laura
(Elizabeth Ingalls)

American. Born Pepin, Wisconsin, 1867 (died 10 February 1957). Educated Walnut Grove, Minnesota; Burn Oak, Iowa; De Smet, Dakota Territory. Married Almanzo James Wilder, 1885 (died 1949), one daughter. Schoolteacher, columnist, writer.

Awards: American Library Association Laura Ingalls Wilder Award, 1954

Fictional autobiographical books usually have little appeal for children, but this series is an exception. Based on her childhood memories as a member of a pioneering family, the books have such an authentic tone that they are all the more memorable. They are, of course, old-fashioned, but they radiate a gentle family happiness which contrasts with the isolated, vulnerable position of the house.

LITTLE HOUSE IN THE BIG WOODS
Windrush, 1987, 167p. – L/P. – 1 85089 913 4
Methuen, 1970, 220p. – 0 416 07130 9
Penguin, 1969, 144p. – Pbk. – 0 14 030194 1

In the same series:

LITTLE HOUSE ON THE PRAIRIE
Windrush, 1986, 252p. – L/P. – 1 85089 900 2
Methuen, 1970, 220p. – 0 416 07140 6
Penguin, 1969, 224p. – Pbk. – 0 14 030204 2

ON THE BANKS OF PLUM CREEK
Windrush, 1988, 276p. – L/P. – 1 85089 941 X
Methuen, 1970, 220p. – 0 416 07150 3
Penguin, 1969, 224p. – Pbk. – 0 14 030228 X

BY THE SHORES OF SILVER LAKE
Windrush, 1990, 272p. – L/P. – 1 85089 994 0
Penguin, 1969, 224p. – Pbk. – 0 14 030303 0
Lutterworth Press, 1961, 304p. –
0 7188 0128 8

THE LONG WINTER
Penguin, 1968, 256p. – Pbk. – 0 14 030381 2
Lutterworth Press, 1962, 352p. –
0 7188 0520 8

LITTLE TOWN ON THE PRAIRIE
Penguin, 1969, 224p. – Pbk. – 0 14 030417 7
Lutterworth Press, 1963, 320p. –
0 7188 0519 4

THESE HAPPY GOLDEN YEARS
Penguin, 1970, 240p. – Pbk. – 0 14 030461 4
Lutterworth Press, 1964, 304p. –
0 7188 0918 1
Age range: 10–12

WILSON, David Henry

British. Born London, 1937. Educated Pembroke College, Cambridge, B.A., M.A. (Cantab.). Married Elizabeth Ayo Amaworo, 1965, two sons, one daughter. University lecturer.

Address: 3 Beech Close, Hope
          Corner Lane, Taunton,
          Somerset TA2 7NZ,
          England

Light, easy books to tempt the reluctant reader to try to tackle full length novels.

BESIDE THE SEA WITH JEREMY JAMES
Pan Books, 1985, 96p. – Pbk. – 0 330 28695 1
Chatto, 1980, 96p. – O/P. – 0 7011 2537 3

In the same series:

DO GOLDFISH PLAY THE VIOLIN?: ADVENTURES WITH JEREMY JAMES
Pan Books, 1987, 128p. – Pbk. –
0 330 29594 2
Dent, 1985, 128p. – O/P. – 0 460 06220 4

ELEPHANTS DON'T SIT ON CARS
Pan Books, 1980, 96p. – Pbk. – 0 330 26005 7
Chatto, 1977, 96p. – O/P. – 0 7011 2273 0

GETTING RICH WITH JEREMY JAMES
Pan Books, 1984, 112p. – Pbk. –
0 330 28383 9
Chatto, 1979, 112p. – O/P. – 0 7011 2441 5

HOW TO STOP A TRAIN WITH ONE FINGER: ADVENTURES WITH JEREMY JAMES
Pan Books, 1985, 112p. – Pbk. –
0 330 28978 0
Dent, 1984, 112p. – 0 460 06150 X
all illustrated by Patricia Drew

A series of amusing stories about a small boy who seems to attract trouble like a magnet. Good for reading aloud.
Age range: 6–9

SUPERDOG
Hodder, 1984, 88p. – O/P. – 0 340 34905 0
Grafton Books, 1987, 96p. – Pbk, O/P. –
0 583 30961 5

In the same series:

SUPERDOG IN TROUBLE
Hodder, 1988, 80p. – 0 340 43061 3

SUPERDOG THE HERO
Grafton Books, 1987, 96p. – Pbk, O/P. –
0 583 30962 3
Hodder, 1986, 96p. – O/P. – 0 340 38872 2
both illustrated by Linda Birch

Woofer belongs to the Brown family. He believes he is very special and proves it by such escapades as falling into the toilet. Very amusing.
Age range: 8–10

THERE'S A WOLF IN MY PUDDING: TWELVE TWISTED, TORTURED, GRIM AND GRUESOME TALL AND TERRIBLE TALES
Pan Books, 1988, 128p. – Pbk. – 0 330 29900 X
Dent, 1986, 128p. – O/P. – 0 460 06240 9

In the same series:

YUCKY DUCKY
Pan Books, 1990, 128p. – Pbk. –
0 330 31044 5
Dent, 1988, 128p. – 0 460 07025 8
both illustrated by Jonathan Allen

Well known stories related with slight differences. Lots of fun.
Age range: 10–12

WRIGHTSON, (Alice) Patricia (née Furlonger)

Australian. Born Lismore, New South Wales, 1921. Educated Correspondence School; St Catherine's College, Stanthorpe, Queensland. Married 1943 (divorced 1953), one daughter, one son. Secretary, editor, writer.

Awards: Australian Children's Book Council Book of the Year Award: *Crooked Snake*, 1956
I.B.B.Y. Honour Award: *I Own the Racecourse*, 1970
Australian Children's Book Council Book of the Year Award: *The Nargun and the Stars*, 1974
I.B.B.Y. Honour Award: *The Nargun and the Stars*, 1976
Australian Children's Book Council Book of the Year Award: *The Ice is Coming*, 1978
Order of the British Empire, 1978
Australian Children's Book Council Book of the Year Award: *A Little Fear*, 1984
Boston Globe–Horn Award: *A Little Fear*, 1984
Dromkeen Children's Literature Foundation Medal, 1986
Hans Christian Andersen Award, 1986

Address: Box 91, Maclean, New South Wales 2463, Australia

An excellent story-teller whose books appeal to the older and more competent reader. A student of Aboriginal mythology, she bases many of her books around its themes.

THE ICE IS COMING
Penguin, 1983, 224p. – Pbk, O/P. –
0 14 031628 0
Hutchinson, 1977, 223p. – 0 09 129150 X

In the same series:

THE DARK BRIGHT WATER
Penguin, 1983, 224p. – Pbk, O/P. –
0 14 031630 2
Hutchinson, 1979, 224p. – O/P. –
0 09 136180 X

BEHIND THE WIND
Penguin, 1983, 168p. – Pbk, O/P. –
0 14 031629 9
Hutchinson, 1981, 158p. – O/P. –
0 09 144620 1

A powerful trilogy centred round Wirrun, an Aboriginal boy, who is struggling to live in modern society, but is unable to turn his back on the ancient knowledge and wisdom. This awareness causes him to interpret events differently. Rather difficult, but rewarding.
Age range: 12–14

A LITTLE FEAR
Penguin, 1985, 112p. – Pbk, O/P. –
0 14 031847 X
Hutchinson, 1983. – O/P. – 0 09 152710 4

A difficult book to classify, for it can be read and enjoyed by both children and adults. Mrs Tucker escapes from the old peoples' home and takes up residence in a lonely cottage with her dog. She finds, however, there is another resident, an evil one, who is trying to drive her out. She vigorously resists. Highly original, more than a little tense, and thoroughly enjoyable.
Age range: 12–adult

CLASSICS

◆

This section has been included because of a firm belief that children's classics are an important part of the heritage bequeathed to children, and one which should be preserved. At a time when reading standards have apparently dropped to a record low, and recognizing that such books are by no means easy to read, it is imperative that attractive editions continue to be made available. Too many editions are dull and difficult. Books have so much competition for children's attention, and to stand a chance of winning must be of a high standard. The titles listed here are all very attractive editions which it is a pleasure to handle. Obviously such books are expensive, ranging in price up to £12, but they guarantee lasting pleasure. This is not a comprehensive list as it includes only books which were available on bookshop shelves at the time of going to press. There may well be many other similar titles.

AESOP

AESOP'S FABLES

Pavilion Books, 1990, 95p. – 1 85145 567 1

Compiled by Russell Ash and Bernard Higton, this version includes a variety of illustrations chosen from editions published during the last 150 years. It is a unique collection, including notes on the tales and their illustrators. A delightful book for children, but also a useful and pleasurable book for adult collectors.

ANDERSEN, Hans Christian

THUMBELINA

Macmillan, 1990, 32p. – Pbk. – 0 333 54184 7

THE WILD SWANS

Macmillan, 1989, 40p. – Pbk. – 0 333 49223 4
both illustrated by Susan Jeffers

Retold by Amy Ehrlich to make them suitable for reading to young children. Beautifully illustrated, with the illustrations occupying the major part of the books.

FAIRY TALES

New Orchard Editions, 1990, 256p. –
1 85079 144 9
illustrated by Margaret Tarrant

Black-and-white and coloured full-page illustrations by an Edwardian illustrator. Large print.

ARDIZZONE'S HANS ANDERSEN: FOURTEEN CLASSIC TALES

Deutsch, 1989, 196p. – 0 233 98372 4
selected and illustrated by Edward Ardizzone;
translated from the original by Stephen Corrin

Small black-and-white plus full-page coloured line-drawings in pastel shades.

FAVOURITE HANS CHRISTIAN ANDERSEN FAIRY TALES

Methuen, 1981, 168p. – 0 416 22080 0
illustrated by Michael Hague

Beautiful large clear print on good paper. Nine stories with full-page paintings. Some are vibrant with colour, others pastel, depending on the tone of the story.

HANS ANDERSEN: HIS CLASSIC FAIRY TALES

Gollancz, 1985, 192p. – 0 575 03558 7
illustrated by Michael Foreman

A book to treasure. Eighteen stories, translated by Eric Haugaard, each introduced by an attractive illustration. Black-and-white illustrations are interspersed throughout, and there are 21 full-page colour plates of differing styles, matched perfectly to the individual story.

BARRIE, Sir James M.

THE STORY OF PETER PAN

Bell & Hyman, 1982, 128p. – O/P. –
0 7135 1351 9
illustrated by Alice B. Woodward; retold from the
play by Daniel O'Connor

Large print with a small amount of text on each page. Lots of full-page colour illustrations which complement the text perfectly.

PETER PAN AND WENDY

Hodder, 1986, 127p.
illustrated by Shirley Hughes

May Byron produced this rather shorter version which Barrie did not object to. Shirley Hughes's black-and-white illustrations are perfectly attuned to the text.

PETER PAN AND WENDY

Hodder, 1989, 123p.
illustrated by Mabel Lucie Attwell

The same re-telling by May Byron with the original Attwell illustrations which many adults will remember from their childhood, and which they may prefer to more modern editions. The large print makes it attractive to younger children.

PETER PAN

Viking Kestrel, 1988, 206p. – 0 670 80862 8
illustrated by Jan Ormerod

The complete text, beautifully enhanced by black-and-white and coloured illustrations.

PETER PAN

Methuen, 1988, 144p. – 0 416 09392 2
illustrated by Michael Hague

Distinctive illustrations in a glorious combination of colours.

PETER PAN AND WENDY

Pavilion Books, 1989, 160p. – 1 85145 449 7
illustrated by Michael Foreman

Imaginative, colourful illustrations, with attractive decorations at the beginning and the end of chapters.

PETER PAN

Random House, 1989, 72p. – 0 394 89226 7

A set consisting of a hardback book edited by Josette Frank, illustrated in colour by Diane Goode, and with a cassette by Lyn Redgrave.

BURNETT, Frances Hodgson

THE SECRET GARDEN

Michael Joseph, 1986, 224p. – O/P. –
0 7181 2664 5

A LITTLE PRINCESS

Michael Joseph, 1989, 129p. – 0 7181 3317 X
both illustrated by Graham Rust

Both contain a variety of illustrations – coloured, sepia, and little snippets of decoration, all interspersed with the text. The period detail is excellent, with clear print and good page design.

THE SECRET GARDEN

Gollancz, 1988, 256p. – 0 575 04168 4
illustrated by Shirley Hughes

Both black-and-white and 16 full-page colour plates in typical Shirley Hughes style make this a very attractive book. The period detail is excellent.

THE SECRET GARDEN

Heinemann, 1990, 314p. – 0 434 93088 1
illustrated by Charles Robinson

A facsimile edition of the original, published in 1911. Excellent illustrations.

CARROLL, Lewis

ALICE'S ADVENTURES IN WONDERLAND

J. MacRae Books, 1988, 128p. – O/P. –
0 86203 324 1
illustrated by Anthony Browne

All the illustrations are coloured, with striking combinations. Typically distinctive.

ALICE IN WONDERLAND

New Orchard, 1990, 256p. – 1 85079 148 1
illustrated by Margaret Tarrant

Full-page coloured illustrations by an Edwardian illustrator. Large print.

ALICE'S ADVENTURES IN WONDERLAND

Dragon's World, 1990, 96p. – 1 85028 105 X

ALICE THROUGH THE LOOKING GLASS

Dragon's World, 1989, 124p. – 1 85028 073 8
both illustrated by Malcolm Ashman

Both books have excellent page design and the illustrations are superb, mainly full-page colour with some small insets. A distinctive and personal interpretation.

ALICE'S ADVENTURES IN WONDERLAND

Gollancz, 1988, 160p. – Pbk. – 0 575 04332 6

THROUGH THE LOOKING GLASS

Gollancz, 1986, 176p. – 0 575 03756 3
both illustrated by Justin Todd

Vivid, memorable pictures, verging on the surreal, and a perfect complement to the stories. Clear print, and good spacing and layout.

ALICE'S ADVENTURES IN WONDERLAND

Hutchinson, 1989, 224p. – 0 09 173764 8
illustrated by Peter Weevers

Beautifully drawn illustrations on every page, some full-page, some smaller. Paintings of Alice were done from life, with the illustrator's daughter sitting for him. Excellent quality paper and clear print.

COLLODI, Carlo

PINOCCHIO

OUP, 1988, 96p. – 0 19 279855 3
illustrated by Victor G. Ambrus

A completely new version, re-told by James Riordan from the original Italian story. Lots of excellent illustrations in both black-and-white and colour.

DICKENS, Charles

A CHRISTMAS CAROL

Cape, 1990, 152p. – 0 224 02900 2
illustrated by Roberto Innocenti

Full-page paintings in glorious colour, good period detail, clear print, beautiful paper and excellent page layout. Total excellence.

A CHRISTMAS CAROL

Gollancz, 1989, 128p. – Pbk. – 0 575 04956 5
illustrated by Michael Foreman

Black-and-white drawings interspersed through the text, plus full-colour plates.

A CHRISTMAS CAROL IN PROSE

Guild Publishing, 1990. – 0 434 934090 9
illustrated by Liz Summers

Also contains *The Story of the Goblins who Stole a Sexton*

Lots of bright, cheerful illustrations, with some black-and-white. The whole book has child appeal as the illustrations have an immediacy which is absent from the more formal illustrations in other editions.

GRAHAME, Kenneth

THE WIND IN THE WILLOWS

Methuen, 1980, 216p. – 0 416 20629 4
illustrated by Cosgrove Hall

Colourful illustrations on decorated pages.

THE WIND IN THE WILLOWS

Gollancz, 1988, 192p. – 0 575 03892 6
illustrated by Justin Todd

A talented artist brings his personal interpretation of the story to the full-page colour paintings. Good quality paper and clear print.

THE WIND IN THE WILLOWS

Methuen, 1951, 178p. – 0 416 53260 8
illustrated by Arthur Rackham

First published in 1939 in America, it is constantly reprinted so that consecutive generations can enjoy Rackham's illustrations.

THE WIND IN THE WILLOWS

Methuen, 1971, 284p. – 0 416 16980 5
illustrated by E. H. Shephard

THE WIND IN THE WILLOWS

Penguin, 1980, 240p. – Pbk. – 0 14 031544 6
illustrated by John Burningham

Although all the illustrations are black and white, there are over 60 humorous sketches which enhance the charm of the story.

GRIMM, Jacob and Wilhelm

FAVOURITE FAIRY TALES FROM GRIMM

Four Winds Press, 1982, 224p. – 0 590 07791 0
illustrated by Mercer Meyer

All the well known stories strikingly and fittingly illustrated in a highly individual style. Good quality paper and clear print with little silhouette decorations interspersed.

POPULAR FOLK TALES

Gollancz, 1990, 192p. – Pbk. – 0 575 04030 0
illustrated by Michael Foreman

Thirty-one stories translated from the German by Brian Alderson, and superbly illustrated with 25 full-colour plates, both humorous and atmospheric, and supported by black-and-white sketches interspersed throughout.

HARRIS, Joel Chandler

THE TALES OF UNCLE REMUS

Bodley Head, 1987, 176p. – 0 370 31089 6
illustrated by Jerry Pinkney

The adventures of Brer Rabbit as told to Julius Lester, illustrated by an award-winning artist. These 48 American folk tales are made accessible to modern children by updating the language without losing the point.

KINGSLEY, Charles

THE WATER BABIES

New Orchard Editions, 1990, 256p. –
1 85079 146 5
illustrated by Harry G. Theaker

Full-page colour illustrations with some black and white, by an Edwardian illustrator. Large print.

THE WATER BABIES

Dragon's World, 1981, 144p. – 0 905895 50 9
illustrated by Susan Rowe

Both black-and-white and water-colour paintings.

THE WATER BABIES

Gollancz, 1986, 224p. – Pbk. – 0 575 03879 9
illustrated by Harold Jones

Attractively illustrated and designed with a variety of illustrations, some small, some L-shaped, and some full-page. The print is very clear.

KIPLING, Rudyard

TALES OF MOWGLI

Heinemann, 1990, 192p. – 0 434 94641 9
illustrated by Patricia McCarthy

Both black-and-white and coloured illustrations in a very distinctive style which resembles batik.

THE JUST SO STORIES

Michael Joseph, 1989, 96p. – Pbk. –
1 85145 454 3
illustrated by Safaya Salter

Beautiful evocative illustrations.

LEWIS, C. S.

THE CHRONICLES OF NARNIA

in reading order:

THE MAGICIAN'S NEPHEW

Windrush, 1986, 198p. – L/P. – 1 85089 094 3

THE LION, THE WITCH AND THE WARDROBE

Windrush, 1986, 177p. – L/P. – 1 85089 084 6

A HORSE AND HIS BOY

Windrush, 1986, 208p. – L/P. – 1 85089 098 6

PRINCE CASPIAN

Windrush, 1986, 209p. – L/P. – 1 85089 099 4

THE VOYAGE OF THE 'DAWN TREADER'

Windrush, 1986, 237p. – L/P. – 1 85089 103 6

THE SILVER CHAIR

Windrush, 1986, 225p. – L/P. – 1 85089 104 4

THE LAST BATTLE

Windrush, 1986, 197p. – L/P. – 1 85089 108 7
all illustrated by Pauline Baynes

Designated as a 'Handi-read', it has large, very clear print, intended for partially-sighted readers, but equally good for children who are put off by small print. Also available as a boxed set.

MASEFIELD, John

THE BOX OF DELIGHTS

Heinemann, 1984, 168p. – 0 434 095952 1
illustrated by Faith Jacques

Abridged by Patricia Crampton, as this is a particularly difficult book for children to read, but she succeeds in preserving the essence of the book. Black-and-white illustrations interspersed with the text, with several full-page colour plates, beautifully painted.

MILNE, A. A.

THE HOUSE AT POOH CORNER

Methuen, 1928, 178p. – 0 416 34180 2
Mammoth, 1989, 176p. – Pbk. – 0 7497 0116 1

WINNIE THE POOH

Methuen, 1928, 158p. – 0 416 39380 2
Mammoth, 1989, 192p. – Pbk. – 0 7497 0210 9
both illustrated by E. H. Shephard

These books are both available in the same edition as originally published. The illustrations are an integral part of the book.

NESBIT, E.

THE RAILWAY CHILDREN

Heinemann, 1989, 188p. – 0 434 95456 X
illustrated by Pamela Kay

A mixture of black-and-white interspersed with the text, and full-colour plates. The pastel colours are very appealing, and there is good attention to period detail.

FIVE CHILDREN AND IT

BBC, 1990, 197p. – 0 563 36065 8
illustrated by John Holder

Excellent illustrations in pastel colours with good period detail. Ties in with the serialization shown on television.

FIVE CHILDREN AND IT

Heinemann, 1990, 192p. – 0 434 95458 6
illustrated by Larry Wilkes

These illustrations, based on research in Aylesford, Kent, where the story is set, capture all the sense of fun and atmosphere of E. Nesbit's story. A pleasing mixture of black-and-white and colour, small, large and full-page. A refreshing new look at an old favourite.

PERRAULT, Charles

CINDERELLA

Hamish Hamilton, 1986, 32p. – 0 241 11780 1
illustrated by Susan Jeffers

Retold by Amy Ehrlich, this is the story of Cinderella at its most basic, and best known. The pastel illustrations on every page, with some double-page spreads, make this a quality picture book.

POTTER, Beatrix

THE COMPLETE TALES OF BEATRIX POTTER

Warne, 1989, 384p. – 0 7232 3618 6
illustrated by the author

A beautiful book for Potter fanatics, containing 23 stories and poems, set out in chronological order with all the original illustrations, printed on good quality paper. There is a brief introduction linking the stories to places and events in the Lake District. Worth every pound!

SEWELL, Anna

BLACK BEAUTY

Gollancz, 1988, 224p. – 0 575 03924 8
illustrated by Charles Keeping

A mixture of black-and-white, half-colour and full-colour, some interspersed with the text, some full-page. Typical Keeping illustrations are a perfect match for this story.

BLACK BEAUTY

Macmillan, 1989, 72p. – Pbk. – 0 333 49334 6
illustrated by Susan Jeffers

Retold by Robin McKinley – an excellent adaptation, keeping as true as possible to the original. As always with the Papermac series, the illustrations are the major part, and are superb.

STEVENSON, Robert Louis

TREASURE ISLAND

Gollancz, 1990, 288p. – Pbk. – 0 575 04840 9
illustrated by N. C. Wyeth

Originally commissioned in 1911, 14

paintings were included. This edition was first published in hardback in 1982. The print is attractive and clear, but not large, and the paintings are striking. Recommended for older children.

TREASURE ISLAND

Heinemann, 1990, 204p. – 0 434 96508 1
illustrated by John Lawrence

An excellent colourful version with illustrations reminiscent of Edward Ardizzone. Clear print on good paper make it easy to read.

TOLKIEN, J. R. R.

THE HOBBIT

Unwin, 1987, 304p. – Pbk. – 0 04 823803
illustrated by Michael Hague

Highly unusual paintings in colours which reflect the atmosphere and mystery of this story.

THE HOBBIT

Windrush, 1990, 384p. – L/P. – 1 85089 805 7
illustrated by the author

This is a large print edition of the original version which will make it more accessible to children who struggle with small print.

WILDE, Oscar

THE FAIRY STORIES OF OSCAR WILDE

Gollancz, 1985, 224p. – Pbk. – 0 575 03614 1
illustrated by Harold Jones

Nine stories, including *The Happy Prince* and *The Selfish Giant*, with lots of black-and-white illustrations, either half or full-page, and very clear print.

CORRIN, Sara and Stephen

THE FABER BOOK OF FAVOURITE
FAIRY TALES

Faber, 1988, 256p. – 0 571 14854 9
illustrated by Juan Wijngaard

Chosen by Sara and Stephen Corrin, the
26 wide-ranging fairy tales are published
in clear print on good paper. The pages
are decorated, and look most attractive.
The award-winning artist has painted 15
full–page pictures of excellent quality.

EHRLICH, Amy

THE WALKER BOOK OF FAIRY TALES

Walker Books, 1986, 208p. – O/P. –
0 7445 0339 6
illustrated by Diane Goode

Nineteen of the best known fairy tales,
adapted by Amy Ehrlich, and
marvellously illustrated on every page,
both black-and-white and full-colour.
Excellent paper and large, clear print. A
superb book.

FOREMAN, Michael

WORLD OF FAIRY TALES

Pavilion Books, 1990, 144p. – 1 85145 466 7
illustrated by the editor

Twenty-two stories from around the
world, some well known, others less so.
The illustrations use vibrant colour on
excellent quality paper. A book to savour,
and guaranteed to make children love
books for life.

FOSS, Michael

A FIRST TREASURY OF FAIRY TALES

M. O'Mara Books, 1989, 160p. – 0 948397 30 6
Macmillan Children's Books, 1988, 80p. – Pbk. –
0 333 48057 0

A SECOND TREASURY OF FAIRY
TALES

Macmillan Children's Books, 1988, 80p. – Pbk. –
0 333 48058 9

Edited by Michael Foss, with illustrations
by such classic illustrators as Arthur
Rackham and Leslie Brook. Good quality
paper, excellent page layout, and lots of
very varied illustrations. Some of the
stories have been slightly abbreviated for
easier accessibility for younger readers.

SERIES

◆

Publishing books in a series is one way of producing good quality material at an economical price. It is also helpful for readers who have found a book enjoyable to have a reliable means of recognizing similar material. Most publishers try to obtain highly regarded authors, first because good material is important at all levels, and second because it is hoped that children will recognize and read the same authors later.

Not all series maintain a consistently high standard. Every book should be examined critically. The entries in this section show for whom the series is primarily intended, followed by examples of the best titles.

ANTELOPE

Hamish Hamilton.

A long established series aimed at 7–9-year-olds, and designed to give young readers practice in order to achieve fluency. Recently given a face-lift with better covers and a new design, the formula remains the same: fairly short chapters, restricted vocabulary, and plenty of illustrations to back up the text, which is in large print. Many of the earlier titles have been re-issued in paperback in the **Young Puffin Story Book Series**

ALCOCK, V.
  The Thing in the Woods

BALL, B.
  Stone Age Magic

BOND, R.
  Night of the Leopard

CURRY, J.
  The Rainbow Trail

DHAMI, N.
  A Medal for Melina

ESCOTT, J.
  Cassie's Soap Opera
  Mystery Money
  Radio Detective
  Radio Reporters
  Radio Trap

GERAS, A.
  The Coronation Picnic
  Finding Annabel

JONES, D. W.
  The Four Grannies
  Chair Person

KING-SMITH, D.
  The Hodgeheg

KINGSLAND, R.
  Harvey's Ark

LAVELLE, S.
  The Strawberry-Jam Pony

McBRATNEY, S.
  The Missing Lollipop
  Zesty Goes Missing

MAYNE, W.
  Netta Next

MITCHELL, P.
  Dadijan's Carrot Halvah

NIMMO, J.
  The Red Secret

PINTO, J.
  The School Hobby Disaster

POWLING, C.
  Elf 61

STORR, C.
  The Spy Before Yesterday

BANANA

Heinemann

A very successful series best suited to 7–9-year-olds. An attractive small format, with colourful illustrations, covering a wide range of interests. They are fun to read, amusing, and not too difficult or long.

AIKEN, J.
  The Erlking's Daughter

COUNSEL, J.
  The Quest of the Golden Dragon

CROSSLEY-HOLLAND, K.
  Storm

FINE, A.
  Scaredy-Cat

HILL, D.
  How Jennifer (and Speckle) Saved the Earth

IMPEY, R.
  The Not-So-Clever Genie
  Who's a Clever Girl, Then?

KEMP, G.
  Crocodile Dog

KING-SMITH, D.
  Lightning Fred
  Yob

LAVELLE, S.
The Big Stick
The Disappearing Granny

LIVELY, P.
Debbie and the Little Devil

PILLING, A.
The Beast in the Basement
No Guns, No Oranges

POWLING, C.
The Phantom Car Wash
Ziggy and the Ice Ogre

URE, J.
Brenda the Bold

MOLLOY, A.
The Christmas Rocket

MORGAN, A.
Christabel

STINTON, J.
Boo to a Goose

WATKINS, P.
David and the Giant

WILLARD, B.
Smiley Tiger

ZOLA, M.
Moving

BLACKBIRD

J. MacRae

Short, interesting novels for the 7–9-year-olds. Divided into easy chapters, with bold print and lots of illustrations, so that new readers will not feel daunted.

ASHLEY, B.
Dinner Ladies Don't Count
Linda's Lie

BOND, R.
Cricket for the Crocodile
Flames in the Forest
Getting Granny's Glasses
Ghost Trouble

CHAMBERS, N.
Stir-about

GARDAM, J.
Bridget and William
Horse

HARVEY, A.
A Present for Nellie

HENDRY, D.
A Camel called April
The Rainbow Watchers

HUDDY, D.
The Nearly Terrible Birthday
The Tale of the Crooked Crab

BLACKIE BEARS

Blackie

Aimed at 7–9-year-olds requiring reading practice. Very attractive and distinctive in bright yellow, but not, however, divided into chapters, which is a pity, for 50 pages is a lengthy read to manage all at once for children just becoming accustomed to a full-length book. Some titles are now available in the **Young Puffin Read Alone Series**

BULL, A.
Green Gloves

ESCOTT, J.
Wayne's Luck
Wayne's Wedding

HARDCASTLE, M.
James and the T.V. Star
The Magic Party

OLDFIELD, P.
Ginger's Nine Lives

PILLING, A.
The Friday Parcel
The Jungle Sale

POWLING, C.
Flyaway Frankie

WADDELL, M.
The Tall Story of Wilbur Small

215

CARTWHEELS

Hamish Hamilton

As children are learning to read, it is important that they find it fun, and feel successful. This series supplies material just right for that purpose, bridging the gap between picture books and full length story books. Bold type, colourful illustrations and stories of a consistently high standard ensure success.

ALLEN, L.
Meeko and Mirabel

BALL, B.
Look out, Duggy Dog!

BARRY, M. S.
Diz and the Big Fat Burglar

DINAN, C.
A Dog would be Better
Eager Beaver

FEIN, E.
Oscar and his Mouse

GERAS, A.
The Glittering River
Little Elephant's Moon

KING-SMITH, D.
Blessa
Dumpling

LAMBERT, T.
The Half-Term Rabbit

LAVELLE, S.
Fetch the Slipper
Harry's Aunt
Harry's Horse

PEYTON, K. M.
Plain Jack

SEFTON, C.
The Day the Smells went Wrong
Flying Sam
Ghost Ship

SUTCLIFF, R.
Little Hound Fox

CHEETAHS

Hodder & Stoughton

The publishers claim that this is 'a series of books characterised by strong storylines and high quality drawings.' Certainly, there is uniformity of appearance, which means the reader can be fairly sure of the length of the book (75 pages). Indeed, many of the books are well written, but each title must be judged on its own merit. Suitable for junior school children.

ALLEN, L.
Crash, Bang and Wallop
A Parrot in the House

ARKLE, P.
The Dinosaur Field

BOON, J.
High Street Witch at the Zoo

DEARSLEY, L.
The Royal Family Next Door

EADINGTON, J.
Jonny Briggs and the Secret Sunflowers
Jonny Briggs and the Silver Surprise

ESCOTT, J.
The Orange Revenge

KAYE, G.
A Dog called Dog

MANGAN, A.
Nan's Palace

MORSE, B.
Sauce for the Fox

PEARSON, M.
Donnabella

COMETS and CRACKERS

Black

Similar to **CHEETAHS**, these two companion series are uniform in length, with attractive covers, lots of illustrations, and clear print, all designed to encourage children aged between 7 and 9 to read. Some are much better than others.

COMETS

DEARY, T.
  The Dream Seller
  A Witch in Time

LEESON, R.
  Hey Robin
  The Reversible Giant
  Right Royal Kidnap

MORPURGO, M.
  Tom's Sausage Lion

PRICE, S.
  A Feasting of Trolls
  Master Tom Katt
  Odin's Monster

SOUTER, A.
  Scrapyard

STRONG, J.
  The Air Raid Shelter
  Dogs are Different
  Liar, Liar, Pants on Fire!

CRACKERS

AHLBERG, A.
  The Vanishment of Thomas Tull

DEARY, T.
  The Ghosts of Batwing Castle
  The Lambton Worm
  The Wishing-Well Ghost

GREEN, P.
  Eating Ice-cream with a Werewolf

PREGER, J.
  The Terrible Trials of Mattie McCrum

STRONG, J.
  The Karate Princess
  Money Doesn't Grow on Trees
  The Wolf

WARBURTON, N. J.
  Saving Grace
  Zartan

GANDERS

Hodder and Stoughton

An outwardly attractive new series for children who have mastered reading, but who need good quality material that will not overwhelm them. The stories are lively and amusing, and the print is large and clear. Coloured illustrations would have enhanced the attractiveness of the series, as the front covers promise more than the contents can yield. Nevertheless, the black and white drawings have charm and humour.

ALLEN, E.
  Emily in the News

DEARY, T.
  Bad Bart and Billy the Brave
  The Skeleton in the Cupboard

FURMINGER, J.
  Hopeless Harry

KAYE, G
  The Baby-Sitting Gang
  The Donkey Christmas

RUSSELL, A.
  The Grand Bristleton Easter Egg

ZABEL, J.
  Wimbleball

GAZELLE

Hamish Hamilton

Aimed at 6–8-year-olds and, like **ANTELOPES**, a well established series which has recently been redesigned to make it more up-to-date and appealing. Small and quite short, (about 50 pages), bold print and lots of illustrations make it a series which will help children gain reading fluency. There are now many titles in the series, some re-issued in paperback, and some are much more worth reading than others.

BOND, R.
Big Business
The Cherry Tree

CLEARY, B.
Here Come the Twins

CRAIG, G.
Pen Pals

CURRY, J.
The Rainbow Trail

ESCOTT, J.
The Joker
Rosabel in Disguise

FINE, A.
Only a Show
Stranger Danger

FORSYTH, A.
The Ginger Tree

GERAS, A.
The Christmas Cat
Through the Darkness, through the Snow

LAMBERT, T.
The Disappearing Cat
No Train for Sam

MATHIAS, B.
Kate's Skates

MAYNE, W.
Netta
Netta Next

SEFTON, C.
The Haunted Schoolbag

HEDGEHOG

Hodder & Stoughton

A relatively new and welcome series designed like **CARTWHEELS** to encourage new readers to practise their new-found skills and achieve fluency. Very enjoyable stories, bold print and lively colourful illustrations all combine to produce excellent reading material.

BAYLIS, J.
Henry's Hallowe'en

BRADMAN, T.
Gary and the Magic Cat

LAMBERT, T.
Dizzy Lizzy

NEWMAN, M.
Horace

PILLING, A.
The Big Biscuit

STRONG, J.
The Everything Machine

WEBB, D.
Bill Buckets

HOPSCOTCH

Hodder & Stoughton

Rather like **GAZELLES**, each title in this series is approximately 50 pages, in large print and with plenty of illustrations. The series is aimed at youngsters aged 7–9 who need lively, exciting stories to encourage reading.

ARKLE, P.
The Adventures of Blunter Button

EADINGTON, J.
Sam the Silver Bus
Sam's Wonderful Week

FORSYTH, A.
Baxter by the Sea

HUGHES, S.
It's too Frightening for me

KAYE, G.
The School Pool Gang

LINDSAY, F.
The Half-Price Bear

JETS

Black – hardback
Young Lions – paperback

This series is aimed at children who can read, but who require practice with lots of encouragement. This is provided by illustrations on every page, both conventional and comic-strip, which appeal more to some readers. The stories are humorous, interesting and imaginative. They are not, however, straightforward to read, as the child has to follow two texts, the story and the 'extras' in bubbles. Authors invited to contribute to the series are well established, and write stories with a clear continuity line.

CHRISTIE, S.
Weedy me

CRESSWELL, H.
Almost Goodbye Guzzler
Two Hoots

GARLAND, S.
Shadows on the Barn

IMPEY, R.
Desperate for a Dog
Houdini Dog

KINGSLAND, R.
Free with Every Pack
The Fizziness Business

MORPURGO, M.
Mossop's Last Chance

POWLING, C.
Hiccup Harry!
Harry's Party

WILSON, B.
Gin Gang Goollie, it's an Alien

KITES

Viking Kestrel

Intended for the age group 7–9, and for children with a certain competence as they are quite long – 100 pages. The print is large, and every page is illustrated with line drawings, but they do look a little dull when compared with new series illustrated in colour. Many of the titles in this series have been re-issued in paperback.

BRADMAN, T.
One Nil

BRANDRETH, G.
The Hiccups at No. 13

GIRLING, B.
Dumbellina

NASH, M.
Rat Saturday

ROGERS, P. & E.
Boneshaker
Boneshaker Rides Again

ROMANES, A.
Red Letter Day

RUFFELL, A.
Sun and Rain

ORCHARD STORYBOOKS

Orchard

There are several mini-series within this group, each written by the same author to ensure reliability and to encourage children to further reading through familiarity. Best suited for the 7–9-year-olds, with short chapters and good illustrations.

ASHLEY, B.
Clipper Street

Six stories set in a South London street, dealing with the problems that face children daily – violence, racism, homelessness.

CROSSLEY-HOLLAND, K.
Folk Tales

Short adaptations of popular British folk stories in four volumes.

LAVELLE, S.
  Jupiter Jane

Four science fiction stories that are also very amusing.

LIMB, S.
  Green Books

Two books about environmental problems dealt with in a humorous way..

URE, J.
  Woodside School

Six stories about the children from Woodside Primary School.

READ ALONE

Viking Kestrel

'Designed for all new readers who want to start reading a whole book on their own.' Attractive covers lead to disappointing interiors, as the illustrations are a dull black and white. However, the print is large and clear, the chapters are short, and the stories, on the whole, are fun to read. Some titles are now available in **Young Puffin Read Alone**

BRADMAN, T.
  Gerbil Crazy

BRANDRETH, G.
  The Slippers that Talked

CASTOR, H.
  Fat Puss and Friends
  Fat Puss on Wheels

CAVE, K.
  Poor Little Mary

CRESSWELL, H.
  Dragon Ride

GORDON, M.
  Help
  Willie Whiskers

HOUGH, C.
  Three Little Funny Ones

JOY, M.
  The Little Explorer
  The Little Lighthouse Keeper

MARK, J.
  The Twig Thing

PILLING, A.
  Dustbin Charlie

WADDELL, M.
  The Ghost Family Robinson

READ IT YOURSELF

Gollancz

A very attractive series, but not as young as the name implies. Approximately 50 pages, not particularly large print, but very clear, lots of coloured illustrations, but not divided into chapters, which is a disadvantage. Lower juniors will enjoy them.

HILL, D.
  Goblin Party

KING-SMITH, D.
  The Jenius

REDWINGS

J. MacRae

Intended as the next stage from Blackbirds, the books in this series are longer, contain more complex sentences, and are in smaller print. The text is broken up, both by chapters and by lots of illustrations, and is not too demanding. The subjects are varied, including historical, supernatural and contemporary life.

ASHLEY, B.
  Boat Girl
  The Caretaker's Cat

ASHLEY, C.
  Songs on the South Bank

BOND, R.
Dust on the Mountain
Tigers Forever

COLE, H.
Kick-off
The Midnight Feast
Our Horrible Friend

GARDAM, J.
Kit
Kit in Boots

HENDRY, D.
Hetty's First Fling
Midnight Pirate
Sam Sticks and Delilah

KENNEDY, N.
Chrysalis

LIVELY, P.
The Stained-glass Window

PARMER, P.
Saturday by Seven

SALWAY, L.
The Haunting of Hemlock Hall

SIMPSON, J. B.
Awful Annie and Perfect Percy
Awful Annie and the Squeaking Chop

SMITH, J.
The Pepper Street Papers

ROOSTERS

Hodder & Stoughton

Designed to 'boost children's confidence in their ability to read "a whole book"'. Good stories of real interest to encourage reluctant readers. The very large, clear print and bold black and white illustrations look quite inviting.

DEARY, T.
Skeleton in the Cupboard

HILL, D.
Matthew's Mog

KING-SMITH, D.
Henry Pond the Poet

LAVELLE, S.
Copycat

MAY, K.
Lenny's Performing Pest

PEARSON, M.
Peter Pepper and the Goblin

SUPERCHAMPS

Heinemann

A series for competent readers who need encouraging to read for pleasure. Small so they do not appear daunting, bright and attractive inside and outside, clear print and unusually good quality paper. The stories are interesting and amusing, not too long and divided into manageable chapters.

CRESSWELL, H.
Rosie and the Boredom Eater

GRANT, G.
The Walloping Stick War

HARDCASTLE, M.
Mark England's Cap

HOFFMAN, M.
Dog Powder

LEESON, R.
How Alice Saved Captain Miracle

MAYNE, W.
The Men of the House

ROSEN, M.
The Class Two Monster

STORR, C.
Dalijit and the Unqualified Wizard

TOPPERS

Deutsch

A highly successful series consisting, unfortunately, of only six titles. Small and attractive, easy to read and well illustrated, they are excellent for encouraging young readers, particularly those who tend to be reluctant readers. First published in hardback in 1986, they have since become available in paperback.

ALCOCK, V.
  Wait and See

CRESSWELL, H.
  Greedy Alice

HOFFMAN, M.
  The Second-Hand Ghost

KING-SMITH, D.
  E.S.P.

LAVELLE, S.
  The Chocolate Candy Kid

PRINCE, A.
  A Job for Merv

TELEVISION TIE-INS

♦

A list of books, details of which can be found in the main text, which have featured on television since 1985. Much has been said about the detrimental effect of television on the reading habits of children. No doubt there is some truth in this, but there is also a positive side. Many good quality books are dramatized, which allows children who would otherwise miss out completely to experience the author's message, and can often stimulate them to read books which they would otherwise have felt unable to tackle.

AIKEN, J.
  Go Saddle the Sea
  Bridle the Wind
  The Teeth of the Gale
    (a trilogy)

ALCOCK, V.
  Cuckoo Sister
  The Sylvia Game
  The Trial of Anna Cotman

ALLEN, J.
  Awaiting Developments

ASHLEY, B.
  A Bit of Give and Take
  Break in the Sun
  Terry on the Fence

BARRY, M. S.
  A variety of stories from 'The Witch . . .'
  series

BAWDEN, N.
  Carrie's War
  The Finding

BLUME, J.
  Starring Sally J. Freedman as Herself

BOND, M.
  A variety of stories from 'Paddington
  Bear' series
  Parsley the Lion

BOSTON, L. M.
  The Children of Green Knowe

BYARS, B.
  Cracker Jackson
  The Night Swimmers
  The Pinballs

CAMERON, A.
  The Julian Stories

CARPENTER, H.
  A variety of stories from the 'Mr
  Majeika' series

CHAMBERS, A.
  The Present Takers

CHRISTOPHER, J.
  The Tripods Trilogy

CRESSWELL, H.
  The Bagthorpe Saga
  Moondial
  The Secret World of Polly Flint
  Time out

CROSS, G
  The Demon Headmaster
  On the Edge

CROSSLEY-HOLLAND, K.
  Wulf

DAHL, R.
  The BFG
  Charlie and the Chocolate Factory
  Danny, Champion of the World
  George's Marvellous Medicine
  Matilda
  The Witches

DE JONG, M.
  Hurry Home, Candy

DICKINSON, P.
  The Gift

DOHERTY, B.
  Children of Winter
  White Peak Farm

EADINGTON, J.
  A variety of stories from the 'Jonny
  Briggs' series

FISK, N.
  Grinny
  Monster Maker
  Starstormers
  Trillions

GARFIELD, L.
  Black Jack
  The December Rose
  Devil-in-the-fog
  The Empty Sleeve

GEE, M.
  The Champion
  The Fire-raiser
  Under the Mountain

HALL, W.
  The 'Antelope' Company Ashore
  The Return of the 'Antelope'

KEMP. G.
  Just Ferret
  Mr Magus is Waiting for you

KING, C.
  Ninny's Boat
  Stig-of-the-dump

KING-SMITH, D.
  Daggie Dogfoot
  Harry's Mad
  Mouse Butcher
  Sophie's Snail

LIVELY, P.
  The Revenge of Samuel Stokes
  The Voyage of QV66

McCAUGHREAN, G.
  A Pack of Lies

MARK, J.
  Hairs in the Palm of the Hand

MORPURGO, M.
  My Friend Walter

MURPHY, J.
  A variety of stories from 'The Worst
  Witch' series

NEEDLE, J.
  Behind the Bike Sheds
  My Mate Shofiq
  The Thief

NESBIT, E.
  Five Children and It
  The Railway Children

NIMMO, J.
  The Snow Spider
  Emlyn's Moon

O'BRIEN, R.
  Mrs Frisby and the Rats of Nimh

PEARCE, P.
  The Way to Sattin Shore

PEYTON, K. M.
  Fly-by-Night
  Who Sir, me Sir?

RANSOME, A.
  Big Six
  Coot Club

SWINDELLS, R.
  Room 13
  A Serpent's Tooth

WALSH, J. P.
  Dolphin Crossing
  A Parcel of Patterns

WILDER, L. J.
  Little House on the Prairie

LIST OF AWARDS
AND PRIZE WINNERS

◆

HANS CHRISTIAN ANDERSEN AWARDS

Made biennially by the International Board on Books for Young People (IBBY), and given to an author in respect of their complete works, judged as a lasting contribution to literature for children. The medal was first awarded in 1956, jointly to Eleanor Farjeon and Jella Lepman – founder of IBBY.

1958	Astrid Lindgen	(Sweden)
1960	Erich Kästner	(Germany)
1962	Meindert Dejong	(USA)
1964	Réné Guillot	(France)
1966	Tove Jannson	(Finland)
1968	James Kruss	(Germany)
	Jose Maria Sanchez Silva	(Spain)
1970	Gianni Rodari	(Italy)
1972	Scott O'Dell	(USA)
1974	Maria Gripe	(Sweden)
1976	Cecil Bodker	(Denmark)
1978	Paula Fox	(USA)
1980	Bohumil Riha	(Czechoslovakia)
1982	Lygia Bojunga Nunes	(Brazil)
1984	Christine Nostlinger	(Austria)
1986	Patricia Wrightson	(Australia)
1988	Annie M. G. Schmidt	(Netherlands)

BOSTON GLOBE–HORN BOOK AWARDS

Co-sponsored by the *Boston Globe* newspaper and the *Horn Book* magazine, awards were first given in 1967. From 1976 there have been awards for *non-fiction* and *illustration* in addition to the *fiction* awards of which the winners are listed here.

Year	Title	Author	Publisher
1967	The Little Fishes	Erik Christian Haugaard	Houghton Mifflin
1968	The Spring Rider	John Lawson	Crowell
1969	The Wizard of Earthsea	Ursula K. Le Guin	Parnassus
1970	The Intruder	John Rowe Townsend	Lippincott
1971	A Room made of Windows	Eleanor Cameron	Atlantic Little Brown
1972	Tristan and Iseult	Rosemary Sutcliff	Dutton
1973	The Dark is Rising	Susan Cooper	Atheneum
1974	M. C. Higgins, the Great	Virginia Hamilton	Macmillan
1975	Transport 7–41–R	T. Degens	Viking
1976	Unleaving	Jill Paton Walsh	Farrar Straus & Giroux
1977	Child of the Owl	Laurence Yep	Harper & Row
1978	The Westing Game	Ellen Raskin	Dutton
1979	Humbug Mountain	Sid Fleischman	Atlantic Little Brown
1980	Conrad's War	Andrew Davies	Crown
1981	The Leaving	Lynn Hall	Scribner
1982	Playing Beatie Bow	Ruth Park	Atheneum
1983	Sweet Whispers, Brother Rush	Virginia Hamilton	Philomel
1984	A Little Fear	Patricia Wrightson	Atheneum
1985	The Moves Make the Man	Bruce Brooks	Harper & Row
1986	In Summer Light	Zibby Oneal	Viking
1987	Rabble Starkey	Lois Lowry	Houghton Mifflin
1988	The Friendship	Mildred D. Taylor	Dial

CANADIAN LIBRARY ASSOCIATION – BOOK OF THE YEAR FOR CHILDREN AWARD

Presented annually since 1947 for an English-language book by a Canadian or permanent Canadian resident.

1947	Starbuck Valley Winter	Roderick Haig-Brown	Morrow
1948	No award given		
1949	Kristli's Trees	Mabel Dunham	McClelland & Stewart
1950	Franklin of the Arctic: a Life of Adventure	Richard S. Lambert	McClelland & Stewart
1951	No award given		
1952	The Sun Horse	Catherine Anthony Clark	Macmillan
1953	No award given		
1954	No award given		
1955	No award given		
1956	Train for Tiger Lily	Louise Riley	Macmillan
1957	Glooskap's Country and Other Indian Tales	Cyrus Macmillan	OUP
1958	Lost in the Barrens	Farley Mowat	Little Brown
1959	The Dangerous Cove: a Story of Early Days in Newfoundland	John F. Hayes	Copp Clark
1960	The Golden Phoenix and Other French Canadian Fairy Tales	Charles Marius Barbeau	OUP
1961	The St Lawrence	William Toye	OUP
1962	No award given		
1963	The Incredible Journey: a Tale of Three Animals	Sheila Every Burnford	Little Brown
1964	The Whale People	Roderick Haig-Brown	Collins
1965	Tales of Nanabozho	Dorothy Reid	OUP
1966	Tikta' Liktak: an Eskimo Legend	James Houston	Longman
1967	The Raven's Cry	Christie Harris	McClelland & Stewart
1968	The White Archer: an Eskimo Legend	James Houston	Academic
1969	And Tomorrow the Stars: the Story of John Cabot	Kay Hill	Dodd
1970	Sally Go Round the Sun	Edith Fowke	McClelland & Stewart
1971	Carter Discovers the St Lawrence	William Toye	OUP
1972	Mary of Mile 18	Ann Blades	Tundra
1973	The Marrow of the World	Ruth Nicholls	Macmillan
1974	The Miraculous Hind	Elizabeth Cleaver	Holt Rinehart & Winston
1975	Alligator Pie	Dennis Lee	Macmillan
1976	Jacob Two-Two Meets the Hooded Fang	Mordecai Richler	McClelland & Stewart

1977	Mouse Woman and the Vanished Princesses	Christie Harris	McClelland & Stewart
1978	Garbage Delight	Dennis Lee	Macmillan
1979	Hold Fast	Kevin Major	Clarke Irwin
1980	River Runners: a Tale of Hardship and Bravery	James Houston	McClelland & Stewart
1981	The Violin Maker's Gift	Donn Kushner	Macmillan
1982	The Root Cellar	Janet Lunn	Lester & Orpen Dennys
1983	Up To Low	Brian Doyle	Groundwood
1984	Sweetgrass	Jan Hudson	Tree Frog Press
1985	Mama's Going to Buy You a Mockingbird	Jean Little	Viking Kestrel
1986	Julie	Cora Taylor	Western Producer Prairie
1987	Shadow in Hawthorn Bay	Janet Lunn	Lester & Orpen Dennys
1988	A Handful of Time	Kit Pearson	Penguin
1989	Easy Avenue	Brian Doyle	Groundwood

THE CARNEGIE MEDAL

The Carnegie Medal is given for an outstanding book for children written in English and contenders are appraised for characterization, plot, style, accuracy, imaginative quality and that indefinable element that lifts the book above the others. Presented annually by the Library Association since 1936.

1936	Pigeon Post	Arthur Ransome	Cape
1937	The Family from One End Street	Eve Garnett	Muller
1938	The Circus is Coming	Noel Streatfeild	Dent
1939	Radium Woman	Eleanor Doorly	Heinemann
1940	Visitors from London	Kitty Barne	Dent
1941	We Couldn't Leave Dinah	Mary Treadgold	Cape
1942	The Little Grey Men	BB	Eyre & Spottiswoode
1943	No award given		
1944	The Wind on the Moon	Eric Linklater	Macmillan
1945	No award given		
1946	The Little White Horse	Elizabeth Goudge	Bockhampton Press
1947	Collected Stories for Children	Walter de la Mare	Faber & Faber
1948	Sea Change	Richard Armstrong	Dent
1949	The Story of Your Home	Agnes Allen	Transatlantic
1950	The Lark on the Wing	Elfrida Vipont	OUP
1951	The Wool-Pack	Cynthia Harnett	Methuen
1952	The Borrowers	Mary Norton	Dent
1953	A Valley Grows Up	Edward Osmond	OUP
1954	Knight Crusader	Ronald Welch	OUP
1955	The Little Bookroom	Eleanor Farjeon	OUP
1956	The Last Battle	C. S. Lewis	Bodley Head
1957	A Grass Rope	William Mayne	OUP
1958	Tom's Midnight Garden	A. Philippa Pearce	OUP
1959	The Lantern Bearers	Rosemary Sutcliff	OUP
1960	The Making Of Man	I. W. Cornwall	Phoenix
1961	A Stranger at Green Knowe	Lucy M. Boston	Faber & Faber
1962	The Twelve and the Genii	Pauline Clarke	Faber & Faber
1963	Time of Trial	Hester Burton	OUP
1964	Nordy Bank	Sheena Porter	OUP
1965	The Grange At High Force	Philip Turner	OUP
1966	No award given		
1967	The Owl Service	Alan Garner	Collins
1968	The Moon in the Cloud	Rosemary Harris	Faber & Faber
1969	The Edge of the Cloud	K. M. Peyton	OUP
1970	The God Beneath the Sea	Leon Garfield and Edward Blishen	Longman
1971	Josh	Ivan Southall	Angus & Robertson
1972	Watership Down	Richard Adams	Collins

1973	The Ghost of Thomas Kempe	Penelope Lively	Heinemann
1974	The Stronghold	Mollie Hunter	Hamish Hamilton
1975	The Machine Gunners	Robert Westall	Macmillan
1976	Thunder and Lightnings	Jan Mark	Kestrel
1977	The Turbulent Term of Tyke Tiler	Gene Kemp	Faber & Faber
1978	The Exeter Blitz	David Rees	Hamish Hamilton
1979	Tulku	Peter Dickinson	Gollancz
1980	City of Gold and Other Stories from the Old Testament	Peter Dickinson	Gollancz
1981	The Scarecrows	Robert Westall	Chatto & Windus
1982	The Haunting	Margaret Mahy	Dent
1983	Handles	Jan Mark	Kestrel
1984	The Changeover: a Supernatural Romance	Margaret Mahy	Dent
1985	Storm	Kevin Crossley-Holland	Heinemann
1986	Granny Was A Buffer Girl	Berlie Doherty	Methuen
1987	The Ghost Drum	Susan Price	Faber & Faber
1988	A Pack of Lies	Geraldine McCaughrean	OUP
1989	Goggle Eyes	Anne Fine	Hamilton

THE CHILDREN'S BOOK AWARD

The Children's Book Award is organized by the Federation of Children's Book Groups and is sponsored by Save and Prosper Educational Trust. The award is an annual prize for the 'best book of the year', judged by the children themselves and has been awarded since 1980. Thousands of children from all over the country help the Federation to test the books.

1980	Mr Magnolia	Quentin Blake	Cape
1981	Fair's Fair	Leon Garfield	Macdonald
1982	The BFG	Roald Dahl	Cape
1983	Saga of Erik the Viking	Terry Jones	Pavilion
1984	Brother in the Land	Robert Swindells	OUP
1985	Arthur	Amanda Graham	Spindlewood
1987	Winnie the Witch	Valerie Thomas and Paul Korky	OUP
1988	Matilda	Roald Dahl	Cape
1989	Room 13	Robert Swindells	Doubleday

CHILDREN'S BOOK COUNCIL OF AUSTRALIA – BOOK OF THE YEAR AWARDS

Started in 1946 to encourage new talent and to recognize outstanding achievement in books of lasting merit; in 1983 a Junior Book of the Year Award was added, and in 1987 the Awards were retitled Book of the Year – Older readers, and Book of the Year – Younger readers. (An Award is also made for picture books.)

1946	Karrawingi the Emu	Leslie Rees	Sands
1947	No award given		
1948	Shackleton's Argonauts	Frank Hurley	Angus & Robertson
1949	No competition		
1950	Whales of the Midnight Sun	Alan Villiers	Angus & Robertson
1951	Verity of Sydney Town	Ruth Williams	Angus & Robertson
1952	The Australian Book	Eve Pownall	Sands
1953	Good Luck to the Rider	Joan Phipson	Angus & Robertson
	Aircraft Today and Tomorrow	J. H. Martin	Angus & Robertson
1954	Australian Legendary Tales	K. L. Parker	Angus & Robertson
1955	The First Walkabout	Norman Tindale	Longmans Green
1956	The Crooked Snake	Patricia Wrightson	Angus & Robertson
1957	Boomerang Book of Legendary Tales	Enid Heddle	Longmans Green
1958	Tiger in the Bush	Nan Chauncey	OUP
1959	Devil's Hill	Nan Chauncey	OUP
1960	All the Proud Tribesmen	Kylie Tennant	Macmillan
1961	Tangara	Nan Chauncey	OUP
1962	Racketty Street Gang	L. H. Evers	Hodder & Stoughton
1963	Family Conspiracy	Joan Phipson	Constable
1964	Green Laurel	Eleanor Spence	OUP
1965	Pastures of the Blue Crane	Hesba Brinsmead	OUP
1966	Ash Road	Ivan Southall	Angus & Robertson
1967	The Min-min	Mavis Clark	Lansdowne
1968	To the Wild Sky	Ivan Southall	Angus & Robertson
1969	When Jays Fly to Barmbo	Margaret Balderson	OUP
1970	Uhu	Annette Macarthur-Onslow	Ure Smith
1971	Bread and Honey	Ivan Southall	Angus & Robertson
1972	Longtime Passing	Hesba Brinsmead	Angus & Robertson
1973	Family at the Lookout	Noreen Shelley	OUP
1974	The Nargun and the Stars	Patricia Wrightson	Hutchinson
1975	No award given		
1976	Fly West	Ivan Southall	Angus & Robertson
1977	October Child	Eleanor Spence	OUP
1978	The Ice is Coming	Patricia Wrightson	Hutchinson
1979	The Plum-Rain Scroll	Ruth Manley	Hodder & Stoughton

1980	Displaced Person	Lee Harding	Hyland House
1981	Playing Beatie Bow	Ruth Park	Nelson
1982	Valley Between	Colin Thiele	Rigby
1983	Master of the Grove	Victor Kelleher	Kestrel
1984	A Little Fear	Patricia Wrightson	Hutchinson
1985	True Story of Lilli Stubeck	James Aldridge	Hyland
1986	The Green Wind	Thurley Fowler	Rigby

JUNIOR BOOK OF THE YEAR AWARD

1983	Thing	Robert Klein	OUP
1984	Bernice Knows Best	Max Dann	OUP
1985	Something Special	Emily Roberts	Angus & Robertson
1986	Arkwright	Mary Steele	Hyland

BOOK OF THE YEAR – OLDER READERS

1987	All we Know	Simon French	Angus & Robertson
1988	So Much to Tell You	John Marsden	Walter McVitty
1989	Beyond the Labyrinth	Gillian Rubinstein	Hyland

BOOK OF THE YEAR – YOUNGER READERS

1987	Pigs Might Fly	Emily Rodda	Angus & Robertson
1988	My Place	Nadia Wheatley	Collin Dove
1989	The Best Kept Secret	Emily Rodda	Angus & Robertson

EARTHWORM CHILDREN'S BOOK AWARD

The Earthworm Award has been set up by Friends of the Earth in order to encourage the writing of children's books which reflect concern about environmental issues. Books eligible are those published during the preceding year, written in English and either published or distributed in the UK.

1987	The Boy and the Swan	Catherine Storr	A. Deutsch
1988	Where the Forest meets the Sea	Jeannie Baker	J. MacRae
1989	Awaiting Developments	Judy Allen	J. MacRae
1990	The Young Green Consumer guide (non-fiction)		Gollancz

THE EMIL/KURT MASCHLER AWARD

The Emil/Kurt Maschler Award was established in 1982 by the late Kurt Maschler for a work of imagination in the children's field in which text and illustration are of excellence and so presented that each enhances yet balances the other. The prize is £1000 and in addition the winner receives an 'Emil' – a bronze figure of Erich Kästner's famous character. It was Kurt Maschler's publishing company, William Verlag, which originally published *Emil and the Detectives* (1929).

1982	Sleeping Beauty and other Favourite Fairy Tales	Angela Carter (selected and translated)	Gollancz
1983	Gorilla	Anthony Browne	J. MacRae
1984	Granpa	John Burningham	Cape
1985	The Iron Man	Ted Hughes	Faber
1986	The Jolly Postman	Allan & Janet Ahlberg	Heinemann
1987	Jack the Treacle Eater	Charles Causley	Macmillan
1988	Alice's Adventures in Wonderland	Anthony Browne	J. MacRae
1989	The Park in the Dark	Martin Waddell	Walker Books

EUROPE AWARD OF LITERATURE FOR CHILDREN AND YOUNG ADULTS

Launched in 1990 by Harper Collins (UK) Ediciones B (Spain), Arena Verlag (Germany) and Editions l'Amitié Rageot (France). The annual competition is aimed at promoting excellence in writing for young readers between the ages of 8 and 16 within the European Community. In addition to a cash prize, the winning manuscript will be published in four languages.

The first award will be made in 1991.

THE KATHLEEN FIDLER AWARD

The Kathleen Fidler Award was set up in 1980 to encourage both new and established authors to submit their work for the 8–12 age group. It is sponsored by Blackie publishers and administered by Book Trust Scotland. The winner is then published by Blackie.

1983	Adrift	Alan Baillie	Blackie
1984	Barty	Janet Collins	Blackie
1985	No Shelter	Elizabeth Lutzeir	Blackie
1986	Diamond	Caroline Pitcher	Blackie
1987	Simon's Challenge	Theresa Breslin	Blackie
1988	Flight of the Solar Duck	Charles Morgan	Blackie
1989	Mightier than the Sword	Clare Bevan	Blackie
1990	Magic with Everything	Roger Burt	Blackie

ESTHER GLEN AWARD

Established in 1944 by the New Zealand Library Association; awarded to the author considered to have made the most distinguished contribution to literature to children during the year. Esther Glen, born in 1881, was a journalist and pioneer writer of children's books in New Zealand.

1945	Book of Wiremu	Stella Morice	Progressive Publication Society
1946	No award		
1947	Myths and Legends of Maoriland	Alexander Reed	Reed
1948	No award		
1949	No award		
1950	The Adventures of Nimble, Rumble and Tumble	Joan Smith	Paul
1951–58	No awards		
1959	Falter Tom and the Water Boy	Maurice Duggan	Paul
1960–63	No awards		
1964	Turi: the Story of a Little Boy	Lesley Powell	Paul
1965–69	No awards		
1970	A Lion in the Meadow	Margaret May Mahy	Watts
1971	No award		
1972	No award		
1973	The First Margaret Mahy Story Book	Margaret May Mahy	Dent
1974	No award		
1975	My Cat likes to Hide in Boxes	Eve Sutton	Hamilton
1976	No award		
1977	No award		
1978	The Lighthouse Keeper's Lunch	Ronda Armitage	Hutchinson
1979	Take the Long Path	Joan de Hamel	Lutterworth Press
1980	No award		
1981	No award		
1982	The Year of the Yelvertons	Katherine O'Brien	OUP
1983	The Haunting	Margaret May Mahy	Dent
1984	Elephant Rock	Caroline Macdonald	Hodder & Stoughton
1985	The Changeover: A Supernatural Romance	Margaret May Mahy	Waiatarua
1986	Motherstone	Maurice Gee	OUP
1987	No award		
1988	Alex	Tessa Duder	OUP

GUARDIAN CHILDREN'S FICTION AWARD

The Guardian Children's Fiction Award has been given annually since 1967 for an outstanding work of fiction for children by a British or Commonwealth author, which was first published in the UK during the preceding year. The award is chosen by a panel of authors and *The Guardian's* children's book review editor. Picture books are not included for consideration.

1967	Devil-in-the-Fog	Leon Garfield	Longman
1968	The Owl Service	Alan Garner	Collins
1969	The Whispering Mountain	Joan Aiken	Cape
1970	Flambards (The Trilogy)	K. M. Peyton	OUP
1971	The Guardians	John Christopher	Hamish Hamilton
1972	A Likely Lad	Gillian Avery	Collins
1973	Watership Down	Richard Adams	Collins
1974	The Iron Lily	Barbara Willard	Longman Young
1975	Gran at Coalgate	Winifred Cawley	OUP
1976	The Peppermint Pig	Nina Bawden	Gollancz
1977	The Blue Hawk	Peter Dickinson	Gollancz
1978	A Charmed Life	Diana Wynne Jones	Macmillan
1979	Conrad's War	Andrew Davies	Blackie
	The Vandal	Ann Schlee	Macmillan
1980	The Sentinels	Peter Carter	OUP
1981	The Scarecrows	Robert Westall	Chatto & Windus
1982	Goodnight Mister Tom	Michelle Magorian	Kestrel
1983	The Village by the Sea: An Indian Family Story	Anita Desai	Heinemann
1984	The Sheep-Pig	Dick King-Smith	Gollancz
1985	What is the Truth?: A Farmyard Fable for the Young	Ted Hughes	Faber & Faber
1986	Henry's Leg	Ann Pilling	Viking Kestrel
1987	The True Story of Spit MacPhee	James Aldridge	Viking Kestrel
1988	The Runaways	Ruth Thomas	Hutchinson
1989	A Pack of Lies	Geraldine McCaughrean	OUP
1990	Goggle Eyes	Anne Fine	Hamilton
1991	Kingdom by the Sea	Robert Westall	Methuen

IBBY HONOUR DIPLOMAS

Awarded every two years, to call attention to some of the best books for children and young people on an international level. Awards for writing are given below; there are also awards for illustration and translation.

1970	I Own the Racecourse	Patricia Wrightson	Hutchinson
1972	Blue Fin	Colin Thiele	Rigby
1974	Josh	Ivan Southall	Angus & Robertson
1976	The Nargun and the Stars	Patricia Wrightson	Hutchinson
1978	The October Child	Eleanor Spence	OUP
1980	A Dream of Seas	Lilith Norman	Collins
1982	Playing Beatie Bow	Ruth Park	Nelson
1984	The Watcher in the Garden	Joan Phipson	Methuen
1986	Dancing in the Anzac Deli	Nadia Wheatley	OUP
1988	Riverman	Allan Baillie	Nelson

LANCASHIRE COUNTY LIBRARY CHILDREN'S BOOK OF THE YEAR AWARD

Awarded to a fiction title suitable for the 11–14 age range, and sponsored by the National Westminster Bank. Judged by 13–14-year-old pupils from Lancashire schools.

1987	Ruby in the Smoke	Philip Pullman	OUP
1988	Redwall	Brian Jacques	Hutchinson
1989	Groosham Grange	Anthony Horowitz	Methuen
1990	Plague 99	Jean Ure	Methuen

THE NEWBERY MEDAL

The Newbery Medal is given annually for the most distinguished contribution to American literature for children. It is named after John Newbery (1713–67), a London bookseller and the first British publisher of children's books. It is administered by the American Library Association and was first awarded in 1922.

1922	The Story of Mankind	Hendrick Willem van Loon	Liveright
1923	The Voyages of Doctor Dolittle	Hugh Lofting	Lippincott
1924	The Dark Frigate	Charles Boardman Hawes	Atlantic Little Brown
1925	Tales from Silver Lands	Charles J. Finger	Doubleday
1926	Shen of the Sea: A Book for Children	Arthur Bowie Chrisman	Dutton
1927	Smoky, the Cowhorse	Will James	Scribner
1928	Gay-Neck, the Story of a Pigeon	Dhan Gopal Mukerji	Dutton
1929	The Trumpeter of Krakow: a Tale of the Fifteenth Century	Eric P. Kelly	Macmillan
1930	Hitty, her First Hundred Years	Rachel Field	Macmillan
1931	The Cat Who Went to Heaven	Elizabeth Coatsworth	Macmillan
1932	Waterless Mountain	Laura Adams Armer	Longman
1933	Young Fu of the Upper Yangtze	Elizabeth Foreman Lewis	Winston
1934	Invincible Louisa: the Story of the Author of 'Little Women'	Cornelia Meigs	Little Brown
1935	Dobry	Monica Shannon	Viking
1936	Caddie Woodlawn	Carol Ryrie Brink	Macmillan
1937	Roller Skates	Ruth Sawyer	Viking
1938	The White Stag	Kate Seredy	Viking
1939	Thimble Summer	Elizabeth Enright	Holt, Rinehart & Winston
1940	Daniel Boone	James Daugherty	Viking
1941	Call It Courage (UK title: The Boy who was Afraid)	Armstrong Sperry	Macmillan
1942	The Matchlock Gun	Walter D. Edmonds	Dodd Mead
1943	Adam of the Road	Elizabeth Janet Gray	Viking
1944	Johnny Tremain	Esther Forbes	Houghton Mifflin
1945	Rabbit Hill	Robert Lawson	Viking
1946	Strawberry Girl	Lois Lenski	Lippincott
1947	Miss Hickory	Carolyn Sherwin Bailey	Viking
1948	The Twenty-One Balloons	William Pene du Bois	Viking
1949	King of the Wind	Marguerite Henry	Rand McNally

Year	Title	Author	Publisher
1950	The Door in the Wall: Story of Medieval London	Marguerite de Angeli	Doubleday
1951	Amos Fortune, Free Man	Elizabeth Yates	Aladdin
1952	Ginger Pye	Eleanor Estes	Harcourt Brace Jovanovich
1953	Secret of the Andes	Ann Nolan Clark	Viking
1954	. . . And Now Miguel	Joseph Krumgold	Crowell
1955	The Wheel on the School	Meindert Dejong	Harper & Row
1956	Carry On, Mr Bowditch	Jean Lee Latham	Houghton Mifflin
1957	Miracles on Maple Hill	Virginia Sorenson	Harcourt Brace Jovanovich
1958	Rifles for Watie	Harold Keith	Crowell
1959	The Witch of Blackbird Pond	Elizabeth George Speare	Houghton Mifflin
1960	Onion John	Joseph Krumgold	Crowell
1961	Island of the Blue Dolphins	Scott O'Dell	Houghton Mifflin
1962	The Bronze Bow	Elizabeth George Speare	Houghton Mifflin
1963	A Wrinkle in Time	Madeleine L'Engle	Farrar Straus & Giroux
1964	It's Like This, Cat	Emily Cheney Neville	Harper & Row
1965	Shadow of a Bull	Maia Wojciechowska	Atheneum
1966	I, Juan de Pareja	Elizabeth Borton de Trevino	Farrar Straus & Giroux
1967	Up A Road Slowly	Irene Hunt	Follett
1968	From the Mixed-Up Files of Mrs Basil E. Frankweiler	Elaine L. Konigsburg	Atheneum
1969	The High King	Lloyd Alexander	Holt, Rinehart & Winston
1970	Sounder	William H. Armstrong	Harper & Row
1971	The Summer of the Swans	Betsy Byars	Viking
1972	Mrs Frisby and the Rats of Nimh	Robert C. O'Brien	Atheneum
1973	Julie of the Wolves	Jean Craighead George	Harper & Row
1974	The Slave Dancer	Paula Fox	Bradbury
1975	M. C. Higgins, the Great	Virginia Hamilton	Macmillan
1976	The Grey King	Susan Cooper	Atheneum
1977	Roll of Thunder, Hear My Cry	Mildred D. Taylor	Dial
1978	Bridge to Terabithia	Katherine Paterson	Crowell
1979	The Westing Game	Ellen Raskin	Dutton
1980	A Gathering of Days: a New England Girl's Journal, 1830–32	Joan W. Blos	Scribner
1981	Jacob Have I Loved	Katherine Paterson	Crowell

AWARDS AND PRIZE WINNERS

1982	A Visit to William Blake's Inn: Poems for Innocent and Experienced Travellers	Nancy Willard	Harcourt Brace Jovanovich
1983	Dicey's-Song	Cynthia Voigt	Atheneum
1984	Dear Mr Henshaw	Beverly Cleary	Morrow
1985	The Hero and the Crown	Robin McKinley	Greenwillow
1986	Sarah, Plain and Tall	Patricia McLachlan	Harper & Row
1987	The Whipping Boy	Sid Fleischman	Greenwillow
1988	Lincoln: A Photobiography	Russell Freedman	Houghton Clarion
1989	Joyful Noise: Poems for Two Voices	Paul Fleischman	Harper & Row
1990	Number the Stars	Lois Lowry	Houghton Mifflin
1991	Maniac Magee	Jerry Spinelli	Little, Brown

THE OTHER AWARD

The Other Award was established in 1975 as a counter-award to the already existing awards and aimed to draw attention to important new or neglected work of a progressive nature from children's writers and illustrators. It took the form of an annual commendation to a number of children's books published during the preceding year and was not accompanied by a prize or money. The award was discontinued in 1988 after 13 years because the administrators chose not to go down the road of sponsorship and because they no longer considered an award an appropriate way to promote 'other' concerns.

1976	Nobody's Family is Going to Change	Louise Fitzhugh	Gollancz
	Trouble with Donovan Croft	Bernard Ashley	OUP
	Helpers	Shirley Hughes	Bodley Head
1977	East End at your Feet	Farrukh Dhondy	Macmillan
	Turbulent Term of Tyke Tiler	Gene Kemp	Faber
1978	Song for a Dark Queen	Rosemary Sutcliff	Pelham
	Goalkeeper's Revenge	Bill Naughton	Puffin
	Gypsy Family	Mary Waterson and Lance Brown	Black
1979	Old Dog, New Tricks	Dick Cote	Hamilton
	Come to Mecca	Farrukh Dhondy	Collins
	Two Victorian Families	Sue Wagstaff	A. & C. Black
1980	Mr Plug the Plumber	Allan Ahlberg	Kestrel
	Green Bough of Liberty	David Rees	Dobson
1981	A Strong and Willing Girl	Dorothy Edwards	Methuen
	Have You Started Yet?	Ruth Thomson	Heinemann
1982	Welcome Home, Jellybean	Marlene Fanta Shyer	Granada
	When the Wind Blows	Raymond Briggs	Gollancz
1983	Nowhere to Play	Karusa	A. & C. Black
	Will of Iron	Gerard Melia	Longman
	Everybody's Here	Michael Rosen	Bodley Head
	Talking in Whispers	James Watson	Gollancz
1984	Brother in the Land	Robert Swindells	OUP
	Who Lies Inside	Timothy Ireland	Gay Men's Press
	Wheel Around the World	Chris Searle	Macdonald
	A Chair for my Mother	Vera Williams	J. MacRae
1985	Our Kids	Peckham Publishing Project	
	Journey to Jo'burg	Beverley Naidoo	Longman
	Vila	Sarah Baylis	Longman
	Motherland	Elyse Dodgson	Heinemann
	Comfort Herself	Geraldine Kaye	André Deutsch

249

AWARDS AND PRIZE WINNERS

1986	Say It Again, Granny	John Agard	Bodley Head
	Starry Night	Catherine Sefton	Hamish Hamilton
	The People Could Fly	Virginia Hamilton	Walker Books
1987	Grandma's Favourite	Peter C. Heaslip	Methuen
	Which Twin Wins?	Peter C. Heaslip	Methuen
	Push Me Pull Me	Sandra Chick	Women's Press
1988	Award discontinued		

SMARTIES PRIZE FOR CHILDREN'S BOOKS

The Smarties Prize for Children's Books has been established to encourage high standards and stimulate interest in books for children. It is sponsored by Rowntree Mackintosh and administered by Book Trust. Eligible books are any published during the preceding year, written in English by a citizen of the UK or an author resident in the UK and the author must be living at the time of publication.

1985	GRAND PRIX AND OVER 7S CATEGORY WINNER		
	Gaffer Samson's Luck	Jill Paton Walsh	Viking Kestrel
	UNDER 7S CATEGORY WINNER		
	It's Your Turn Roger!	Susanna Gretz	Bodley Head and Fontana
1986	GRAND PRIX AND 7–11 YEARS CATEGORY WINNER		
	The Snow Spider	Jenny Nimmo	Methuen
	6 YEARS AND UNDER CATEGORY WINNER		
	The Goose that Laid the Golden Egg	Geoffrey Patterson	André Deutsch
1987	GRAND PRIX AND 9–11 YEARS CATEGORY WINNER		
	A Thief in the Village	James Berry	Hamish Hamilton
	6–8 YEARS CATEGORY WINNER		
	Tangle and the Firesticks	Benedict Blathway	J. MacRae
	5S AND UNDER CATEGORY WINNER		
	The Angel and the Soldier Boy	Peter Collington	Methuen
1988	GRAND PRIX AND UNDER 5S WINNER		
	Can't You Sleep Little Bear	Martin Waddell	Walker Books
	6–8 YEARS WINNER		
	Can It Be True?	Susan Hill	Hamish Hamilton
	9–11 YEARS WINNER		
	Rushavenn Time	Theresa Whistler and Brixworth Primary School	
1989	GRAND PRIX AND UNDER 5S WINNER		
	We're Going on a Bear Hunt	Michael Rosen	Walker Books
	6–8 YEARS WINNER		
	Bill's New Frock	Anne Fine	Methuen
	9–11 YEARS WINNER		
	Blitz Cat	Robert Westall	Macmillan
1990	GRAND PRIX AND 9–11 CATEGORY WINNER		
	Midnight Blue	Pauline Fisk	Lion Publishing
	6–8 YEARS WINNER		
	Esio Trot	Roald Dahl	Jonathan Cape
	0–5 YEARS WINNER		
	Six Dinner Sid	Inga Moore	Simon & Schuster

WHITBREAD LITERARY AWARD CHILDREN'S NOVEL

The Whitbread Literary Award Children's Novel was first awarded in 1972. The award is for a book for children of seven and up, published in the UK or Republic of Ireland and written by a British or Irish author or one who has been settled in Britain or Ireland. It is sponsored by Whitbread and administered by the Booksellers' Association.

1972	The Diddakoi	Rumer Godden	Macmillan
1973	The Butterfly Ball and the Grasshopper's Feast	William Plomer	Cape
1974	How Tom Beat Captain Najork and his Hired Sportsmen	Russell Hoban	Cape
1975	No award		
1976	A Stitch in Time	Penelope Lively	Heinemann
1977	No End to Yesterday	Shelagh Macdonald	André Deutsch
1978	The Battle of Bubble and Squeak	A. Philippa Pearce	André Deutsch
1979	Tulku	Peter Dickinson	Gollancz
1980	John Diamond	Leon Garfield	Kestrel
1981	The Hollow Land	Jane Gardam	J. MacRae
1982	The Song of Pentecost	William Corbett	Methuen
1983	The Witches	Roald Dahl	Cape
1984	The Queen of the Pharisees' Children	Barbara Willard	J. MacRae
1985	The Nature of the Beast	Janni Howker	J. MacRae
1986	The Coal House	Andrew Taylor	Collins
1987	A Little Lower than the Angels	Geraldine McCaughrean	OUP
1988	Awaiting Developments	Judy Allen	J. MacRae
1989	Why Weep the Brogan	Hugh Scott	Walker Books
1990	AK	Peter Dickinson	Gollancz

LAURA INGALLS WILDER AWARD

Awarded by the Association for Library Services for Children in the American Library Association to an author or illustrator whose books, published in the USA, have made a substantial and lasting contribution to literature for children over a period of years. Now awarded every three years.

1954	Laura Ingalls Wilder
1960	Clara Judson
1965	Ruth Sawyer
1970	E. B. White
1975	Beverly Cleary
1980	Theodor Giesl (Dr Seuss)
1983	Maurice Sendak
1986	Jean Fritz
1989	Elizabeth Speare

AUTHOR INDEX

◆

TITLE INDEX

♦

TITLE INDEX

GENRE INDEX

♦

(Readers should refer to the Title Index to find page numbers.)

ADVENTURE

Adrift
Another fine mess
BFG, The
Big Six
Black Jack
Box of nothing
Charlie and the chocolate factory
Charlie and the great glass elevator
Clancy's cabin
Confidence man
Coot Club
Different dragons
Digital Dan
Dr Jekyll and Mr Hollins
Dragon days
Finn gang
Fox hole
Going home
Great Northern?
Gumble's Yard
Handful of thieves
Henry Hollins and the dinosaur
Inflatable shop
Jack Holborn
James and the giant peach
Last bus
Last vampire
Minnow on the Say
Missee Lee
On the run
Peter Duck
Picts and the Martyrs
Pigeon post
Pippi Longstocking
Pirates' mixed-up voyage: dark doings in the Thousand Islands
Prisoners of September
River man
Runaway summer

Secret water
Short voyage of the 'Albert Ross'
Silver's revenge
Summer of the dinosaur
Swallowdale
Swallows and Amazons
Tom Tiddler's ground
We didn't mean to go to sea
Wheel of danger
Where the wind blows
White Horse gang
Winter holiday
Witch's daughter

ANIMAL

Ace
Adventures of the railway cat
Almost all-white rabbity cat
Along came a dog
Animals of Farthing Wood
Battle of Bubble and Squeak
Beach dogs
Blitzcat
Cat called Max
Christmas with Tamworth Pig
Creature in the dark
Daggie Dogfoot
Dog days and cat naps
Dog so small
Flight from Farthing Wood
Fly-by-night
Fox cub bold
Fox-busters
Fox's feud
Great escape
Harry's Mad
Hodgeheg, The
House of Wings
Hurry home, Candy

GENRE INDEX

I, Houdini: the autobiography of a self-educated
    hamster
In the grip of winter
Jo-Jo, the melon donkey
Just Nuffin
Keeping Henry
King of the vagabonds
Little foxes
Lost and found
Magnus Powermouse
Martin's mice
Midnight fox
Mouse butcher
My dog Sunday
Mystery pig
Olga da Polga
One-eyed cat
Peppermint pig
Prime of Tamworth Pig
Puffin book of pet stories
Railway cat
Railway cat and Digby
Railway cat and the horse
Railway cat's secret
Ram of Sweetriver
Rats!
Rescuing Gloria
Saddlebottom
Seal secret
Sheep-pig
Siege of White Deer Park
Superdog
Superdog in trouble
Superdog the hero
Tamworth Pig and the litter
Tamworth Pig saves the trees
Tamworth Pig stories
Team, The
Toby man, The
Tom's sausage lion
Travellers by night
Uncle Charlie Weasel and the cuckoo bird
Uncle Charlie Weasel's winter
Voyage of QV66
Walk on the wild side
Watership Down
Wild wood

CONSERVATION

Animals of Farthing Wood
Awaiting developments
Chinaman's Reef is ours
Flight from Farthing Wood
Fox cub bold
Fox's feud
Green book
In the grip of winter
M.C. Higgins the Great

On the flip side
Rebel on a rock
Rescuing Gloria
Serpent's tooth
Siege of White Deer Park
Someplace beautiful
When the wind blows
Why the whales came

FANTASY

Antar and the eagles
'Antelope' Company ashore
'Antelope' Company at large
Archer's Goon
Black hearts in Battersea
Bongleweed
Cart and Cwidder
Charlie, Emma and Alberic
Charlie, Emma and Dragons to the rescue
Charlie, Emma and the Dragon family
Charlie, Emma and the juggling dragons
Charlie, Emma and the school dragon
Charmed life
Cuckoo tree
Daymaker, The
Dido and Pa
Diggers
Dragon hoard
Dragon in Class 4
Dragon in spring term
Dragon in summer
Drowned Ammet
Dwarfs of Nosegay
Eight days of Luke
Elidor
Fairy rebel
Fantasy tales
Farm that ran out of names
Fattest dwarf of Nosegay
Finnglas and the stones of choosing
Finnglas of the horses
Gift from Winklesea
Greedy Alice
Halfmen of O
Homeward Bounders
In a nutshell
Indian in the cupboard
Iron man: a story in five nights
Karlson flies again
Karlson on the roof
King of Copper Mountain
Lives of Christopher Chant
Magicians of Caprona
Midnight is a place
Moon of Gomrath
Moon's revenge
Motherstone
Mouse and his child

Mr Magus is waiting for you
Night birds on Nantucket
Ogre downstairs
Paddy's pot of gold
Pangur Ban: the white cat
Power of three
Priests of Ferris
Prince on a white horse
Return of the 'Antelope'
Return of the Indian
Secret of the Indian
Serpent of Senargad
Shape-shifter:the naming of Pangur Ban
Shon the Taken
Skybreaker, The
Snowman
Spellcoats, The
Spellhorn
Stig of the dump
Stolen lake
Tom's midnight garden
Town that went south
Transformations
Truckers
Under the mountain
Unicorn trap
Virgil Nosegay and the cake hunt
Virgil Nosegay and the Hupmobile
Virgil Nosegay and the Wellington boots
Warlock at the wheel, and other stories
Weirdstone of Brisingamen
Whispering mountain
White horse is running
Wings
Winter players
Witch week
Wolves of Willoughby Chase
World around the corner

FAMILY

All about the Bullerby children
Animal, the vegetable and John D Jones
Bagthorpe saga
Bagthorpes abroad
Bagthorpes haunted
Bagthorpes liberated
Bagthorpes unlimited
Bagthorpes versus the world
Blossom promise
Blossoms and the Green Phantom
Blossoms meet the vulture lady
By the shores of Silver Lake
Cherry time at Bullerby
Christmas at Bullerby
Crummy mummy and me
Day at Bullerby
Dear Mr Henshaw
Friends and brothers

Goodbye, Chicken Little
Granny project
Happy days at Bullerby
Little house in the big woods
Little house on the prairie
Little town on the prairie
Long winter
Lotta
Lotta leaves home
Lotta's bike
Lotta's Christmas surprise
Mardie
Mardie to the rescue
Mischievous Martens
Not-just-anybody family
On the banks of Plum Creek
Peppermint pig
Ravensgill
Six Bullerby children
Springtime at Bullerby
Tatty Apple
These happy golden years

FAIRY STORIES, FOLK TALES AND TRADITIONAL STORIES

Anancy – Spiderman
Bag of moonshine
British and Irish folk tales
Dead moon and other tales from East Anglia
    and the Fen country
Faber book of favourite fairy tales
Faber book of Northern folk tales
Fairy tale treasury
Ghosts at large
Hindu world
How the whale became, and other stories
Listen to this story: tales from the West Indies
Mouth open, story jump out
Old Peter's Russian tales
People could fly: American Black folk tales
Pineapple child, and other tales from Ashanti
Tales of an Ashanti father
Three Indian princesses: the stories of Savitri,
    Damayanti and Sita
Web of stories

HUMOUR

Beezus and Ramona
Bill's new frock
Blood and thunder adventure on Hurricane
    Peak
Boy with illuminated measles
Bunnicula
Celery stalks at midnight
Country pancake
Emil and his clever pig

HISTORICAL

MYSTERY

GENRE INDEX

Round behind the ice-house
Stone menagerie
Summer of the swans
Thunder and Lightnings
Witch's daughter
You two, The

SOCIAL SITUATIONS: SIBLINGS

Cuckoo sister
Hi there, Supermouse
Superfudge
Tales of a Fourth Grade nothing

SOCIAL SITUATIONS: STEP-FAMILIES

Break in the sun
Frankie's Dad
Goggle-eyes
Ogre downstairs
Scarecrows, The
Trouble half-way

SOCIAL SITUATIONS: WITHDRAWAL

Cartoonist, The
Swan, The
TV kid
Trouble with Donovan Croft

SCIENCE FICTION

Another Heaven, another Earth
Antigrav
Beware of the Brain Sharpeners
Bewitched by the Brain Sharpeners
Beyond the burning lands
Blade of the poisoner
Blue misty monsters
Brain Sharpeners abroad
Catfang
Caves of Klydor
Children of Morrow
City of gold and lead
Computer nut
Dark sun, bright sun
Day of the Starwind
Deathwing over Veynaa
Delikon, The
Devil's children
Evil eye
Exiles of ColSec
Fireball
Galactic warlord
Grinny
Heartsease

Huntsman, The
Last legionary quartet
Lost star
Lotus caves
Master of fiends
Megan's star
Mindbenders
Monster garden
Mr Browser and the Brain Sharpeners
Mr Browser and the comet crisis
Mr Browser and the mini-meteorites
Mr Browser and the space maggots
Mr Browser in the space museum
Mr Browser meets the burrowers
Mr Browser meets the mind shrinkers
New found land
Planet of the warlord
Pool of fire
Prince in waiting
Quest of the Quidnuncs
Rag, a bone and a hank of hair
Rains of Eridan
Revenge of the Brain Sharpeners
Robot revolt
Shepherd Moon
Skiffy
Skiffy and the twin planets
Space hostages
Starstormer saga
Starstormers
Sun burst
Sword of the spirits
This time of darkness
Thousand eyes of night
Trillions
Warriors of the wasteland
Weathermonger, The
Wheelie in the stars
White mountains
Wild Jack
World-eater
Xanadu manuscript
Young legionary
Z for Zachariah

SCHOOL

Behind the bike sheds
Class that went wild
Demon headmaster
Fibs
Fighting in break, and other stories
Flames
Foxcover
Ghost dog
Gowie Corby plays chicken
Hanky Panky
In a class of their own: school stories
Mintyglo Kid

GENRE INDEX

SHORT STORIES

Arabel and Mortimer
Bad boys
Beside the sea with Jeremy James
Birthday burglar and the very wicked
  headmistress
Boy who bounced and other magic tales
Catch your death and other ghost stories
Chewing-gum rescue and other stories
Chocolate porridge and other stories
Clothes horse and other stories
Creepy-crawly stories
Daredevils or Scaredycats
Do goldfish play the violin?: adventures with
  Jeremy James
Dog days and cat naps
Door in the air and other stories
Downhill crocodile whizz and other stories
Elephant party
Elephants don't sit on cars
Even naughtier stories
Faithless Lollybird and other stories
Fantasy tales
Feet, and other stories
Fighting in break, and other stories
Fingers crossed: stories for nine-year-olds
First Margaret Mahy story-book
Fog hounds, wind cat, sea mice
Fred the angel
Getting rich with Jeremy James
Ghostly laughter
Great piratical rumbustification, AND The
  Librarian and the robbers
Harp of fishbones
High days and holidays
How to stop a train with one finger: adventures
  with Jeremy James
Imagine that! Fifteen fantastic tales
In a class of their own: school stories
Julian, secret agent
Julian stories
Julian's glorious summer
Kingdom under the sea
Last slice of rainbow and other stories
Leaf magic and five other favourites
Letters of fire and other unsettling stories
Librarian and the robbers
Listen to this story: tales from the West Indies
Little bookroom
Little car
Little Pete stories
Lizzie Dripping
Lizzie Dripping again
Lizzie Dripping and the little angel
Lizzie Dripping by the sea
Magic Orange tree and other stories
Magician who kept a pub and other stories
Mahy magic

Mark the drummer boy
Mice and Mendelson
Mists and magic
Modern fairy tales
More stories for seven year olds
More stories for under-fives
More stories Julian tells
More stories to tell
Mortimer says nothing and other stories
Mortimer's cross
My naughty little sister stories
Naughty stories: tales of terrible children
Necklace of raindrops
Never meddle with magic
Nonstop nonsense
Nothing to be afraid of
Old man who sneezed: read aloud stories
Old nurse's stocking basket
Past eight o'clock: goodnight stories
Puffin book of Christmas stories
Puffin book of pet stories
Round the Christmas tree
Runaway shoes: Puffin bedtime story chest
School stories
Second Margaret Mahy story-book
Shadow-cage
Small pinch of weather
Sophie's snail
Stories for eight year olds and other readers
Stories for five year olds and other young
  readers
Stories for nine year olds and other young
  readers
Stories for seven year olds
Stories for six year olds and other young readers
Stories for tens and over
Stories for under-fives
Tale of a one-way street
Tales for telling
Tales of Arabel's raven
Tell me a story
Tell me another story
Ten in a bed
There's a wolf in my pudding
Thief in the village and other stories
Things in corners
Third Margaret Mahy story-book
Time for one more
Time to laugh: fifteen funny stories
Topsy Turvy tales
Treasury of stories for five year olds
Treasury of stories for seven year olds
Treasury of stories for six year olds
Up the chimney down
Warlock at the wheel and other stories
What the neighbours did and other stories
Who's afraid? and other strange stories
Wrestling princess
Yucky ducky

THRILLERS

Baker Street Irregulars
Bang! Bang! You're dead
Candle in the dark
Day of the dragon
Death knell
Devil-in-the-fog
Devil's doorbell
Falcon's Malteser
Henry's leg
Leadfoot
Night of the scorpion
On the edge
Silver citadel
Silver crown
Snatched
Sound of propellers
Stan

Tea-leaf on the roof
Worm charmers

WAR

Carrie's war
Conrad's war
Dolphin crossing
Fireweed
Fly west
Game of soldiers
House of sixty fathers
Journey of 1,000 miles
Kingdom by the sea
Little brother
Thunder in the sky
Waiting for Anya
War horse